George T. Wolz

St. Charles College

May 21, 1954

THE CHRISTIANITY OF SHOLEM ASCH

THE
CHRISTIANITY
OF
SHOLEM ASCH

AN APPRAISAL
FROM THE JEWISH VIEWPOINT

by

Chaim Lieberman

PHILOSOPHICAL LIBRARY
New York

From the Yiddish

by

Abraham Burstein

Typography by the Polyglot Press, New York.

Manufactured in the United States of America.

TABLE OF CONTENTS

THE CHRISTIANITY OF SHOLEM ASCH

Preface

*"And every tongue that shall rise against
thee in judgment thou shalt condemn"*
(Isaiah LIV, 17)

The present work, besides offering a Jewish view of the Christological writings of Sholem Asch, reflects the reaction of the overwhelming majority of Jews all over the world to these writings and their apostatic character. This reaction is of supreme significance as a religious and cultural manifestation in general, and as a revelation of the state of mind of contemporary Jewry in particular.

For close to half a century Sholem Asch has been a leading light in Yiddish literature to which he made many notable contributions. Half a dozen or so of its permanent classics have come from his pen. He occupied a position of eminence wherever the Yiddish language is spoken and Jewish literature held in esteem. True, he was also known as the enfant terrible of Yiddish literature. Making the most of poetic license, he all too often kicked over the traces. Yet this on the whole did not impair his literary fame or diminish his large and grateful audience.

However, all this changed completely the moment Asch turned to the Christian theme and emerged with *The Nazarene*, followed by *The Apostle, Mary* and even *Moses*.

Avowedly a mediator who only sought to cement friendship between Christians and Jews, he undertook a veritable crusade among Jews on behalf of the Christian faith. With one intoxicating work after another on the Christian theme, and to the plaudits of all the missionaries of all the churches, he carried on in the course of years a missionary activity, on a scope never before known among Jews. Jews have become used, and inured, to the missionaries who century after century have laid siege to the Jewish people, but who beleaguer them from without. Sholem Asch however worked from within, as a Jew among Jews. While claiming that he was a more fervent Jew than ever before, he

1

sang the praises of Christianity and as will be seen in the following pages, misrepresented, distorted, debased and degraded Judaism, polluting its pure waters at their source. His prestige as a celebrated Jewish writer endowed his activity with a deadly potency on immature and, in matters Jewish, ignorant readers. His effectiveness has been notably strong with regard to Jewish youth in America, where his works were published in English, thus striking at the very roots of Jewish national existence. His influence has also extended to other lands, where his works appeared translated into the native tongues. What was more painful was the fact that he began his baneful activities just at the time when the Nazis began their crusade of extermination against the Jewish people.

Jewish reaction was swift and stern. Everywhere among Jews his new works were received in a mood of bitter resentment. A dark, forbidding abyss opened up between the people and Sholem Asch. An instinctive, mutual estrangement developed, which intensified with the passing of the years. Time was when Asch's tall, picturesque figure was a feature of every important Jewish gathering, particularly those of national importance, whether in Warsaw, Paris, London, or New York. He was much in evidence on all the various fronts of Jewish life. There was seldom a Jewish undertaking of any significance at which Asch failed to take his place or make himself heard.

Of all this only a memory now remains. Asch no longer appears where Jews foregather and no longer participates in Jewish affairs. He cut himself off from his people as though with a knife. No one planned it that way and no one called for it, but by a spontaneous attitude of rejection on the part of the Jewish public, he was retired from Jewish life as thoroughly as if he were to withdraw to some lonely island. He no longer has a hold on Jewish public opinion, except in a negative sense. As if in some great spiritual upheaval, he has been deposed from his place of eminence and allowed to sink into oblivion as far as the Jewish people was concerned. This attitude is fully shared by the religious and non-religious Jew alike.

The process of demolition of the Asch reputation was as inexorable as it was painful. For a period of over three decades, he was a contributor and star novelist in The Jewish Daily Forward, one of the great Yiddish newspapers of New York, but now could no longer continue in that position. He was a member

2

of the Jewish Agency for Palestine, and has quietly dropped out. A solitary sympathizer among Yiddish writers made a motion at a meeting of the Yiddish PEN Club of New York to send Asch greetings on the occasion of some literary anniversary: the motion was voted down. There was a Yiddish school in Brooklyn that bore the name of "Sholem Asch": the parents refused to send their children unless the name was removed.

But his Waterloo he met in Israel. Three times he strained to make the trip to the State of Israel, where apparently he hoped to stage a comeback. Twice he turned back in the middle of the journey, presumably sensing that he was not welcome. The third time he crashed in, but with mournful results. He was met at the boat by a committee of just one. The Society of Hebrew Writers took no notice of his stay in the country. He was not dined or wined at receptions or banquets. He was thoroughly ignored by press and public. A call upon the aged and ailing President, Dr. Chaim Weitzmann, brought cries of "shame!" and "desecration of the flag!" from the rostrum of the Kneset. A typical report on his visit to the Jewish state is the following, written, it is to be noted, by a sympathizer:

"Sholem Asch has visited our country. He spent several weeks here. The local press as well as Radio Kol Israel maintained silence and made almost no mention concerning the greatest Jewish writer of our generation.

"I say, *almost* made no mention, since an inconspicuous brief notice regarding Sholem Asch's arrival in the country did appear, printed in small type and tucked away among other unimportant announcements. Nothing further was reported concerning the great master, and it goes without saying, that no articles on him or evaluations of his work appeared in the local press. Also, neither were there any receptions nor banquets tendered in his honor. And when Sholem Asch left the country, as far as I know not even an announcement concerning his departure was made in the newspapers.

"And although our Israeli press is torn with dissension, in the case of Sholem Asch, however, there was consummated the great unification" ("Freie Arbeiter Stimme," New York, June 20, 1952).

On the other hand, as regards the Christian world, Asch did not go unrewarded for his arduous exertions as self-appointed Apostle to the Jews. He was richly endowed with fame and

3

fortune among the Gentiles. The religion of poverty brought Asch great wealth.

Indeed, Asch won a treasure, but he lost a people. And true to the tradition of Jewish backsliders, he was even already beginning to show a vindictive spirit towards his "former brethren," as will be shown hereafter.

Yet in all the above, the Jews dealt with Asch in nowise differently from the way other peoples dealt in similar, perhaps less onerous circumstances.

Our generation, the generation of communism and fascism, has been particularly distinguished in spawning renegades and traitors. They have teemed, these turncoats, in all countries and in all fields: in politics, in science, and in literature. America has had its Ezra Pound; Norway its Knut Hamsun; France its Charles Maurras, England its Dr. Allan Nunn May. Their names are legion. They all met their day of reckoning.

The Jewish people, too, did not escape this plague: the Jews have had their Sholem Asch. And he, too, has had his day of judgment.

All of which goes to prove that the Jewish heart is in the right place, despite some defections due to the general laxness of the times. The reaction to Asch was in its own way a reaffirmation of faith and a rededication to the values of Judaism. And it was necessary to state all this plainly and bluntly in order to give the lie to the missionaries and apostates who go ahunting among Jews, pointing to Asch as their prize trophy, and spreading tall tales of the "crumbling walls" of Judaism and such. Sholem Asch himself more than once assured the Gentiles, that the Jews are accepting a new orientation as regards the Christian saviour.

In the present work, the reader will see why it was that Sholem Asch met with so sharp a rebuff on the part of Jews. The book in the Yiddish original, the major portion of which appeared during the course of Asch's career as advocate of Christianity played a definite role in the crystallizing-out of this reaction. The work, greatly augmented, is here published in English translation with the hope that it may reach a part, even if only a small one, of that Jewish public which has been affected by Asch's works, and undo at least some of the evil he has perpetrated upon the Jewish community.

4

CHAPTER I

The Nazarene

Through his works on the Christological theme, beginning with the Nazarene down through Moses, Sholem Asch has been guilty of a grievous sin against the Jewish people. For he has forced upon it anew the ancient Judaeo-Christian controversy, which is best left undisturbed.

At no time in history have Jews willingly entered any controversy concerning the Nazarene and his teaching. There were many cogent reasons why Jews have avoided religious disputations. In the first place, they have never actively sought to win converts from other faiths. The dictum of Micah (iv, 5) —" for let all the peoples walk each one in the name of its god, but we will walk in the name of the Lord our God forever" — has been more than a mere phrase for the Jew. It has in truth and in fact been a basic historic principle of our existence. Jewish religious tolerance was rendered even more extensive by the prophetic declaration that even the heathen peoples who sacrificed to strange gods were, in their blundering way, actually serving the true God. With patience and trust the Jews awaited the day when all men would acknowledge the lofty sublimity of Judaism, and they would of themselves come unto the Lord, as foretold by Isaiah (xlv, 14) : "They shall fall down unto Thee, they shall make supplication unto Thee; surely God is in Thee, and there is none else." As for Christianity, Jews have always considered it a notable advance in the moral development of mankind, as contrasted with the moral condition of the pagan world. This attitude is perhaps best demonstrated by a saying long popular among Jews in Eastern Europe, which enjoined the Jew not to take to the road alone with a non-Jew who fails to cross himself or doff his hat when passing a church or a cross by the wayside.

5

There is another reason for Jewish positive aversion to disputations concerning the Christian faith. We can neither lose nor win such debates. We cannot lose, because ours is the truth; and we cannot win, because theirs is the might. In past ages such public controversies often proved catastrophic for the Jews, frequently ending in violence and with the burning of the Talmud. The more patently the Jews demonstrated the errors of the other faith, the more horribly did the others take their vengeance. For this reason, too, Jews rarely indulged in writing of the Nazarene, and whatever they did set down on that subject was generally done under the exigencies of self-defense. During medieval centuries, when Christianity was establishing itself throughout Europe and the Jews stood like a rock, a living denial of and reproach to the new faith, priests, with the connivance of Jewish converts, frequently compelled the rabbis to discuss with them the merits of their respective religions in the market place. The Jewish renegades were in fact more insistent than the priests, anxious as they were to prove their worth to their new masters and patrons. They were mostly men over whom there hung a moral cloud, shady, mercenary characters, who, to ingratiate themselves with the Gentiles, would undertake to overwhelm the rabbis and prove from Jewish sacred lore itself that Jesus was in truth the messiah. The rabbis went most reluctantly, both because they feared that the Jews might suffer much thereafter, and because they had no desire to stand in the contaminated presence of the renegades. But compelled to attend by royal or ecclesiastical command, they did so for the sanctification of the Name, prepared to die if need be in defense of their beliefs.

In this day Jewry stands, just as in the Middle Ages, a living refutation of Christianity. And so will it abide for all time. There are always elements in Christendom ready once more to fan the flames of the Christian-Jewish argument. One need but glance into some of the text books used in the instruction of millions of children in Christian schools, and note the prejudice, contempt and hatred contained therein against the Jew; one need but read the Gospels, in order to realize that the Christian attitude toward the Jew is a matter of utmost delicacy and precariousness.

When Sholem Asch published his first Christological work in 1939, on the very eve of World War II, Jews occupied an even more perilous position than during the Middle Ages. The anti-Jewish agitation unleashed by the Nazis reached an all time peak

6

in the western world. All the medieval decrees against Jewry had been revived, with many new restrictions, invented by a truly Satanic mentality, added. A mighty torrent of anti-Jewish propaganda, as never before experienced, was engulfing the world. The greatest massacre in history, engineered by the Nazis, was in process of preparation. The enemy was sharpening his knives for the total extermination of the Jewish people.

It was in such a time when the sword threatened from without and consternation reigned within, that Sholem Asch, a leading spirit of Jewish literature, chose to come forward with *The Nazarene,* to provoke afresh the old Christian feud with the Jew, thus placing himself in the ranks of the Jewish renegades of medieval times.

The Jewish public was shocked and scandalized as by no other literary event before or since. It was a sword plunged into the very vitals of the people. The brutal thrust was felt all the more keenly since the people were led to expect something quite different. For some years prior to the publication of this book Asch had been dabbling in religion, and religious Jews had watched the new manifestation with optimistic curiosity. For Asch had long been the spoiled playboy of Yiddish letters, and had often kicked over the religious traces. Very early in his career, for instance, he scandalized the Jewish world by an open assault upon the ancient rite of circumcision. Then he wrote a piece, the God of Vengeance, where he blasphemously introduced the Scroll of the Law into a house of ill fame. Now it was bruited about that his forthcoming opus would not only herald the return of the prodigal author to a loyal recognition of his Jewish heritage but would uphold the Jewish side in the old yet ever new and vital problem of the Church versus the Synagogue.

At last the long heralded moment arrived, but the mountain gave birth to—a cross! No one had suspected that the fruit of Asch's labor was to be a tome on the Christian Saviour and an obvious missionary tract.

Jews were confronted with a sharp dilemma. One could not remain silent, since Asch's work was too clearly a conversionist effort. Yet taking up the challenge was dangerous, for it could only mean stirring up the hot ashes of an ancient controversy that might better be left dormant. For this awful predicament Sholem Asch was entirely responsible; it was he who brought his people to the edge of an abyss.

7

How are we to deal with this problem, which must endure at least as long as Asch's work will endure and will be used by missionaries to undermine the Jewish faith? For a solution we must draw upon the wisdom of our forebears, who we have seen sought in every possible way to avoid Christian-Jewish disputations, but who, once upon the scene, feared no peril and spoke without restraint or reservation. It would be well here to refer to one such dispute between a distinguished rabbi and a renegade. The participants were the great Rabbi Nahmanides (Ramban) and the convert Pablo. The disputation took place in 1263 before the King of Aragon in Barcelona. The renegade was clearly vanquished after several days of debate. But the church could not accept defeat. One sabbath morning the King, with a large retinue, suddenly presented himself at the synagogue where the Jews were gathered for the Sabbath services, mounted the pulpit, and bade the Jews acknowledge Jesus the messiah and Son of God.

One can imagine the consternation of the congregation, faced with the King in the synagogue uttering a royal decree commanding belief in the basic Christian dogma—and this in the thirteenth century, amidst the darkest gloom of the dark ages. The life of the community hung by a hair.

Then Nahmanides arose and boldly addressed the King:

"My Lord King! You are assuredly a mighty ruler, a wise sovereign, whose words are exalted, but we must respectfully oppose your dictum that Jesus was the messiah. He lived his life in our land, and there offered proofs to our ancestors that he was God; and they denied his claims in his very presence. If he really had been God, as you assert, he could have demonstrated that fact in those days better than you today. And if they refused to believe him even when he was alive among them, how then should we be expected to believe and agree with the King, who knows nothing of the matter except what has been transmitted to him distantly by men who never laid eyes on Jesus and did not dwell in his country as did our own ancestors—living witnesses to the facts?"

It is from such instances as this, of which Jewish history is replete, that we must draw our strength. If Rabbi Nahmanides refused to be frightened by a Spanish renegade, should we today have fear of a Sholem Asch? And if the Jewish sage could venture to talk as he did in the benighted thirteenth century, should we tremble

8

in the "enlightened" twentieth century? Our sacred No shall not be silenced!

Thus, as we enter upon the present discussion we cannot over-emphasize the fact that there is not the least desire to disturb the Christian in his faith but rather to defend our own heritage against marauders from within and without, and particularly against the insidious domestic menace of the popular novelist.

Now the question posed by Nahmanides is the first good question to place before Sholem Asch. Why indeed did our ancestors of that day deny both Jesus and his teachings? They saw him, heard him, carried on discussions with him; why did they repudiate him so utterly and determinedly?

Asch's reply, gathered from his novel of the life of Jesus, is a curious one. He denies the very premise, maintaining that the overwhelming majority of the people in Jesus' day did not repudiate him, but accepted him with great love, mystic wonderment, and deep faith. Every page of the Asch opus is filled with depictions of the entire populace enthusing over Jesus, pursuing him to kiss his footprints and to draw inspiration from his teachings. We see not only the masses thus adoring him, but some of the great sages and scholars, including leading Pharisees. It appears that the corrupt family of the High Priest were alone in rejecting Jesus—and they carried the day. They persecuted him, tried and convicted him, and finally handed him over to the Romans for execution. Why? Because he was dangerous to their reign of corruption, to their exploitation of the poverty-stricken Jewish masses.

This is the foundation upon which Asch's volume is constructed.

The implication of Asch's magnum opus is that over a period of two millennia countless Jewish generations who have preferred death at the stake and sword to acceptance of the Jesus cult have acted thus not as a result of religious, theological, or philosophical convictions; of loyalty to Torah, Prophets, and Talmud; but as an outgrowth of the knavery of an ancient priestly clique which once embarked upon a devious anti-Christian path out of selfishness, sordidness, and crass materialism. Two thousand years of Jews including those living today, are therefore but the foolish, befouled victims of a loathsome conspiracy of priestly malefactors bent only on preserving their putrid profits!

9

It is hardly necessary to comment that this assumption is utterly false and ignorant. Suffice it to say that no serious Christian scholar, no honest Christian believer, has ever entertained or offered so preposterous, so insulting, an idea of the Jewish attitude toward Jesus. Even the most anti-Jewish of the four Gospels gives an idealogical basis for Jewish resistance to the founder of Christianity. We read in John, 33: "The Jews answered him: For a good work we stone thee not, but for blasphemy; and because that thou, being a man, makest thyself God." Paul writes: "For I bear them witness, that they have a zeal of God but not according to knowledge" (Romans 2). He charges them with error but not malice. What Asch has done is to take the world's gravest and loftiest problem, a conflict overshadowing all history, the noblest drama of man, the supreme tragedy of all time, and reduce it to criminal folly, to some wicked, worthless human vice or foible.

No less fantastic are Asch's ideas concerning the Pharisaic sages and leaders who repudiated the Nazarene and did so, according to him, out of scholarly pride, and in order to maintain their power over the people which the teachings of Jesus threatened to undermine. True to the spirit of the New Testament, he disparages the Pharisees that he might the better exalt Jesus. And just as there is no historical warrant whatever for the Asch depiction of countrywide enthusiasm for Jesus, so there is not the remotest truth in his presentation of general popular antagonism toward the sages and Pharisees. The exact opposite is the case. The people had turned away from the priesthood and royalty, rendered corrupt by the Roman imperium, and devoted their love and loyalty to the men dedicated to the upholding and preservation of the Torah of Moses.

Sholem Asch apparently has made no distinction in approach and treatment between the Jesus story and an ordinary novel. The free reign he has given to his creative imagination in his secular romances, he has employed in *The Nazarene* as well, which cannot be justified by any manner of reason. In handling ordinary fiction, one may employ any twist of the imagination and direct the plot hither and thither. But one may not capriciously invent in a world historical theme, every detail of which has been duly recorded, thoroughly plumbed, and overlaid with meaning which itself acquired world historic significance.

It may be seriously questioned on general principle whether

10

the subject of Jesus and the historic controversies concerning him are a matter for free belletristic treatment. The professional fictionist is a free agent, who may employ his material and his fancy as he pleases. He can vary his chiaroscuro at will. But the slightest variation of light and shade on a single point in a matter of such tremendous values as are involved in the historic Jewish-Christian controversy may well spell the difference between orthodoxy and heresy, or belief and disbelief. The result may mean the difference between life and death for countless multitudes. Because of a single stroke of a Greek letter, great bloody wars have been fought in Christendom.

Every potential fallacy inherent in a fanciful handling of the Jesus story has in very fact been committed by Sholem Asch. And all of them, strangely enough, are tipped against the Jews and consequently in favor of their Christian adversary. The dice have been loaded for the benefit of the Christian partner in the fateful game. So completely has Asch been carried away by his enthusiasm for the subject that nothing, evidently, has been able to restrain him—neither his woefully inadequate knowledge of Judaism, nor a sense of responsibility to his people. In his furore he has even outdone the Gospels, which are the only source for the Jesus narrative. Where the Gospels register one, Asch registers ten. Where the Gospels have a grey coloration, Asch lays on black. Where the Gospels cry, Asch wails. And his is an impasto technique. He even invents new episodes, never thought of in the Gospels.

Asch employs every literary stratagem to bias and intoxicate the reader in favor of the Jesus theme. The highly romanticized story of Jesus, for which some claim there is no historical warrant whatever, bears in Asch's book the sharp flavor of stark realism. The trick is well known to romantic writers and to liars—for romancers, as Plato pointed out, are in a certain sense tellers of untruths. When a skilled liar recounts a fabrication, he provides so many plausible details and minutiae as to create the impression of truth. Such is the method employed by Asch in his book on Jesus. A story basically supernatural and non-natural he fills to the brim with natural and realistic data as detailed and as numerous as the dust of the earth. His precise descriptions of the land of Judea —mountains, valleys, rivers, flora, odors, people—are juxtaposed with tales of the tumultuous activity of and around Jesus, the ecstasy of the masses following him, the intrigues and conspiracies of the priests and Pharisee sages; scene after scene is described to

11

the last detail, and all is recounted with such a fierce vitality that the reader is numbed into accepting as reality every fantastic invention presented in the seven hundred long pages.

Now it is, of course, quite true that the cities and the mountains and the valleys and the rivers are historic and real. It is also true that in those distant days rain fell on the land of Judea, grass grew there, the sun shone by day and the moon by night, and not vice versa. But to give the impression, as Asch tries to do, that most of the nation were madly partisan toward Jesus and his teachings, and were fully prepared for conversion, and that the teachings and observances of the scribes and Pharisees—meaning Judaism itself—were thoroughly despised by the people, is a loathsome, revolting mockery of historic truth. Even the Gospels know of no such cleavage between the people and their spiritual leaders.

Intelligent Jews reading this holy hokum may dismiss it with a smile. But when naive men and women, ignorant of the facts, are misled by what they take to be a legitimate historical novel, it ceases to be a laughing matter. The prestige of a noted Jewish author may, in the case of Christians, intensify old prejudices and create new ones against the Jews. If the readers happen to be untutored Jewish boys and girls lacking a proper Jewish education and background, as they all too frequently do, the results may be grave indeed. This type of book is liable to induce a morbid state of mind in them and torment them with a problem they are not prepared to cope with. It may prejudice them against their own people and make them accept with Asch the thesis that the Jewish rejection of Jesus was an historical error, for which the Jew is properly punished. They may be imbued, gratuitously, with a sense of a historic guilt and fall into brooding, tormenting self-analysis, self-doubting, and finally self-denial. They may become victims to some of the psychological effects of anti-Semitism, in the sense of the retribution preached by the Church and sustained by Sholem Asch. For his book from end to end fairly shrieks to high heaven: Behold what wrong the Jew has done to the redeemer of man and the evil he has wrought thereby! It is, moreover, liable to lower their estimation of their people and even estrange them from it. The confused Jewish youth may well be inclined to pose the query, Why should we not make good today the ancient error of our ancestors?

The churches keep their portals ever open and await with eagerness the coming of the Jew.

12

It is this that makes Sholem Asch's *The Nazarene,* as well as his subsequent Christological works, so deadly a crime against the Jewish people.

2

Transmigrations

The Nazarene opens in Warsaw with a demented Polish "professor," bearing the name of Pan Viadomsky—which name may imply "the knower," "the thinker." Viadomsky is the prime mover, the hero of the narrative; it is around him that the larger first portion of the work revolves. Viadomsky is a very queer character. To begin with he is a fiery anti-Semite, although that alone would not render him unusual, since that prejudice has been the normal thing in a Pole. He is a scholar of a sort, a researcher, or rather a bibliomaniac, in the classical tongues, known to the world of learning as an eccentric old gentleman who often created diversions with his half-mad delvings into the ancient cultures of Greece and Rome. He is a kind of bookworm luxuriating in bibliophilic dust, pursuing books old and forgotten and manuscripts all but unknown. As a special hobby, he writes anti-Semitic books and hatches anti-Semitic conspiracies.

Either because of his Christian loyalties or because of his hatred of the Jews, he is a passionate researcher in the history of Christianity. Through his partly aberrant studies in Roman civilization and early Christianity, he has developed the fantastic notion that through early transmigration of souls he walked the earth during Jesus' lifetime as a high Roman official in Judea, known as Cornelius. He has lived through the active career of Jesus, from his rise to his crucifixion; and, having played an important part in these events, heard all and seen all, he now often remembers all that happened. Quite frequently and unexpectedly, there fades into forgetfulness the current personality of the Pole Viadomsky, and the transmogrified personage of old rises from the unconscious to the surface. Sometimes he even induces that state. As the Roman Cornelius, his favorite topic of conversation is Judea, the Nazarene and the dramatic events of those ancient days.

Delving through the dust of an old Jew's antique shop, Viadomsky discovers a secret Hebrew manuscript of olden times. Not

13

knowing Hebrew himself, he seeks out a teacher of the language. For this purpose Sholem Asch is recommended—and thus do their paths cross.

Asch, completely swept off his feet by the tales related by Viadomsky as he reverts to his old Roman existence, retells these episodes; thus the Jesus story finds its place in *The Nazarene*. Gradually, however, under Viadomsky's influence, Asch becomes obsessed by the illusion that he, too, is a soul transmogrified from a former Sholem Asch who lived in ancient Judea and that as Johanan, he was a witness of Jesus' entire career. As he indulges in his own reminiscences, we are treated to a second retelling of the New Testament story.

The manuscript, which is deciphered only with great pain on the part of both men, turns out to be a record of the Jesus affair by the traitorous apostle, Judas Iscariot. The complete "manuscript" is presented; thus, the same story is told for the third time.

We shall not pause to discuss the artistic side of this manipulated and clumsy device of transmigration with its complicated arrangement of flashbacks within several different memories, a device, by the way, adopted from "The Legend of Thomas Didymus" by J. F. Clarke. But one cannot pass lightly over the symbolic character of such a rendition which is surely intended to convey some "profound" meaning. The technique provides the first indication of Asch's methodology in his Christological works, whereby he takes from the Jewish scale of the balance and loads over onto the Christian scale. Beauties, ideas, symbols, parables, and aphorisms from Judaism of which Christians never previously had any inkling, are carried over and woven into the texture of the Christian theme. Christian readers are misled into believing that these are original with Asch, products of his own creative imagination, and are impressed with his greatness as artist, thinker, and scholar. As a result Asch has gained the reputation of a great Hebrew scholar. Some American reviewers, in their enthusiasm have even dubbed him "the greatest Hebrew scholar of our time."

There is a Jewish tradition that the souls of Jews of all eras stood gathered at the foot of Mount Sinai when the Law was given —a symbol that every Jew has a share in the Law and that the Law is binding upon every Jew in all generations to come. "Neither with you only," spoke Moses, "do I make this covenant and this oath; but with him that standeth here with us this day before the Lord our God, and also with him that is not here with us this day" (Deut. xxix, 13-14).

This beautiful gem of Jewish lore set in the background of the two-storied, flashback structure of the Asch opus, with its device of the transmigration of souls, is intended to convey the idea that though Asch lives here and now, he nevertheless feels himself a living participant in the tragedy of the crucifixion, having been actually present there and then, and thus bearing his share of blame and responsibility. The same naturally, goes for Pan Viadomsky. This is further to signify, symbolically, that all human beings, Jews and Gentiles, all the Asches as well as all the Viadomskys of all ages, were present in spirit at the crucifixion, are guilty of Christ's blood and must therefore make amends.

The novel is constructed as taking place simultaneously in two worlds and two periods. The locales are Warsaw and ancient Judea; the eras, antiquity and the present. A hodgepodge of time and place, the story takes us on a merry-go-round between modern Warsaw and ancient Jerusalem, from Sholem Asch consorting with Pan Viadomsky to Johanan bustling about the Roman officer Cornelius. We are now in the world as we know it, and now in other worlds of supernatural incident: the Jesus story is an event for all places, and for all times.

However, Pan Viadomsky, as indicated above, is an anti-Semite to the marrow of his bones. Every remark he utters concerning the Jews reeks with venom. One might call him a two-level anti-Semite for he is a Jew-hater both as Pole and as Roman. When he is a Polish aristocrat there flows from his lips all the poison common to a Polish anti-Semite; and when his soul is transmuted into that of the Roman officer he bestrews the people of Israel with all the vituperations of the contemporary Roman against the Jew. Compounded together, the result is a goodly sum. *The Nazarene* thus may be termed a veritable anthology of anti-Semitism, ancient and modern. On the very first page one is apprised of the "time-honored" complaints that Jews are troublesome gnats, sneaks, disturbers, grabbers, and destroyers of the morals of every nation among whom they live. In the course of the story we are treated to the most delightful titbits of the anti-Semite—from the accusation of the ritual murder to the "smart" dig that Polish Jews smell of onion and garlic.

At the time, the very time, Sholem Asch conferred upon the

world the blessing and the glory of his Jesus story the Polish Jews did indeed emit a powerful odor; however, it wasn't of onion and garlic, but of their burning flesh. They burned to the tune of six million. At the hands of good Christian folk.

This brings us to the cardinal query concerning Asch's first Christological work: why did he elect to make Pan Viadomsky an arch anti-Semite, and in both transmigrations? Why should it have pleased him to render his version of the Jesus story, and incidentally of Jewish history in general, specifically through the mouth of a virulent Jew-hater? There was no such compulsion in the logic of his narrative. The central character might just as well have been a Judaeophile. After all, there were Poles who were friends of the Jews, and among the Romans, too, there were numerous friends, even enthusiastic partisans of the Jews. Some of them became converts and as such came to occupy a high place in Jewish history. Why could not Asch have chosen for his ancient "gilgul" of Viadomsky one of this class? Why could he not have chosen Eliza Orzeszko, a Polish writer, who wrote admiringly of the Jews? This treatment would have been far more in keeping with the hero and core and aim of the book, for the novel as it stands reveals not only a disharmony, but a fundamental inner defect. In a volume intended to portray the emergence of the "God of Love," His scion Pan Viadomsky, stands as a living symbol of the deep hatred toward the people out of whose loins the God of Love sprung. While we are told of the rise of a hope, we read simultaneously of its tragic failure!

But even assuming that there had to be a Jew-hater in the story, why could not Asch at least have presented a countervailing character? He describes himself and Viadomsky creeping through all the Jewish slums in Warsaw,—the poor filthy streets, the market places and the wretched shops. We see the darker side of Jewish existence; why does he never take his anti-Semitic comrade, in his researches on Judaism and Christianity, to, let us say, the home of a Warsaw rabbi? There were in Warsaw, in the time of which Asch writes, though alas, no more today, rabbis, men of brilliance, scholars of the law, to say nothing of outstanding laymen of culture and character, who could tell a thing or two about Jesus, the Messiah, and Judaism to both Asch and Viadomsky. In Asch's book Jesus bears the title "rabbi." Could the novelist not have introduced a contemporary rabbi to present and represent the Jewish side of the eternal controversy?

16

Had Asch allowed some representative Jew to join battle with Viadomsky on the merits of Judaism and Christianity, the result would surely have been exciting and rewarding. Above all—fair. The introduction of a friend of Israel as antidote to the enemy of Israel might have justified the presence of the latter. As Asch's work stands, the Jew and Judaism have no friend or defender; both are delivered up to ignorance and contumely, to contempt and derision.

There are two obvious reasons, one lesser, one greater, for the particular way Asch chose to handle the subject. First, when a Jewish author begins to cast eyes toward Gentile recognition, the general rule is that he begin by doing some Jew-baiting himself. This has proved a sure-fire success. Non-Jews seem to derive special delight out of watching a Jew castigate his brethren.

Second, anyone entering the door of Christianity at one end is likely to emerge through the door of anti-Semitism at the other end. The tragic experience of our history has taught us that Jews who desert to Christianity rarely are satisfied with the mere forsaking of their people and their faith, and almost invariably have joined with the oppressors and persecutors of the Jews. This has been the case throughout the Middle Ages. Frequently they became the instigators and leaders of persecution, supplying non-Jews with slanders against the Jews, instigating disputes concerning the Talmud, "exposing" "secrets" and books, often even carrying out the burning of those books.

The strange phenomenon is even the subject of a popular jest among the Jews. Two poor, ragged, starving Jews, passing the residence of a priest, saw a sign in the window promising any Jew who would enter and accept conversion a reward of fifty rubles. "Let's go in," urged one, "we are famished." "It's forbidden!" protested the other. "But it wouldn't hurt to go in just to see what it's all about." "It's wrong to yield to temptation!" Ignoring the objurgations of his friend, the first did enter. In half an hour he emerged and started off without even so much as a glance at his friend. The latter ran after him, crying, "Well, Shmerl, what happened inside?"

Upon which came the reply: "Get away, damned Jew!"

This has been the standard "formula" for Jewish converts throughout the ages. Something inexplicable ignites a burning animus in them as they turn away from their people and make their exit from the synagogue. They are at once caught up in the

17

anti-Jewish spirit of Christianity, which is itself an apostate from Judaism and is animated by the same mysterious animus. For Christianity by its own definition doomed itself to eternal antipathy toward Judaism. It views its emergence from Judaism, not in the manner of a graft from a tree, planted in separate soil and growing up to lead its own, independent arboreal existence, but rather in the manner of an oak from an acorn: the acorn is consumed in the process and loses its identity as the oak develops.

Judaism on the other hand regards Christianity as only a stage in the long march of mankind to the pure monotheism of Judaism, as it is said: "In that day will the Lord be one, and His name one."

Thus Christianity is sworn to war with Judaism from generation to generation until it is ultimately submerged. It may tolerate any other religion under the sun, but Judaism must be blotted out. This doctrine, rehearsed in the ears of Christendom from century to century, has generated an enmity "which may be felt" and which has become a part of normal Christian living.

The Jewish convert, anxious to prove his loyalty to his new faith, tries to outdo his newly acquired confreres in his anti-Jewish zeal, which gave rise to the popular Jewish saying: "A Jewish convert (Meshumed) is worse than a heathen (goy) ."

Some such metamorphosis must have taken place in Sholem Asch: he has remained true to the tradition.

There was a time when Asch was looked upon in Yiddish literature as the glorifier and idealizer of Jewish life. Such of his works as *A Town* and *Shloime Nagid* are fairly oozing with sweetness and light. But as one begins to read his Christological works, one becomes uncomfortably aware of a complete change of atmosphere.

Embarking upon a venture to find favor with the Christians, Asch inevitably had to adopt this anti-Jewish attitude towards Judaism, making Viadomsky his mouthpiece.

So inexhaustible is the odium spewed upon the head of Jewry from the mouth of Pan Viadomsky and his ancient counterpart Cornelius that the reader is forced to pose the question—"why should God have chosen these loathsome people, this ethnic abomination, wherewith to reveal Himself unto humanity? Why should the pure stream of redemption have to course down so polluted a channel?" I shall not here repeat all the relevant anti-

18

Semitic utterances of the book. Why give them further dissemination? A few samplings will suffice.

Cornelius, a Roman hegemon in the Jewish land, scorns the entire people. He despises them in all their strata—high and low, rich and poor, proletarian and aristocrat, fool and sage, ignoramus and scholar. He remains always the proud Roman, with nothing but contempt and abhorrence for every Jew. Yet note his reaction when he comes upon Jesus:

"Caught up in that atmosphere of wonder, I approached, and for the first time in my life made obeisance to a Jew" (p. 171).

Not a single Jew in all Judea could elicit the respect of this representative of Rome, the implication being that only in Jesus has the Jewish people achieved real stature, and only through him was the nation deserving of the respect of other nations.

A second example: The scene is the Jewish market place in Warsaw; the time is Passover eve; there is much tumult among last minute purchasers of holiday needs. Sholem Asch and Pan Viadomsky stand by as observers. Viadomsky, finding himself suddenly in the grips of his alter ego, is reminded of other Jews long ago in the land of Israel on another Passover eve in the days of Jesus, and he delivers this "pathetic" outburst:

"Oh, Israel, Israel, what has become of thee!. . . Shoemakers, peddlers, hucksters, dealers in old clothes and rusty iron, that's what's become of you! You sit in the gutters of an alien, barbarous city, steeped in mud and snow. The Jochanans, the Simons, the Judahs, the Jacobs, the Josephs. . . Do they not see their own faces? Do they not hear their own voices? Israel, what art thou become?" (p. 387).

The tirade continues in the same vein. Asch finds nothing of worth, of Jewish greatness and glory to display to his companion all through his association with Pan Viadomsky. He takes him to the backyards of Jewish Warsaw, to the slums, to the lower depths, never to where is sunshine, light, burning candles in shining candelabras. He doesn't even take him to eat gefilte fish, which proverbially will make the mouth water of the most ardent anti-Semite and make him ask for a second helping. Yet Warsaw for generations was a seat of Jewish glory.

Why then did Sholem Asch so assiduously avoid the brighter side?

Asch is here only following the historic policy of the Church

19

of portraying the Jew in a fallen state of degradation, as a witness to the Christian Saviour, as this policy has been expressed by Pascal in his incomparable manner: "The condition in which one sees the Jews," he wrote, "is, moreover, a great proof of the Religion. For it is an astonishing thing to see that people subsisting for so many years, and to see them always in a state of misery; it being necessary for the proof of Jesus Christ both that they subsist as a proof, and that they be wretched, because they crucified him" (Pensées). Thus, Asch's treatment came right out of the Church's books.

In his "conversion" Asch did not follow in the footprints of those righteous from among the Gentiles who acknowledged the greatness and beauty of Judaism. Instead, he concluded a pact with the devil, ganging up with an anti-Semite, and presenting a caricature of Judaism!

The Talmud tells of a curious holiday the early Christians used to hold in Rome in celebration of the ascendence of Christianity and the "downfall" of Judaism:

"There is a holiday in Rome, once in seventy years, on which a sound man mounts the shoulders of a lame man. The sound man represents Esau, the lame man, Jacob. The first is richly appareled, with diamonds about his neck and ankles. The pair are led through the streets, while the cry is raised, Jacob's plot has played him false! He cheated the blessings from Esau, but the blessings have been turned back to us (Abodah Zarah 10b)."

That is exactly the kind of "Roman Holiday" Sholem Asch is celebrating in *The Nazarene.*

3

"A Hebrew Scholar"

We have already indicated the circumstance, a fateful one, that led Sholem Asch to make the acquaintance of Pan Viadomsky. The "Angel of Hebrew" is to be thanked for that. In his later years, we are told, the Polish anti-Semite decided to learn a little of the language of the Bible, the traditional tongue of Judaism, in order—as he makes clear—to penetrate more easily into the "con-

20

spiratorial world" of the Jewish people. Sholem Asch was recommended to him as one who knew Hebrew, or better, as a "Hebrew scholar." But what was to have been a mere fictional role assumed by Asch for purposes of his narrative has been mistaken by readers for living reality. And how that characterization has grown! The tremendous circulation of the English version has gained Asch wide acclaim as a Hebrew scholar, even as "the greatest living Hebrew scholar."

One can blame neither the ordinary English reader nor the literary reviewer for making this association. Most readers have but a cursory acquaintance with the fundamentals of Christianity and a still scanter knowledge of Judaism. *The Nazarene* moves within the orbits of both. The average English reader finds the Jewish elements new discoveries, and in his naive wonder he is ready to hail the author as a great scholar.

This mistaken belief, for obvious reasons, was eagerly seized upon by pious Christians and missionaries, who received the work with enthusiasm. To them *The Nazarene,* coming as it did from the pen of a famous Jewish author, was proof of the truth and triumph of Christian doctrine. Now that the "greatest *Jewish author*" has become the "greatest *Hebrew scholar*" as well, the "greatest authority on Jewish lore," the "preeminent Jewish thinker," etc, etc., Sholem Asch has become a name to conjure with. Missionary groups have found the book a God-send, and they have had a field day among those vulnerable Jewish youths who have felt religious yearnings but have lacked proper instruction in their own faith.

Sholem Asch could not but feel flattered at the unexpected homage accruing to him from this unlooked for quarter, and he has done his best to aid and assist in the dissemination of the strange belief. He used the various newspaper interviews to which he now fell heir to drop insinuations and suggestive hints as to his profound learning in Talmud, in Hebrew, in Aramaic, etc. Which brings us face to face with one of the most extraordinary episodes in all literature. For it is all nothing but "a delusion, a mockery and a snare," a huge joke, a colossal hoax!

It is indeed a pity to explode this illusion, cherished as it is by so many well-meaning Christians and naive Jews; but it is a piece of surgery that has to be performed! The truth of the matter is that among Jews Sholem Asch has always been known as a

21

simple, unlearned, unschooled, uneducated man, shocking as it may seem to say it. A gifted author, yes, but a mere plebe as far as any learning either general or Jewish is concerned.

To the Freudian psychologist, Asch's adoption in his book of the personal role of "Hebrew scholar" will not appear strange. It is the result of a decided inferiority complex gnawing away at his colossal vanity. For not only does he fall short of a scholar, but his reputation in Yiddish literature is that of a *downright ignoramus*. And he has been told so openly and repeatedly.

Asch could convince only a Polish anti-Semite, or a naive English-reading public, of the fairytale of his Hebrew scholarship. But the cognoscenti know, and know well, that the only Hebrew word he may be expected to spell correctly is the "Sholem" of Sholem Asch!

Now lest it apear too fantastic, too unbelievable, to charge Asch with complete ignorance of Hebrew and consequently of Hebrew learning with which the language is intimately bound up, let it be added here—incredible as it may sound—that even in Yiddish, his mother tongue, the very instrument of his creativity, he is far from adept!

Tragic indeed is this recapitulation of Sholem Asch's short-coming in Hebrew, in Yiddish, and in other fields. His ignorance has long been a matter of bitter comment in the Jewish literary field. It has been pointed out, sometimes with pity, sometimes with disgust, that it is a blemish on the entire Yiddish literature that a writer of Asch's rank and stature should lack the proper command of the language he writes in! It is not infrequently that an artist's talent remains a rough diamond, never polished by the clarifying abrasives of culture. Such artists may often rise to great heights in the realm of intuitive creation. But it is another matter when, like Sholem Asch, they dip their pens into other inks than those of pure belles-lettres to invade fields where other qualifications than mere talent are required. There they are liable to cause harm and fearful confusion among the unlearned and uncultured.

Let me now quote what the leading critic of Yiddish literature, Samuel Niger, has to say concerning Asch's cultural qualifications. In two indignant articles (The Day, June 12 and 13, 1937) he takes the novelist to task for a multitude of sins, not least among them being his lack of an elementary knowledge of Yiddish grammar.

22

"I declare," says Mr. Niger, "and I am doing so purposely in plain, clear, frank terms, with complete unceremoniousness, that one encounters in Asch's writings scores upon scores of sentences that are devoid of either taste, or substance, or life. . . phrases and expressions with no grammatical coherence whatsoever."

Lo, behold the master!

Irritated by Asch's frequent self-pitying wailings, the noted critic continues:

"Why is he trying to befuddle us with old-wives' tales? Does he not recall reading, as far back as 1902, the first review by Baal Machshavot, to the effect that he, Asch, was not yet proficient in his use of language? Did he not read these words in plain Yiddish, and was it not an admonition that he must needs acquire some elementary knowledge?"

Lo, hail the scholar!

Mr. Niger then proceeds to quote a number of sentences culled out of Asch's works, analyzes them grammatically and syntactically, points out the errors and discusses for Asch's benefit the manner in which they should have been written. Asch is publicly and pitilessly tongue lashed, as by a teacher scolding a schoolboy.

This writer at the time took issue with Mr. Niger, contending that it was too late in the game to treat a mature writer like a beginner. But on the basic point Mr. Niger was perfectly right.

This transpired in 1937. Only two years later, in 1939, appeared *The Nazarene*, translated from the Yiddish manuscript, launching Asch upon his career as a giant of learning, colossus of knowledge of Judaism, arbiter of the historic Judeo-Christian dispute, a Daniel come to judgment!

Other critics were even more severe in taking Asch to task for his abysmal ignorance of the language in which he wrote. The late distinguished talmudist and historian of Jewish law, Professor Chaim Tchernowitz (who, I might add, until the publication of *The Nazarene* was a close friend of Asch's) blasted Asch from another angle. Aroused by the novelist's intrusion into the theological field, he wrote with profound disgust of his vaulting ignorance and vainglory. In his Hebrew pamphlet, "Other Gods," directed against *The Nazarene*, discussing Asch's frequent excursions into philosophical discourse, the noted scholar says: "Asch's philosophy is derived from the introductions to school readers or from cheap encyclopedias, or it is plain unintelligible

23

prattle and senseless drivel" (p. 7). In bitter and scornful language he denounces him as an upstart and with sardonic play on words predicts a heap of ashes of Asch's missionary pursuits.

Of Asch's Christological endeavors Professor Tchernowitz says: "Most of his utterances are taken from Christian theology, acquired from cheap booklets handed out freely in the streets" (ibid 9).

The eminent scholar maintains that Asch was unable to read the New Testament except in Yiddish translation, having scarcely any workable knowledge of any other tongue. The professor thus explains some gross errors in Asch's opus, which access to other sources could have prevented.

For the edification of those who understand some Hebrew I offered in the Yiddish original of this work several delectable examples of Asch's Hebrew "erudition," culled from the Yiddish version of *The Nazarene,* which for obvious reasons could not be given here. These specimens may be found in the appendix to this volume.

Now if this is the sad case as regards elementary training, what can we expect to find as we move along to higher levels of Biblical and Talmudic scholarship? Indeed, we here encounter an astonishing lack of knowledge of the most basic principles of Jewish teaching. Combining ignorance with zeal, Asch produces the grossest misrepresentation of the very problems at issue between Judaism and Christianity, which he took it upon himself to umpire. A few examples will illumine the point.

We read in *The Nazarene* of the Jews marveling at Jesus and asking, "What, is he a prophet sent of God that he can remit sin?" (227). Now this is a query that Jews were never able to pose, for a prophet in Judaism never was granted the power to remit sin. The prophet explained sin, fulminated against it, warned of inevitable punishment, demanded penitence, but never did he, in his own capacity or as a representative of God, provide indulgences for sin. This is one of the fundamental differences between Judaism and Christianity; only in the latter can the church, through the priest, exonerate the sinner. In Judaism God alone can grant that pardon. Where the transgression involves another human, forgiveness must also be granted by the aggrieved person.

Again, in *The Nazarene,* in describing the modifications and innovations which Jesus ventured to introduce into the Law and the fundamental teachings of the sages, portrays the Jews express-

24

ing amazement and continually querying: Is he a prophet that he dares speak thus, or is he the messiah? Why does he offer no proof, and why does he not tell us from whose authority and from what source he derives this power? This is a recurrent motif of Asch's work, indeed the chief cornerstone upon which his Jesus story is erected. It is based upon the notion that revision of the Torah was the peculiar right of the prophets. As to the ultimate annulment of the whole of the Mosaic Law and its substitution by a new law or "authority," that right, according to Asch, was reserved for the Messiah alone.

Accordingly, it is the sense and contention of Sholem Asch that had Jesus offered the Jews satisfactory proof of his messiahship, they would have accepted his innovations in the Torah and ultimately his abrogation of the Mosaic Law, and the Jesus drama might have had a happy ending. However, all the miraculous deeds performed by Jesus hit a blind spot in the minds of the Jews, with all the tragic consequences as we know them today.

This conception is developed theoretically in *What I Believe* (1941) and worked into the structure of *The Nazarene*. Says Asch: "Only he who can meet the obligation laid upon the prophets will be recognized by the Jews as the King Messiah, and his will be the right to cancel the previous authority and to introduce his own" (What I Believe, 109-110). And lacking proof the Jews "misunderstood" the message and aim of Jesus.

Now, this "magnificent" ideological structure, erected with prodigious exertion, collapses like a child's house of cards when subjected to the verities of Jewish law. All would be fine, if it were not all wrong. For it is a basic and fundamental precept of Jewish law that neither the prophets nor the messiah has any power to alter the authority of the Torah or to introduce a new authority. The Torah is eternal and immutable for laymen, prophet and messiah alike. From the final passage in Leviticus (xxvii, 34): "These are the commandments which the Lord commanded Moses for the children of Israel in Mount Sinai"—the sages derive the precept, "We learn from this that no prophet may introduce new laws from this time on" (Shabbat 104a). The prohibition became operative at the very moment of the promulgation at Sinai and unto eternity.

The Messiah like any other Jew will be subject to the Law and its precepts. Indeed, one of the proofs of the messiah will be his strict observance of the old Law, sure disproof of his attempt to introduce a new one. The true teaching about the messiah is thus summed up by the Rambam: "That he will study the Torah, perform the divine commandments like his ancestor David, in accord with both the Written and the Oral Laws" (Maimonides, Laws of Kingship, ch. 11).

So it was not because the Jews "misunderstood" the proofs, but rather because they understood them all too well that they could not accept Jesus either as prophet or as the Messiah. No miracle, however impressive, could sway the Jews towards recognition of Jesus in face of his claim of authority to change the Law or "fulfill" it, meaning abolish it, as it was ultimately abolished in Christianity. And these reasons are as valid today as they were then.

No, it was not the Jews who misunderstood, but Sholem Asch.

This should dispose of the myth of Sholem Asch as "Hebrew Scholar." As has been stated above, it is not incumbent upon a belletrist to be a man of learning or scholarship. But unless one is both learned and endowed, he dare not proclaim himself an authority and undertake to pontificate in so tremendous a matter as the dispute between Christianity and Judaism.

That Sholem Asch should have passed himself off as a "Hebrew scholar" is the literary joke of the century. The wonder is that he walked as surely as he did down the road through such heavy darkness. It is a case of what might perhaps be called "literary somnambulism."

It was noted above that Asch's appropriation of the role of scholar might best be explained in Freudian terms. Modern psychology also helps to enlighten another feature of *The Nazarene,* the bitter, venomous hatred Asch evinces toward the Jewish sages, scholars, and scribes figuring in his Christian tale. It is the well-known, deep-rooted hate of the ignoramus for the man of learning, that hate which the Talmud so vividly describes. Asch's hatred obscured his vision, and in his own blindness he has misled others into a misconception of some of the most precious values in Judaism.

Obviously, a framework for expressing his hatred is provided in the New Testament. There, the Pharisees are the antagonists of Jesus and his teachings, and Jesus propels his sharpest arrows at them. His favorite epithet for them is "hypocrites." In the mouths of Christians, therefore, the word "Pharisees," so highly

26

honored and justly revered among the Jews, becomes synonymous with "hypocrites." This aberration puts the New Testament ethics into a sharp misbalance. The Nazarene had kind words for all, mercy and affection for the worst of sinners, for the dregs of humanity, not excluding the execrated tax-gatherers. Only for the honorable and high principled Pharisees he had nothing but gall and wormwood.

The New Testament supplies Asch with a precedent for his vituperation of the Pharisees. True to the maxim that the servitor is often more extreme than the man he serves, he outdoes his master. Jesus takes the line of the Pharisee versus the virtuous sinner or the Pharisee versus the poor man, Asch names the opposing forces as the learned man and the ignoramus. To him the word "Pharisee" is synonymous with the sage, scholar and scribe, while the ignorant man (amhaaretz) is identified with the poor, oppressed, and persecuted.

The concepts of "sage" and "ignoramus" seem to weigh upon his mind above all else. In reading Asch, one might gain the impression that Jesus appeared solely to redeem the ignorant from the learned. One would think that the ignorant "man-of-the earth" among the Jews was not unlike the "untouchables" of India. We read:

"There were present many heads of synagogues, Rabbis and judges of local religious courts. They kept at a certain distance, these chaverim, from the common men-of-the-earth, who might contaminate them; and the latter did not dare to approach them. But the plain folk felt that this was their day, for it was their Rabbi Jesus whom the learned had assembled to hear" (166).

Elsewhere, Asch recounts the visit of Jesus to the home of the Pharisee Simon, where the sages have gathered to interrogate him. The common men are not permitted to enter, and are in fact driven from the house with sticks. Jesus, beholding this, asks of Simon, "Why will not thy servants and thy slaves permit the people to enter thy house?"

"And Simon answered: 'The people of the land are ignorant, the ritual is not strong in their hands, and they know not the laws of purity and impurity, therefore we are afraid that they may contaminate the house, the vessels or the bread'" (223).

Elsewhere Jesus is made to exclaim, "Behold and see, O my Father in heaven, how they have divided thy children into clean and unclean, pure and impure" (238).

27

On another occasion, Simon, son of Jonah, later to be known as Peter, stands before the rabbinic court, protesting:

"I am a simple man, a fisher of Kfar Nahum, not learned in the Law, but my heart yearneth toward my Father, the Creator . . . but the ways were twisted and many-branching whereby the learned men would have led me to the Creator of world. Who shall master them? Ye have divided God's Law into a thousand parts; who shall gather them up and hold them in his hand, save the learned who are occupied therewith day and night? For us, the unlettered and heavy-laden, God's word is closed with many seals. We wander lost in darkness, we beat our bodies like blind men against the walls without number which you have put up about our Father in heaven. And we hear from you only the warning words, 'Ye unclean hands, come not nigh to touch us!'" (245).

In another encounter with the populace, Jesus says, "Let us pray to our Father in heaven!" To which one responds, "Rabbi, we are ignorant men; we have not been taught to pray" (158).

Such is the manner in which Asch, with poor grace, indicts the Judaism of that far-off pre-Christian era, whereas within Christendom itself, almost two millennia later, untold millions remain totally ignorant and illiterate.

Scholarly pride and lust for power are attributed to the learned as the motives determining their attitude toward the men-of-the-earth, and toward Jesus, as well, whom he pictures as the redeemer of the unlearned. It would thus appear that learning was for the sages, as priesthood was for the priests, only a means for power and domination, oppression and exploitation. The sages allegedly saw in Jesus a peril to their status, a menace to the hegemony of the intellectual aristocracy. In flaming words Asch portrays the contempt of the rabbis for the unlearned.

Now one difficulty in reading Asch is that often one is at a loss to determine whether he says what he says out of ignorance or out of rancor. In either case he is deceitful and a teacher of error. He distorts Jewish history and maligns the Jewish faith.

To portray the Jewish sages as enemies of the ignorant masses —no greater distortion or libel is imaginable. The Jewish sages abhorred not the ignorant, but ignorance. The greatest ideal of the learned men of Israel in all ages was to spread the knowledge of Torah among the people. There was no more important divine command than "to learn and to teach." For the fact alone that the very being of the nation is rooted in *The Book*.

28

Among the pagan peoples in all ages it has been the tradition to keep science and culture from the common people. The priests alone were the guardians of wisdom. Only they were required to know the religious statutes, while the ordinary folk were not permitted to look into the divine "mysteries." This for many centuries has been true of the Catholics in regard to the Bible.

Pope Gregory VII of the eleventh century expressly thanked God that the Bible was written in Latin, a dead language, so that the common people would not be able to read it (Sheldon, *History of the Church*). It is a historical fact that from A. D. 325, when creed-making began, there was practically no Bible study in Christendom for 1260 years. Gogol, the noted Russian novelist (1809-1852), a good Christian, wrote: "To give a peasant school education in order to enable him to read the shallow pamphlets published by our European humanitarians is sheer nonsense." Never so among the Jews. The Torah directly and explicitly commands, "And thou shalt teach them unto thy children." It is incumbent upon every Jew both to learn the Law himself and to teach and transmit it to his descendants. This command has been observed by the entire people throughout all ages with such devotion, diligence, and love; so enthusiastically, passionately, fanatically, and withal so methodically, that no parallel thereto can be discovered in any other people. Nor will an alien and outsider ever be able to appreciate the full depth and import of so remarkable a phenomenon.

The Talmud relates of King Hezekiah: "He fixed a sword at the door of the Temple, exclaiming, 'Whoever does not study Torah shall be impaled on this sword!'" This is a hyperbolic expression of the rigorous commandment to study and acquire learning; "whoever" implying no distinction of caste or class. The result was, we are told further, that in the era mentioned "A search was made from Dan to Beersheba, and not a single illiterate was discovered; and further search was instituted from Gabbath to Antipatris, and they found no boy or girl, no man or woman, unacquainted with the laws of purity and impurity" (Sanhedrin 94).

This is a report of the state of affairs as far back as the days of the First Temple. Concerning the period of the Second Temple, the Talmud reveals:

"But for Joshua ben Gamala the Torah would have been forgotten from Israel. For at first if a child had a father, his father

29

taught him, and if he had no father he did not learn at all. . . . They then made an ordinance that teachers of children should be appointed in Jerusalem. . . . Even so, however, if a child had a father, the father would take him up to Jerusalem and have him taught there, and if not he would not go up to learn there. They therefore ordained that teachers should be appointed in each prefecture. . . . At length Joshua ben Gamala came and ordained that teachers of young children should be appointed in each district and each town, and that children should enter school at the age of six or seven" (Baba Bathra 21a).

The very sages misrepresented by Asch as monopolizers of Torah and wisdom were the men who ordained that a town which did not provide schooling for its young be outlawed and razed. They decreed that such a municipality be stringently warned, and if the warning be ignored that it be excommunicated, and placed in the category of the "banned city" of the Bible.

Was a similar state ever even remotely approached among any other people in history? Consider the law of "Hasagat gevul," providing against encroachment upon the business or trade of a person by invading his territory with a similar business or trade. It is a very strict law. Yet one activity is exempted from its provisions: instructing the young. No limit can be placed upon the number of teachers or schools in any one neighborhood.

Similar laws and decrees, too many to record here, from earliest times were directed towards the fulfillment of the sacred duty of propagating Torah knowledge and dissipating ignorance in the camp of Israel.

This was the situation in the period immediately preceding the appearance of Jesus. With utmost solicitude the sages saw to it that the children of the poor and the unlearned especially be given instruction in Jewish lore. The Talmud declares: "Be heedful of the children of the poor for from them proceedeth the Torah" (Aboth) ; and further: "Be heedful of the children of the ignorant, for from them proceedeth the Torah" (Sanhedrin 96a). Far from despising these elements, the sages looked to them as the national source of strength for Torah-learning and Torah-living.

As to the extent to which the sages strove to promulgate the Torah and to prevent its becoming the monopoly of one intellectual class, one may note the talmudic injunction against ac-

30

cepting fees for teaching Torah ("since you obtained it without cost, you must give it without price"), and the command that the Torah never become "the inheritance of the children of the sages." A large portion of the early sages were themselves poor workingmen and toiled laboriously for their bread.

As to the caste system of learned and unlearned that Asch saw in his imagination, let us again refer to the Talmud:

"The rabbis of Jabneh used to say: I was created by God, and my friend the ignorant man (man-of-the-earth) was created by God. I perform my labor in the city, and he performs his labor in the fields. I arise early to my work, and he rises early to his work. I cannot excel in his work, and he cannot excel in my work. If you should say that I receive greater reward and he (being less learned than I) lesser reward, we have learned that there is no difference whether one receives more or less, so long as one's devotion is turned toward God" (Berakhot 17a).

Even the most culturally mature nation of antiquity, Greece, knew nothing of such democratization of education and learning. There is a Greek legend that tells of the Muses reproaching a philosopher who had dreamt of their appearing before him in a brothel. They accused him of wishing to keep them there under the subterfuge of rendering them "popular." The moral of the legend is that there is something essentially aristocratic in learning and culture, and that popularizing them is prostituting them.

The exact opposite has been the Jewish approach to Torah or learning in ancient days and in all times thereafter. It was held to be a national tragedy when the Torah lay deserted in "a corner." When the child is only three, the Jewish father is obligated to teach him the first words of Hebrew lore. Never was the Torah intended for "philosophers" alone. It has been said that the Torah is not too small for the greatest, nor too great for the smallest. At a time when it was considered a near disgrace in Europe to be able to read and write—the true vocation was the ability to wield a sword—Jewish tots sat within ghetto walls and studied the Talmud. Judaism can best be described as a democracy of Torah. Nothing is more striking in the five books of the Mosaic Law than the constant reiteration of the need of learning.

"Moses commanded us a law, an inheritance of the congregation of Jacob" (Deut. xxxiii, 4). Not a legacy or possession of individuals or a class, but the inheritance of the entire congregation. This has been the teaching and the transmitted rule of all our wise men to the present day. The Jewish people have maintained the injunction in sanctity in all ages. Were the world not so filled with prejudice against the Jew, men would perceive here the greatest marvel of human history—a people that has succeeded in permeating all classes and strata of the population, high and low, rich and poor alike, with a high degree of culture and learning. The child in the cradle hears a Yiddish song proclaiming that Torah is the "best of all wares." Tuition fee has always been considered the most sacred expenditure in the budget of the Jew, the first item on it. Jews lacking the means to pay for education receive aid from the community.

An ancient Jewish law decrees that should two Jews be captive, one a king and the other a teacher, and there is money enough to redeem only one of the two, the teacher must be preferred to the king. What other ethnic group would promulgate such a law?

Rabbi Shimon ben Yohai said: "If thou hast seen cities uprooted from their places in the land of Israel, know thou that it was because they failed to maintain instruction in Torah, Scripture and Mishnah" (Eichah Rabbah).

When many nations still had no alphabet, and other nations had not yet come into existence, the Jews were already possessed of a system of popular education. It was compulsory, but maintained not by governmental power, but by moral force alone. Through mere moral force Jews have proved more successful in maintaining a high standard of popular education and culture than many more pretentious modern nations with all the powers of state.

This sanctified tradition of culture, for the people, the entire people, from the aristocracy down to the masses, was an established norm in Jewish life long before the Nazarene appeared in the world.

Disregarding all this, out of ignorance or malevolence, or both, Sholem Asch casts a shadow over the truest and most profound characteristic of Jewish democracy—a democracy utterly unique in its spiritual essences and holy ways.

Asch, clothed in belletristic righteousness, tries to create an aversion for Judaism through horror pictures of the practice of the laws of purity and impurity, clean and unclean. Certain laws in this category chiefly concerned the man-of-the-earth, who

32

was not sufficiently tutored or heedful in their observance. But "tahor" and "tame" have other connotations than "clean" and "unclean." A learned man, too, becomes unclean after coming in contact with a corpse or an unclean vessel, and another person, learned or ignorant alike, may not then touch him, on peril of transferring the state of impurity to himself. These laws were purely ritualistic, involving religious ideas, and had nothing to do with caste distinctions among humans. There is no purpose or justification, therefore, in the lament Asch places in the mouth of Jesus: "Behold and see, O my Father in heaven, how they have divided Thy children into clean and unclean, pure and impure!"

It is, of course, perfectly obvious that despite all efforts by the sages to disseminate learning, some of the people could not but remain backward. In those ancient days, with printing still in the distant future, it was not easy to reach into the more obscure corners or to carry culture to out-of-the-way places. As a result the existence of some cleavage between the wise and the unknowing was inevitable as it has been in all times and in all countries. One notes a poignant example of this during the bolshevik revolution in Russia, when the word "intelligent" or "intellectual" became a term of reproach, and the intelligentsia were persecuted to near annihilation. The Talmud frequently refers to this mutual suspicion and dislike. The learned man disapproved of the unlearned, but the ignoramus abhorred the sage. The Talmud describes the hatred of the ignorant for the learned, and especially the hatred of the wives of the ignorant for the sages, as greater than the hatred of the heathen for Israel (Pesahim 49).

A pointed reference to the mutual dislike between the learned and unlearned is carried in a remarkable utterance of Rabbi Akiba, who did not begin his education until he was forty years old. Said Rabbi Akiba, "When I was an ignorant man, I used to think that if I could get hold of a learned sage I would bite him like a donkey."

To this his disciples rejoined, "Don't say like a donkey, rabbi! Say, like a dog!"

To which Akiba replied, "When a dog bites he does not break the bones beneath the flesh, but the donkey does break the bones" (Pesahim 49).

The bite that under-educated, complex-ridden Sholem Asch took at the sages of Israel was indeed the bite of the donkey.

It was to be expected that Asch would, as a matter of course, propound the ethics taught by the Nazarene as superior to those espoused by Judaism, as is usual with uncritical Christian writers. This attitude dominates the book. All wickedness, real or imagined, he ascribes to the upholders of the Torah and the Sanctuary; all virtue, in deed and intent, he ascribes to the person of the Nazarene. The purpose is to support and prove the Christian doctrine that at the emergence of Christianity the Mosaic Law had already outlived its usefulness, had indeed accomplished the task assigned to it in the divine scheme, and could no longer influence humanity for the better. The times were ripe for a new dispensation, a New Testament, and the Nazarene had come down from heaven to provide it.

In contrasting Christian with Jewish ethics Asch is not unlike the country child on his first visit to a city department store. He is bewildered and taken in by the glitter of gold and silver tinsel. Indeed, wherever the Nazarene makes his appearance in the story, Asch, who figures in it as an ardent youth, manages to be on hand where any important utterance is made, and thickly exudes a juvenile sentimentality. Never profound, always prone to the decorative and grandiose, at times amusingly stentorian, he here plays on all his instruments of pathos and bathos, and employs his best hyperbolic style of frills and flourishes, which he strains to an insufferable shrill. With boyish recklessness, he toys with the destinies of the gods, and sets himself up as arbiter in a conflict as big as the world, a conflict in which are involved all the depths and heights of which the human spirit is capable.

He becomes as enthusiastic as a schoolboy over The Sermon on the Mount, rhapsodizing over it as though he were the first man to discover it, entirely oblivious of the fact that behind him lie two thousand years of experience, analysis, and criticism of the whole system of "Christian ethics," criticism emanating not only from Jews, but from clear-eyed Christians, some of whom are quite frank in admitting that the Nazarene introduced no useful innovations. Ernest Renan, who was a great admirer of the Nazarene, was nevertheless honest enough to acknowledge that Jesus added nothing to the teachings of Hillel the Elder. The Nazarene improved in no way on the moral fundamentals of Judaism. What was new in his doctrines on closer examination is revealed to be so extreme as actually to border on the immoral.

Again it is necessary to repeat that it is not our intent here, nor has it ever been a Jewish aim, to carry on an ideological strife with Christianity. If only the Christian attitude toward Judaism had been the same! But when one of our own rises up and lifts his hand against Judaism, whether in behalf of Christianity or of any other faith or philosophy, it becomes our sacred duty not only to ward off his blow, but to retaliate with all our might.

Christianity, which proclaimed itself the heir of Judaism, from the beginning set its wits to work to emulate Judaism in all things, ingeniously providing a scheme of parallelisms to events in the development of the Jewish faith. The focal point of the Old Testament is Mount Sinai and the giving of the Law: hence the Christian Bible also provided for a mountain, which the Nazarene ascended and from which he promulgated the fundamentals of his faith in a "Sermon on the Mount." We shall examine some of its provisions.

We read (Matthew v, 38-39): "Ye have heard that it hath been said, An eye for an eye and a tooth for a tooth. But I say unto you, that ye resist not evil: but whosoever shall smite thee on thy right cheek, turn to him the other also. . . . " Here we have a "declaration of war" by the new morality upon the old. The passage quoted has been uiversally recognized as the most beautiful and precious gem of Christian morality. Every Christian points proudly to this passage as the noblest expression of human morals. The Nazarene puts forth as an example of inferior morality to be discarded and superseded the opposed precept, the Torah's "eye for an eye, tooth for a tooth."

Because of the glaring light focussed by Jesus upon this precept, singling it out for special condemnation, the Jewish people have never been able, in the eyes of the Christian world, to exonerate themselves of the charge of clinging to a cruel morality. It has been of no avail to protest that both in the Torah itself and in the interpretation of the sages this phrase has meant payment in money, not an actual eye for an eye or tooth for a tooth. Suppose that one injures his neighbor's eye, causing it to lose, say, fifty percent of its vision. How can the culprit be made to pay in retaliation exactly fifty percent of the vision of one of his own eyes?

35

In spite of his objections to the old axiom, Jesus, in the same Sermon on the Mount, proceeds to dispose of eye and limb in the same "cruel" manner, but for a far lesser reason. We read:

"And if thy right eye offend thee, pluck it out and cast it from thee . . . and if thy right hand offend thee, cut it off and cast it from thee; for it is profitable for thee that one of thy limbs should perish, and not that thy whole body should be cast into hell"(29-30).

It would seem from this that for the sake of one's well-being in the world to come it is perfectly proper to pluck out an eye or cut off a hand; but to attain justice in this world, it is not. Which is the superior morality?

Let us now take a closer look at the principle of turning the other cheek. How does it work out, or rather, how would it work out in practice? Who will deny that from the first this has remained but an empty phrase among the Christians? No one has ever practiced it, no Christian in his right mind has ever adopted it as a mode of conduct.

Were the principle to be fully effectuated in daily life, society could not exist. Common sense and instinct taught the Christians in all generations that this was only a pretty phrase, beautiful but not to be used. Quietly, yet resolutely, they have ignored it, regarding it as morally inconsequential. From their first generations onward Christians have fought and slaughtered one another just as savagely as the ancient pagans. In all Christendom it is a "matter of honor" never to ignore an insult or a blow. Any aggrieved person who does not punch the jaw or blacken the eye of the aggressor is branded a worthless coward. The irony is even greater when one recalls that the Christians have even waged war in the name of the Nazarene.

Let us, however, assume that somewhere is to be found a Christian who has undertaken to observe this glorious precept, and determined never to return a blow for a blow. It is apparent that practical application of the precept would involve him in no end of complications. Where his own person is involved, the problem is, no doubt, simple enough. But what if, while enjoying a pleasant promenade, he beholds a wicked man beating another man, a sinner thrashing a saint, a strong man striking a weakling, a big fellow slapping a little chap? Shall he interfere to restrain or punish the aggressor, or shall he continue his walk unperturbed? If he comes to the rescue of the weaker and helps

36

him fight off the assailant, he is violating the Christian precept. But if he stands off indifferently, he is guilty of violating another command, albeit one from the Torah, "Thou shalt not stand idly by the blood of thy brother," but "thou shalt surely help him." It is to be assumed that the Christian would not choose to abandon one in distress.

It is possible to envisage still another situation. Two good Christians, both holding to the principle of turning the other cheek, are set upon by a wicked man who slaps one and then the other on the right cheek. Like the good Christians that they are, each will meekly offer his other cheek. But remembering that they are equally bound to come to the rescue of one in trouble, A may return the blow to the assailant for B, and B for A. The result will be somewhat as follows:

Each of the two offers his other cheek on his own behalf but delivers a blow for his friend. Meanwhile the assailant avails himself of the two other cheeks offered to him, and so blows are flying in all directions, while all the time the sacred admonition of Jesus is being dutifully observed by the two good Christians: is it not all reduced to an absurdity in the end?

Granting then that the good Christian is in duty bound to come to the rescue of his neighbor, there rises another question. If one may exercise violence, on behalf of another, why not in behalf of one's self? Is my soul of less worth simply because it is mine?

This is not the first time this and similar analyses have been made of the turn-your-other-cheek philosophy, to prove its logical faultiness, practical inadequacy and lack of justice. Yet Sholem Asch apparently never heard about it.

The turn-your-other cheek precept has often been probed in the light of the problem of war, when an enemy invades one's country. According to the Nazarene's teaching self-defense is forbidden. But when have Christians ever followed this course? Christian nations have not only failed to observe the law of nonresistance, but they themselves have often started wars on any pretext, just or otherwise. Since Europe was won over to Christianity, it has not become any less belligerent than it was before, and in recent centuries it has been the most martial of all the continents. Wars have been carried on not only by temporal governments, but also by papal states over which the Church enjoyed civil control.

37

The commandment of non-resistance to attack, and its even more difficult concomitant of turning the other cheek, prove on analysis to be in essence immoral, insomuch as such conduct gives a free hand to the wicked. The way is left open for the criminal; the innocent sufferer is bound hand and foot. Evil-doing is easy and attractive. Such a rule, if observed, would not tend to lessen but would be certain to increase the evils of the world. It would prove a blessing to all evil forces, particularly those that make a cult of evil and ridicule the morals of virtue. It is a principle that disarms justice and puts the good conscience in chains. It turns over the world and all therein to the wicked, the thief, the robber, and the murderer. If this is the moral norm of human co-existence, then all ideals of justice and righteousness, as we are wont to understand them, fall by the wayside; all teaching of reward and punishment, all our concepts of human and divine justice, lose their meaning.

Now, what has Judaism to say concerning the turning of the other cheek? In offering this and subsequent queries, it is not my intention to call Judaism to the witness stand, and by means of some clever questions and answers prove its "good character" and respectability. Judaism is too great and too immense to unlock, at the mere waving of a wand, the majestic portals of its many mansions and the doors leading to its store houses of wisdom. Its heights and depths cannot be unfolded in a single sitting. It is rather my purpose to place Sholem Asch on the witness stand and to show, albeit in barest outline what he has neglected and omitted, falsified and dissembled in his story with the evident intent of debasing Judaism and glorifying Christianity at its expense. From the ensuing argument the reader will understand that Asch's opus, despite any artistic merits it may possess, is but the outcrop of dishonest intent, and is, therefore, at bottom a fraudulent and sinful work.

Let us return to the point under consideration, the question of what Judaism has to offer anent the focal Christian commandment. As opposed to the unnatural and essentially immoral Christian precept of turning the other cheek, Judaism is concerned with the *first* cheek. The Talmud (Sanhedrin 58) says: "He who smites the cheek of his neighbor is even as one who smites the cheek of God." Not only the person is smitten, but his Maker, also, for man was created in God's image. Although the actual wording of this apophthegm is not "neighbor" but "Israelite," in keeping with Hebrew phraseology, it applies to all mankind.

In the same tractate (58b) it is said: "He who lifts his hand against his neighbor (here the actual word is used), even if he did not smite him, is called a wicked man and a sinner. In the end his hand will be broken."

How much nobler is the Jewish principle than the Christian! The onus here falls not upon him who gets slapped, but upon the slapper; not upon the victim, but upon the transgressor. The Jewish precept is the very opposite of the Christian: by implication a man is forbidden to turn the other cheek, or the first one either for that matter. In offering his cheek for assault he is as one who would offer the cheek of God to human mistreatment, thus subjecting the Lord to a creature of flesh and blood.

The Jewish commandment is directed not against the righteous man, but against the wicked man, the sinner. The sinner is reminded of the sacred concept that man was created in the image of God, and by the same token the victim is elevated to the virtual status of Godhood. The divine element in man is brought to the forefront, while at the same time no violence is done to human nature. The offender is warned of divine punishment, while the way is left open for punishment by man.

In practice all Christendom orders its life according to the Jewish principle, not the Christian. No Christian, whether gentleman or common man will suffer a blow with impunity. When abused he will strike back. The court will provide punishment for the culprit, not because pain has been suffered—for the pain may itself be of slight consequence—but because human dignity has been insulted.

Nevertheless, the Jewish principle, noble in its practicality, and practical in its nobility, remains unsung and unhonored in the Christian world. And it is not even mentioned in Asch's work in the appropriate passages of dispute between Christianity and Judaism. For his obvious purpose is not to defend Judaism, much less to extol it, but to disparage it in contrast with Christianity.

Judaism not only refused to accept the doctrine of non-resistance to evil and subjection to the wicked, but it proclaimed to the fullest the need for meting punishment to the transgressor who corrupts God's wonderful world. The sages of the Mishnah say (Aboth V) : "With ten Sayings (words of the Lord) the world was created. What does this teach us? Could it not have been created with one Saying? It is to make known that severe

39

punishment will befall the wicked who corrupt the world that was created with ten Sayings, as well as the goodly reward that will be bestowed upon the just who preserve the world that was created with ten Sayings."

Once more let us inquire: According to which system of ethics is the life of Christian nations conducted—the Christian or the Jewish? The United States of America is customarily termed a "Christian country." But the Declaration of Independence does not declare it the duty of the people to yield to tyranny, but rather states that their duty is to rise against it.

Every Christian land has its system of criminal law, its police and courts and judges, its prisons; and in most countries there is capital punishment. All these systems have been established on a principle that completely negates and repudiates the Nazarene's teaching of turning the other cheek. Christendom conducts itself according to the Jewish principle of crime and punishment, even though its specific statutes are not those of Judaism, nor is its spirit that of the Jews.

We may cite here another much tooted principle of Christian ethics, belonging in the same category, the commandment—Love thine enemy. Never has Christianity succeeded in showing, in theory or in practice, how this form of conduct, so completely at variance with human nature, is possible of realization. An obvious objection is, if we must love our enemies, what are we to offer our friends? Besides, this, too, is a teaching that in all respects favors the wicked: he enjoys the advantage of his hatred toward me, plus the added advantages of the love I am bidden to bear for him.

More modest but not flying in the face of normal human nature is the Jewish principle concerning a personal enemy (Proverbs xxiv, 17): "Rejoice not when thine enemy falleth, and let not thy heart be glad when he stumbleth; lest the Lord see it and it displease him, and he turn away his wrath from him (unto thee)" (Aboth iv, 24).

In the same Book (xxv, 21) we find: "If thine enemy be hungry, give him bread to eat; and if he be thirsty, give him water to drink." Exodus (xxiii, 4-5) commands: "If thou meet thine enemy's ox or ass going astray, thou shalt surely bring it back to him again. If thou see the ass of him that hateth thee lying under its burden, thou shalt forbear to pass by him; thou shalt surely release it with him." With human nature what it is, even

40

this may be difficult of accomplishment, but it is not beyond human capacity.

Yet, how much of this is fulfilled by the Christian world, which vaunts itself against Judaism because of its "love thine enemy" attitude?

It should be noted, however, that among Christians, too, one occasionally comes upon clear-eyed men with courage to take a sane and realistic estimate of that strange withdrawal from the world called "Christian ethics." Rev. Lou Ray Call, minister of the South Nassau Unitarian Church, Baldwin, N. Y., in a sermon on the Sermon on the Mount praised it as the "Christian ideal embodying many fundamental moral principles," but he opposed any overly literal interpretation of it.

"When you tear that great sermon out of its context," he asserted, "and apply it in our place, time and circumstance, it is woefully impractical. Those who preach it do not practice it and they have no expectation of trying to practice it, for if they did they would be summarily entombed in wards for the mentally ill." (N. Y. Times, June 30, 1952).

In brief, Christians only pay lip service to the florid pronouncements and sparkling dicta of their own Christian morality, abusing the Jews at the same time. But their lives, their conduct, and their manners are firmly grounded in the ethical principles of Judaism.

Yet along comes Sholem Asch with the stale wares of a firm long bankrupt, and presents them to the Jews as an extraordinary, unique treasure!

5

Poverty and Wealth

Addressing ourselves to other phases of Christian morality—the ethics of property, of poor and rich, of labor and pleasure, of the world and its glories, of life and its joys—we find the same gulf separating the two faiths in their outlook and philosophy, and the same tragic contradiction between Christian pronouncements and Christian practice.

Nothing is so completely berated and condemned in Christian lore as is wealth. Not only errant wealth, gained through ex-

41

ploitation, rapine, or chicanery, but even honestly earned riches. The Nazarene's ideal state was that of poverty. By his very possession of wealth, the rich man is automatically evil; while solely because of his indigence, the poor man is a saint. There is a parable in the Gospels of a rich man and a poor man. The rich man has committed no transgressions, done no one any injury. He has performed many good deeds. Nevertheless, on his death, he is at once dispatched to hell. On the other hand, the poor man, whose only virtue is his poverty, at his death goes straight to paradise.

"It is easier for a camel to go through the eye of a needle, than for a rich man to enter into the Kingdom of God," runs a New Testament saying of the Nazarene (Matthew xix, 24). Also: "Blessed are ye poor! For yours is the Kingdom of God. . . .But woe to you that are rich! For you have your consolation" (Luke vi, 20, 24).

The rich are also bidden to take their possessions and distribute them among the poor. And that is just what the earliest Christians had to do. No one was admitted into the fraternity without first relinquishing all his belongings to the communal store; for the first Christians lived in a commune.

Thus it is obvious that Christianity's highest virtue is poverty, and its most grievous sin is riches. One would, therefore, expect to find Christians cherishing poverty. One would expect a Christian civilization to be based upon the ideals of simplicity and renunciation of wealth. But what is Christian reality?

An honest, forthright Christian scholar, William Rathbone Gregg, author of "The Creed of Christendom," offers this answer:

"Yet in spite of this emphatic warning, riches have been the most general pursuit of Christians in all ages and among all classes. . .among the accredited teachers of the Gospel as well as among the mere following flock of lay disciples. Nay more, the most really Christian nations have been, and still are, the most devoted to the pursuit of gain. Nor do they even affect to fancy that they are wrong or disobedient in thus eagerly striving for that wealth which their Master so distinctly ordered them to eschew and dread; they put aside or pass by his teaching with a sort of staring unconsciousness, as if it in no way concerned them. . . .The most respectable of the religious world give one day to their Saviour, and six days to their ledger; the most pious banker, the purest liver, the most benevolent nobleman, never

42

dreams of despising riches, or of casting from him his superfluous possessions. On the contrary, he is grateful to God for them."

Riches in themselves are not the ideal of the Jew. Moderation is the outstanding aim of Jewish ethics. "Who is rich? He who rejoices in his portion" (Aboth iv). Declares the Talmud: "One of eight things of which too much is unhealthy and little is good, is riches, for it keeps one from studying the Law. Through possession of too much gold and silver did the Jews come to make the Golden Calf" (Yoma 86). Elsewhere it says: (Bets. 92): "The wealthy folk of Babylon will descend to Gehinnom"—but not because of their mere possession of riches, but for their niggardliness toward the poor.

The wise men of Israel considered poverty the greatest human curse. They compared the poor man to one dead. The man afflicted with poverty, they said, is one to whom all the world's agonies seem to have attached themselves. And again: If one were to place all the afflictions on one scale and poverty on the other, the latter would outweigh them all. The underlying idea being that the poor man, unable to perform good deeds, is incapable of becoming a complete man, of realizing a full life of human dignity. The best part of man, the generous and constructive pattern of personality, must wither at the root. Perhaps this is the motive behind the teaching of the sages that the poor are also under obligation to give to charity.

Jesus taught: "And if a man will contend with thee in judgment and take away thy coat, let go they cloak also unto him" (Matthew v, 40). "If thou wilt be perfect, go sell what thou hast, and give to the poor and thou shalt have treasure in heaven" (ibid. xix, 21).

Against the above sparkling dicta the Mosaic Law offers far more modest fare: "Each man as the gift of his hand (according to his possessions)"; "according to the blessing that God hath given thee." The sages, specifically Maimonides (Deoth 5), aver: "One is not permitted to dedicate or disown all one's possessions, so as thereafter to become a burden on the community."

Yet despite this more modest formula, honest Christians recognize, with envy, that the Jews from time immemorial have exceeded all other nations in the extent of their charitable giving. The idea of charity is the peculiar gift of Judaism to the world.

Of labor the Nazarene said: "Therefore I say to you, be not

solicitous for your life, what you shall eat, nor for your body, what you shall put on. . . . Behold the birds of the air, for they neither sow, nor do they reap, nor gather into barns, and your heavenly Father feedeth them. Are not you of much more value than they?" (Matthew vi, 25, 26).

We must reiterate the same old question: does this accord with the actual life of Christians? Does it at any point touch Christian reality? Is this more than just a glittering phrase? In real life Christians do exactly the opposite. They continually preach the virtue of providing for one's future, of putting something away for a rainy day. In most Christian lands the people are provided with savings banks and every sort of social security and insurance. The lot of the person who lives from hand to mouth, expends all his earnings, and gives no thought for the morrow is an unfortunate one. He is in a bad way indeed when he is compelled to apply for aid, to borrow, or request charity.

This much of the poorer classes. As to the wealthy, it is quite evident they do not rely on miracles. They amass goods from generation to generation until a family fortune is accumulated. The gigantic banks found in every city and town in Christian lands are proof that the Christians do not heed the command of their Messiah and God, that one give no thought for the morrow. Yet this command is part of the Sermon on the Mount, which the Christians pronounce the most sacred declaration of their faith.

The Jewish teaching is the exact opposite. Says the Talmud (Kiddushin 82a): "A man should always teach his son a cleanly craft, and let him pray to Him to whom riches and possession belong, for there is no craft wherein there is not both poverty and wealth; for poverty comes not from a man's craft, nor riches from a man's craft, but all is according to his merit."

Thus did the sages establish the notion, that though the extent of a person's livelihood is guided by Providence, nevertheless each man must learn how to earn a living, lest the reliance on the divine become unnatural. Thus a fine balance is established between the real and the ideal.

Of course, all bounty and all earthly goods have their origin in the merciful goodness of God, and Providence provides all creatures with their needs. "The eyes of all wait upon Thee, and Thou givest them their food in due season" (Psalms cxiv, 15). Says the Psalmist: "Cast thy burden upon the Lord, and He will

44

sustain thee" (lv, 23). But this does not mean that man need do no labor. Contrarily, it is also said in Psalms (cxxviii, 2): "When thou eatest the labor of thy hands, happy shalt thou be, and it shall be well with thee." To this the sages have added that he who lives by the labor of his hand is greater than one who is pious and Godfearing.

Christianity, preaching as it does a carefree existence, at least by implication, deprecates labor. But Judaism has always glorified and sanctified labor. "Great is labor—which is attested in the fact that even Adam tasted no food before performing labor. For God first put Adam in the Garden of Eden 'to dress it, and to keep it,' and then followed the command: 'Of every tree of the Garden thou shalt eat,'" etc.

"Great is labor"—said Rabbi Tarphon (Abot de Rabbi Nathan, xi) "for God did not cause his Divine Presence to dwell among the Jews until they had performed labor; for it is said: 'And they shall make me a sanctuary, and I will dwell in the midst of them'" (Exodus xxv, 8).

The Christian is bidden to rely for food on miracles, but Judaism teaches: "One is not permitted to rely on a miracle." And further: "How lowly was this Man, that the order of the Creation was changed on his account." In other words, a miracle on one's behalf is a mark of demerit rather than merit. For heaven is not content to disturb the orderly processes of nature, except in moments of great divine revelation such as the crossing of the Red Sea, that man may recognize God's greatness.

Once again we pause to ask: Does the Christian world, in its pursuit of food, in its industrial and commercial activities, in its creative achievements in general, live its life in accordance wth the passive spirit of Christianity, or with the active, energizing spirit of Judaism?

The Christian citations here adduced are by no means singular instances only superficially alike. They are not rare growths in scattered acres but samples of a vast pattern covering the entire field of man's life on this earth. They are spurts of one source, limbs of one body, part of a philosophy of life even more fully expressed in passages like the following:

"Love not the world, neither the things that are in the world. If any man loves the world, the love of the Father is not in him. For all that is in the world, the lust of the flesh and the lust of the

eyes and the pride of life, is not of the Father, but is of the world"
(I John xi, 15-16). Or:

"Ye adulterers and adulteresses, know ye not that the friendship of the world is enmity with God? Whosoever, therefore, will
be a friend of the world is the enemy to God" (James iv, 4).

These expressions by John and by James, brother of Jesus,
are the basic formulation of the Christian spirit, the real soul of
the Christian faith. It is a spirit essentially antagonistic to the
world and to all manifestations of human living. As a weltan-
schauung it is deeply pessimistic, with overtones of Buddhist
abnegation of all existence.

In contrast, note the joyousness which marks the Jewish outlook. God created the world and saw that it was good. All creation
chants hymns of praise—"When the morning stars sang together,
and all the sons of God shouted for joy!" (Job xxxviii, 7): "The
sun is as a bridegroom coming out of his chamber, and rejoiceth
as a strong man to run his course" (Psalms xix, 6) : "He is God,
that formed the earth and made it, He established it, He created
it not a waste, He formed it to be inhabited" (Isaiah lxv, 18).

The Torah commands all to observe the laws and statutes
"in order that thy days be long and it be well with thee."

The Midrash asserts that the Torah begins with the letter
"beth" and not with "alef," because "alef" is the first letter of
"arur" (accursed) while beth is the first of "baruch" (blessed).
Creation, the earth, is a blessing.

"Whoever despises the good life in this world, is marked by
an evil omen," says the Tana D'be Elijahu. His punishment will be
great, for he denies the goodness of God and despises His gifts.

The Midrash tells of God's determining to create man and of
the ministering angels protesting, saying, "Sovereign of the universe! 'What is man that Thou art mindful of him, and the son of
man, that Thou thinkest of him?" (Psalms viii, 5). "If so," said
He to them, " 'sheep and oxen, all of them' (ib. 8), why were
they created; why were 'the fowl of the air and the fish of the
sea' (ib. 9) created? A tower full of good things and no guests—
what pleasure has its owner in having filled it?" (Genesis Rabbah
viii, 6).

The Jewish view is not that to glorify God one must deny
the world, but rather that we glorify God when we accept the
world and make it holy. The extent to which the sages forbade
self-imposed restraints against enjoying the pleasures of the world

46

can be gleaned from references such as the following, of which there is no end in the literature of Judaism:

"Every man will have to give a full accounting to heaven for all permitted foods his eye looked upon, and he did not eat of them" (Jer. Talmud).

"God showed His love for Israel, in that He adjured them not to stultify themselves by too great restraint" (Yalkut Torah).

The philosophy of Judaism is essentially a joyous one. Joy in God, in His universe, in its bounties and uses, in the Law and its divine commands. The noblest joy of all is that which comes from performing these commands.

The cult of joy in Judaism found its highest expression in the movement called Chassidism. It is related that the chassidic Rabbi Aaron Karliner wore beautiful garments not, God forbid, out of pride, but because when poor clothes cover the body they induce depression of spirit and sadness; and the Holy Presence does not descend to dwell where sadness dwells.

Furthermore, said Rabbi Aaron Karliner, "When it is said that a man must bear joy in his heart, the real meaning of this is— a Jew must be completely happy for the fact alone that he is a Jew. This is the chief joy. The Jew who has no such feeling is rebellious to the God who created him a Jew. Such a man has never understood the full meaning of the blessing, 'that Thou hast not made me a heathen.' "

The late Lubavitcher, Rabbi Joseph Isaac, was once asked by Sigmund Freud, *"What is Chasidus?"* He replied, "There are two large continents, the intellect and the heart—the theory and the practice. But the stormy ocean of daily life divides them— Chasidus is the bridge that unites them. It not only teaches us and shows us the beauty and the holiness of the world but it helps us to translate our ideal into reality. Above all, it shows us very clearly what a Jew's purpose in life is."

The sacred, Torah-sanctioned idea of enjoyment of life allowed the Jew normal satisfaction of natural desires. Natural desires dammed up by excessive prohibitions and asceticism drive man toward unnatural channels. Jewish life, with its measured rituals, especially its graceful and mannered family life, has often been the envy of those hostile to the Jewish people.

The difference in outlook of the two religions is so vast and irreconcilable that the juxtaposition of single passages from either sometimes is sufficient to illuminate the gulf separating them.

47

It is like contrasting black and white, light and darkness to contrast the following passages emanating from the supreme source in either faith:

Moses: "It (the Law) is not in heaven" (Deut. xxx, 12).

Jesus: "My Kingdom is not of this world."

From which flow logically, like a corollary from a mathematical theorem, the following:

The Psalmist: "The meek shall inherit the earth."

Jesus: "Blessed are the poor in spirit: for theirs is the Kingdom of Heaven" (Matthew v, 3), though the preceding is also embraced.

Or: "Do not keep aloof from the community" (Hillel, Aboth ii, 5). "And be not conformed to this world" (Paul, Romans, xii, 2).

Indeed, the two faiths are as far apart as heaven and earth. The vast implications of the two outlooks are self-evident. Some Christian philosophers have declared in despair that the Christian ideal—the Kingdom of God—cannot be realized within the limits of the earthly life and earthly community. But the Jew, despite his cruel fate at the hands of all peoples in all ages, has not ceased to pray, hope and strive that he may speedily behold. . . "When the world will be perfected under the Kingdom of the Almighty" (daily prayer).

Only one who bears in mind that the *leitmotif* of Jesus' teaching was the imminent end of the world can comprehend the true meaning of Christianity. Jesus came on the scene to preach that the universe was on the verge of extinction, and that only those who believed in him would be saved, salvation meaning eternal life in the hereafter. His apostles and disciples were, in his own days, awaiting the end of the world, and were prepared for it at every moment. From their attitude derived the pessimistic outlook of Christian teaching, with its adjurations to desist from labor, saving, ordinary care, and to relinquish property. Nothing, of course, could be taken along to the other world, and here below no one to whom one might bequeath his possessions would remain.

"Verily I say unto you," Jesus warned, "that there be some of them that stand here, which shall not taste of death till they have seen the Kingdom of God come with power" (Mark ix, 1). On one occasion, while dispatching his emissaries abroad to preach his doctrines, Jesus spoke: "Verily, I say unto you, Ye shall not have gone over the cities of Israel, till the Son of man be

48

come" (Matthew x, 23). And again: "Verily, I say unto you, that this generation shall not pass, till all these things be done" (Mark xiii, 30).

Similarly, Paul writes: "But this I say, brethren, the time is short; it remaineth, that both they that have wives be as though they had none; and they that weep, as though they wept not; and they that rejoice, as though they rejoiced not; and they that buy, as though they possessed not; and they that use this world, as not abusing it; for the fashion of the world passeth away" (I Corinthians vii, 29-31). They believed implicitly, and therefore preached that the existing world was passing; that the physical world as created in the first six days would cease to exist; that believers in Christ remaining in it at the day of doom would be transported to the "kingdom of heaven"; those dead would rise from their graves; that those saved would live on, not in body but in spirit. As Paul said: "Now this I say, brethren, that flesh and blood cannot inherit the kingdom of God. . . . Behold, I show you a mystery: We shall not all sleep, but we shall all be changed . . . and the dead shall be raised incorruptible, and we shall be changed" (I Corinthians xv, 50-52). Therefore, from the earliest times, the true Christian inclined toward asceticism and abnegation of all existence for himself and all humanity.

To escape mundane temptations, some early agitators, later to become the early Christian saints, went to live in the wilderness. Some saints who desired even more separation from worldly concerns lived for years atop pillars. Later the institution of the monastery arose, providing the true Christian with seclusion, with removal from the world—"not alone from pleasure and possessions and honor, but also from family life, citizenship, and society." To this day such conduct has remained the true ideal of Christianity.

Similar denial and negation of the world has been impossible in Judaism. The Torah found a place for those inclined to asceticism, condoning it but never encouraging it. When a man chose to be a "nazarite," he was called "holy to the Lord"; but he was commanded to offer three sacrifices at one time, "for that he sinned by reason of the dead" (also translated: "for that he sinned against a soul") (Numbers vi, 11). The Talmud (Nedarim 10a) comments: "That is because he afflicted himself through abstention from wine. This, then, can be argued from the minor to the major. If one who afflicted himself only in respect of wine

49

is called a sinner, how much more so one who ascetically refrains from everything? Hence one who fasts too often is called a sinner."

Professor Vincent A. McCrossen, Christian author of *The New Renaissance of the Spirit* (1949), (with the imprimatur of high American Catholic Church dignitaries), writes nostalgically of the Christian Middle Ages:

"The emphasis of the medieval world was, therefore, away from everyday reality. . . . No age has been less devoted to the matters of earth than was the medieval period at its height. Its very soul was Christian. . . . The business and commerce and money making in which Rome had gloried were no longer held to be the most admirable pursuits of men. The ancient Roman cities, the arenas and aqueducts and bridges, fell into decay. . . . Hundreds of thousands of men and women, following the advice of Christ and the teachings of St. Paul, that virginity is a state preferable to marriage, entered the convents and cloisters and monasteries, to spend their lives in fasting and prayers, in self-mortification and penance. . . . There are numerous examples of kings and queens, princes and princesses, who gave away all that they had, kingdoms and powers and riches, to become humble workers in the vineyard of the Lord."

The historian's comment that the expression "Christian civilization" is a misnomer is fully justified, insomuch as the world and Christianity negate each other. "Christianity completely cancels out the world," writes Carl Lowith in "Meaning of History" (144), adding: "If Jesus is the example for the Christian to follow, the world will never go in his ways." The same judgment has been pronounced throughout the generations, by great and small, pious, "neutral," and heretical. Soren Kierkegaard, the great Danish theologian who regarded himself as "a missionary to the Christian world itself whose aim was to bring Christianity to the Christians," wrote: "Most people believe that the Christian commandments were by design made too difficult, just as one sets the clock a half hour ahead to be certain not to rise too tardily."

But they seem to have overwound the clock.

The Swiss historian, Jacob Burckhardt, called Christianity an ascetic faith which had its early success among the heathen because its upholders were able to negate the world and its goods and become "heroes of the wilderness." But later Christianity made its compromise with the world and thereby lost its influence. The discrepancy between Christian profession and Christian practice has long been the target for devastating criticism by the atheistic and unbelieving, constituting a major cause for the decline not only of Christianity but of religion generally throughout the western world. Witness Karl Marx:

"Is not every minute of your practical life a denial of your religious theory? Do you consider it wrong to appeal to a court when someone swindles you? The apostle declares you may not do this. Do you turn your right cheek when someone smites your left, or do you complain to the authorities? The Gospels prohibit the latter . . . Are not the majority of your laws and civil regulations concerned with property? Yet you have been admonished that your treasures are not of this world" (Marx-Engels Miscellany, I, 242). Friedrich Nietzsche's glib tongue expressed the matter most concisely and artfully: "The last Christ died on the cross."

The result is that Christianity, which is not a religion of life and which preaches commandments in eternal conflict with man and the universe, has created a permanent, unbridgeable contradiction between Jesus, Christianity, and the Christian, exposing the Christian to the inescapable charge of hypocrisy, while causing a dichotomy within the Christian soul itself, that tragic tension which sometimes has been termed "the agony of Christianity."

Christianity boasts no trace of that feeling of completeness and spiritual wholeness which is the heritage of the Jew within Judaism. In the deepest and truest sense of the terms, Christianity is the Law of Death, Judaism the Law of Life.

But of all this greatness and glory of Judaism there is not a trace in Asch's work on the Nazarene, not a sound nor the echo of a sound.

6

"Human, All Too Human"

It is not surprising that ordinary people have been unable to realize the supernatural and superhuman commandments of the Nazarene, since, when confronted by an actual test of his precepts, Jesus himself transgressed them.

He preached the doctrine of turning the other cheek, but when, according to the Gospels, a servitor of the high priest smote

51

him on the cheek, he did not turn the other, but asked, "Why smitest thou me?" (John xvii, 23).

In the Sermon on the Mount he bade men love their enemies and bless those who cursed them. But on lower ground Jesus uttered a parable concerning himself: "But those mine enemies, which would not that I should reign over them, bring hither, and slay them before me" (Luke xix, 27). Vindictively Jesus said, "For judgment I am come into this world, that they which see not might see, and that they which see might be made blind" (John xi, 39). Belligerently he declared: "Think not that I am come to send peace on earth; I came not to send peace, but a sword" (Matthew x, 34).

The most awful abuse, maledictions, and threats of dire punishment he poured upon the heads of his antagonists. "Woe unto you, scribes and Pharisees!" was his sole reaction to those who sought to defend their ancestral faith; "Ye serpents, ye generation of vipers! . . . That upon you may come all the righteous blood shed upon the earth, from the blood of righteous Abel unto the blood of Zacharias, son of Borachias!" (Matthew xxiii, 29, 33, 35).

Not just his immediate opponents, the scribes and the Pharisees, but all those who would not believe in him were branded outcasts and were subjected to divine punishment: "He that believeth on the Son has everlasting life; and he that believeth not on the Son shall not see life; but the wrath of God abideth on him" (John iii, 36). This is stated in another form (John iii, 5): "Verily, verily, I say unto thee, except a man be born of water and the Spirit, he cannot enter into the Kingdom of God."

In amazing contrast, the Pharisees, whom Jesus hated with such stinging hate, made the broadminded and humane pronouncement: "The righteous of all nations have a share in the world to come"—and not the Jews alone.

King Solomon said: "As for the alien, who does not belong to thy people Israel but who came from a distant land . . . when he comes and turns in prayer towards this temple, then do thou listen. . . ." (I Kings viii, 41-43); while in glaring contradiction the Nazarene showed himself highly prejudiced to aliens, members of other nations: "These twelve Jesus sent forth, and commanded them, saying, 'go not into the way of the Gentiles, and into any city of the Samaritans enter ye not but go rather to the lost sheep of the house of Israel'" (Matthew x, 5, 6).

Compare also the teaching of the soundly accursed Pharisees;

"Despise not any man" (Aboth iv, 3); and of the Talmud in Abodah Zarah: "Even a heathen that studies the Torah is equal to a high priest"; with the terrible sentence of the Nazarene: "If a man abide not in me, he is cast forth as a branch, and is withered; and men gather them, and cast them into the fire, and they are burned " (John xv, 6). This terrible pronouncement was later to be employed by the Church to establish the theory of the Inquisition and justify the practice of burning at the stake.

"Ye have heard that it hath been said, thou shalt love thy neighbor, and hate thine enemy. But I say unto you, Love your enemies, bless them that curse you" (Matthew v, 43-44), said Jesus in the Sermon on the Mount. But the Gospels are aflame with words of hatred for Jesus' enemies, or those considered his enemies. On occasion he displayed an appetite for sweet revenge as any mere mortal, as we shall discover in the parable of the Good Samaritan.

The Torah (Leviticus xviii, 19; quoted in Matthew without credit) commands: "Thou shalt love thy neighbor as thyself"—which has always been proclaimed by the sages as the basic tenet of the Law. Jesus, who joined the sages in praise of the principle, was once asked: "And who is my neighbor?" This well known parable was his reply: A man traveling along the road was assailed by two robbers who plundered and beat him, leaving him half dead on the way. A priest who happened to pass saw the injured man and promptly crossed the road to avoid him. Then came a Levite who also looked and crossed the road. When a Samaritan passed, however, he was touched by pity; he bound the stranger's wounds, carried him to a secure spot, and tenderly cared for him. Thus, the Samaritan was the exemplary neighbor.

Let us note the three persons mentioned in the narrative who beheld the unfortunate victim. They are a priest, a Levite, and a Samaritan. Since the first two are Jews of the two "higher" subdivisions in the hierarchy of Jewish peoples, one expects the third to be a Jew as well, and an ordinary Israelite to complete the succession. However, the moral exemplar is neither an Israelite, nor even a Jew but a Samaritan, a member of a tribe which hated the Jews, and which they despised. Jesus exalts even above the priests a tribe whose very name was anathema among ancient Jews, implying at the same time that a Jew was incapable of a simple act of mercy.

Thus, in a simple parable Jesus found occasion to exercise

his spite against Jewry. "Good Samaritan" has remained a byword among Christians to this day, and many churches bear the name, "Church of the Good Samaritan." Because of Jesus' vindictiveness, there is no possibility of Christians ever naming a house of worship, "Church of the Good Israelite."

And the Nazarene was not above exercising vindictiveness even against a tree. When Jesus was suffering the pangs of hunger, he was unable to restrain his earthly human emotions. Once, "In the morning, as he turned into the city, he hungered; and when he saw a fig tree in the way, he came to it, and found nothing thereon, but leaves only, and said unto it, Let no fruit grow on thee henceforward forever. And presently the fig tree withered away" (Matthew xxi, 18-19). In another version in the Gospels, it is made plain that it was not the season for figs.

Did the innocent tree deserve this cruel punishment? It only fulfilled its nature that at that time of year it bore no fruit. If it were the intention of the Nazarene to display a miracle through the incident, he could just as readily have shown his powers by commanding the tree at once to bring forth fruit, out of season. He could have acted like the son of Rabbi Jose, who, wishing to provide food for his father's workers, approached a fig tree and cried: "Fig tree, fig tree, send forth your fruit, so that my father's workers may eat thereof!" Upon which, says the Talmud (Taanit 24), the tree produced fruit before its time, and the men ate thereof.

"A certain woman, whose young daughter had an unclean spirit, heard of him, and came and fell at his feet. The woman was a Greek of Syro-Phoenician ancestry; and she besought him that he would cast forth the devil out of her daughter. But Jesus said unto her, Let the children first be filled; for it is not meet to take the children's bread and cast it unto the dogs" (Mark vii, 25-27).

But the Psalmist, many generations before Jesus, spoke differently: "The Lord is good to all, and, His tender mercies are over all His works" (Psalms cxlv, 9).

The much maligned Pharisees declared: "It is incumbent upon one to feed the poor of the Gentiles as one does the Jewish poor" (Gittin 61a); and the midrashic scholars said (Tana D'be Elijahu): "I call upon heaven and earth as witness that, whether Gentile or Jew, man or woman, manservant or maidservant, upon everyone rests the Divine Presence in accordance with his actions."

54

There is no limit to the number of contrasts that can thus be offered between Jewish and Christian ethics; with always a comfortable margin on the credit side of Judaism.

In the nineteenth century there lived in Europe a great Christian poet and thinker, Soren Kierkegaard. His characterization of Christianity is penetrating. He said: "It is easier to become a Christian when one is not a Christian than to become a Christian when one does already belong to them."

It apparently was difficult for even "Christ" to be a Christian.

7

Man as "God"

With the cunning stealth of a nocturnal marauder Sholem Asch insinuates the principle of Jesus' divinity into his book, knowing well that in attempting to shatter the principle of Divine Unity he is attacking the very foundations of the Jewish faith and Jewish existence.

The unity of God is the central absolute of Judaism; its beginning and end. This principle is enunciated in the profession of faith—"Hear, O Israel, the Eternal is our God, the Eternal is one"—which is Israel's declaration to the world. God is one, single and indivisible, and beside Him there is no other. The "one" in the Shema is the Jewish denial of any other form of religion, whether polytheism, dualism, or pantheism. "One" is the focal principle, from which derive all the other ideas in Judaism—the unity of the universe, the unity of mankind, the unity of morality. The entire Jewish consciousness, individual and collective, depends upon it. The Jew is born with the One and dies with the One. The One is with him in his rising up and in his lying down. Twice a day, in the morning and in the evening prayers, he recites the Shema with its emphasis on One. This belief is also enunciated in the benediction for the opening of the ark and the reading of the Torah on Sabbath and festivals. The Mishnah and the Talmud open with the question, "From what time does one begin the reading of the evening Shema?" And when the Jew offers the highest and most magnificent manifestation of his Jewishness, when he goes to his death for the sake of his faith, his

55

last words betwixt earth and heaven constitute the flaming outcry, "Hear, O Israel, the Eternal is our God, the Eternal is one!" The Jew utters the "One" with a special intonation and with a fervor into which he pours his entire soul.

The Shema with its sacred "One" has not remained a mere abstraction, a belief, or a prayer. The Jew has found it imbedded in the structure of his body, woven into the very web of his flesh. We learn:

"In the three portions that comprise the Shema there are eighteen mentions of the name of God, corresponding to the eighteen vertebrae of the spine; there are also 248 words, to correspond with the 248 members of the human body:—in consonance with the words of Psalms, 'All my bones declare, Who is like unto Thee among the gods, O Eternal'" (Sefer Haeshkol i, 5).

And under this Judaic structure, abuilding from Abraham to the last Jew who this very evening will retire with the Shema on his lips, Asch, like a marauder in the night, sneaked up to burrow and undermine, intent upon setting up the Nazarene alongside the Divine Being.

In his later Christological writings he does this quite openly and directly. In *The Nazarene* he is still hesitant and cautious; the idea of the divinity of Christ is insinuated, slyly, stealthily, yet quite recognizably. The book is written with pious trepidation, as if by a man overwhelmed by the awe one feels in rare moments of religious ecstasy as one stands in a sacred place and is aware of the immediate presence of the Creator. Asch describes Jesus revealing himself to the world as a heavenly being; and how the conviction slowly dawns upon his followers that he is indeed an incarnation of God, descended to earth. The subtle atmosphere thus created penetrates the pores of the reader, and as the story unfolds before him he is affected in the same manner.

Asch has Mary, mother of Jesus, speak words that imply his divine origin: "It seemed to me that the heavens covered themselves with glory, and peace and good will descended to all men with the coming forth of the child. And I called to my husband: I know not how it is with you, but meseemeth that I see a great light, and singing reacheth my ears, and sweet odors like those of Eden surround me" (257).

On the night of the last supper, one of Asch's heroes remarks: "Do you see that light in heaven? It is the light of the creation,

56

the light which God has concealed in heaven from the beginning" (602).

Asch quotes complete, detailed portions of the Nazarene's discourses, lifted literally from the Gospels, or sometimes, slightly paraphrased, propounding the notion that the Nazarene is the son of God, come down from heaven to redeem the world. He elaborates the wonders and miracles that abound in the Gospels to prove the divine power of Jesus. He relates the exploits of Jesus in making the sick well, the blind to see, and the dead to live again. He gives a vivid description of the Transfiguration, portraying Jesus at times as pure light, and at other times as flaming fire, though he avoids using the specific term.

As has been noted, Asch himself appears in the work as the reincarnation of a previously existing soul. He, and another authorial mouthpiece of a former existence, by the name of Rufus, follow the Nazarene about the country, fairly swooning with ecstasy. They behold him mounting to the upper storey wherein the Last Supper is about to be held; and when Jesus appears before them in an extraordinary vision, Rufus speaks to Asch's incarnation:

"I tell you, it is none other than an angel of heaven come down to attend service."

To which transmogrified Asch replies, "You are right, my friend. This day it was our privilege to stand face to face with an angel of the lord" (602).

With such descriptions, dialogues, declamations, and worshipful intoxication, Asch ceases to be the writer of pure belles-lettres and becomes an avowed partisan of the Christian cause. Lacking in objectivity as well as in truth, he transgresses not only before God and before the Jewish people, but also before the very theme of his narrative.

As a partisan of the Christian attitude, Asch adopts the full Christian pattern in which are portrayed two kinds of Jew in Jesus' time: the kind that recognized and accepted Jesus, those are for Asch the good and worthwhile Jews; and the kind that repudiated him, hence they are the base, hypocritical, sycophantic sinners and rascals of Israel. Among these are the Pharisees and the scholars, the defenders of the faith.

Were Asch worthy of the theme of "Judaism-Christianity" he would realize that the focal point lies elsewhere. He would realize: Here is a people, the Jewish people rooted in, based on, and eternally committed to the concept of a single God, One without form or body, eternal, creator and governor of the universe and everything therein. Upholding that idea, the people suffer the enmity of a world sunk in repellent paganism and monstrous idol-worship. Then the nation finds itself under the rulership of Rome, whose Caesars proclaim themselves gods, and are so worshipped—all of which is revolting and abhorrent to Jewish consciousness. In such a community there suddenly appears a man, a Jew called Jesus, who announces himself the son of God, putting forth the claim that the divine power and glory have been transmitted to him. And he demands divine recognition for himself! He speaks thus:

"The Father is in me and I in him" (John x, 38).

"I and my Father are one" (John x, 30).

"Verily, verily, I say unto you 'Before Abraham was, I am'" (viii, 58).

"He that hath seen me hath seen the Father" (John xiv, 9).

"He that seeth me seeth him that sent me" (John xii, 45).

"He that hateth me hateth my Father also" (John xv, 23).

Indeed, God himself bows to Jesus: "It is my Father that honoreth me, of whom ye say, that he is your God" (John viii, 54).

When the Jews protest that Jesus, a man, has proclaimed his own divinity, he does not deny the charge though he speaks evasively. He replies with "proof" from Holy Writ: "Is it not written in your Law, 'I said, ye are gods'" (Psalms lxxx, 2) (John x, 33-4).

In John, we read that God has granted Jesus power over all flesh (xvii, 2).

Nowhere does Asch display a normal Jewish attitude toward these extraordinary claims. Nor does he ever depict the immense amazement which the claims of Jesus must have aroused among the Jews as they heard them directly from his lips. Here we are assuming that there was a Jesus, although many scholars have denied his existence. For two thousand years Jews have now been hearing these statements from Christian sources, and their astonishment is very great every time they hear them. It must have been even greater in those ancient days when they were first propounded. But Sholem Asch fails to evince any reaction to these claims either as a Jew or as a literary artist. Let us try for a moment to visualize the scene for ourselves:

Yonder on a street corner in Jerusalem stands a pale young

58

man expounding: "I am the son of God, I and my Father are one —all power in heaven and earth has been given me"—which in straightforward language means: I am God.

A Jew watching from across the way scrutinizes the strange declaimer and ponders: "This melancholy youth claims he is God. He says all things were made by him, the world was made by him (John 1: 3, 10). It is he who created the heaven and the earth, and all its creatures; it is he who brought on the Deluge to drown out most of his creation; it is he who spoke to Abraham and promised the Land for his children; it is he who led the Jews out of Egypt; it is he who divided the Red Sea; it is he who, speaking from Mount Sinai through thunder and lightning, proclaimed, 'I am the Lord your God!' All these feats have been accomplished by this melancholy speaker now crying in the streets of Jerusalem and demanding recognition."

The Jew engages the speaker in dispute. "You say, 'I and my Father are one' and 'The Father is in me and I am in the Father.' But it is written: 'The Lord, He is God in heaven above and upon the earth beneath; *there is none else*' (Deuteronomy iv, 39). It is written: 'See now that I, even I, am He, and there is no god with Me' (Deut. xxxii, 39). It is written: 'That ye may know and believe Me, and understand that I am He; before Me there was no God formed, neither shall any be after Me' (Isaiah xliii, 10), covering all three possibilities, past, present and future."

Thus would continue a long series of objections.

Said the Nazarene: "He who has seen me has seen the Father." But this conflicts with the basic doctrine of Judaism—the idea of the pure spirituality of God. As Moses instructed his people: "And the Eternal spoke unto you out of the midst of the fire; ye heard the voice of words, but ye saw no form; only a voice" (Deuteronomy iv, 12). And Isaiah said (xl, 18): "To whom then will ye liken God? Or what likeness will ye compare unto Him?"

Another declaration of the Nazarene is: "And I will do whatever you ask in my name" (John xiv, 13). But Jewish Holy Writ proclaims: "Besides Me there is no God. Turn to me and you are saved in all ends of the earth! For I am God, and there is none else" (Isaiah xlv, 21-22).

Once more in John (v, 22) we read: "For the Father judgeth no man, but hath committed all judgment to the son." But Deuteronomy (i, 17) says, "For the judgment is God's."

Matthew (xxviii, 18) says of Jesus: "All power is given unto me in heaven and in earth." In Isaiah (xliii, 11), however, we are told: "I, even I, am the Lord; and beside Me there is no saviour."

Whereas Jesus proclaims that no one may come to the Father except through the son, the prophet says (Hosea xiii, 4): "Yet I am the Lord thy God from the land of Egypt; and thou knowest no god but Me, and beside me there is no saviour."

Said the Nazarene: "For the Father judgeth no man, but hath committed all judgment unto the Son: That all men should honor the Son, even as they honor the Father" (John v, 22-3). Whereas God proclaims (Isaiah xlii, 8) : "I am the Lord, that is My name; and My glory I will not give to another."

And so on interminably. The Jewish teaching of divine unity in the Bible is so sternly and mightily hewn that it can no more be swept away than the sun can be swept from the heavens. Neither the avowals of the Nazarene and the Gospels nor the millennial repetitions of the Church have been able to move Judaism from its position by a hairbreadth. The Jewish sages, and such philosophers of later periods as Saadia Gaon, Ibn Gabirol, Judah Halevi and Maimonides have intensified and clarified the Jewish concept of unity until not the slightest vestige of anthropomorphism remains. "Inconceivable is He, and unending is His unity" is regularly recited by the Jew in prayer (Yigdal).

Such were the proofs a Jew might have offered Jesus in rejecting his claims. And what could the Nazarene say in rebuttal? This is of the essence of the story. The duelling and sparring could have been made supremely interesting. They could have filled the story with the rolling of thunder and flashing and crackling of lightning. Yet Asch avoids the issue completely. His story is very tame on that point.

But it must be noted that the New Testament itself is very reserved in this respect. Never is the Jewish argument met in a head on collision, but only evasively and very far from the mark.

Equal in magnitude with infringing upon the unity of God is the offence of infringing upon the eternity of The Law. The Nazarene made himself guilty of that, too. Sholem Asch willingly yields up to him on this score also. Although it is generally accepted that it was Paul who brought about the final break between Judaism and Christianity, in truth the breach can be traced back to the Nazarene himself. Jesus spoke concerning the Torah:

"Think not that I have come to destroy the Law, or the

prophets; I am not come to destroy, but to fulfil. For verily I say unto you, Till heaven and earth pass, one iota or one tittle shall in no wise pass from the Law, till all be fulfilled" (Matthew v, 17-18; Luke xvi, 17). But immediately following, in Luke (xvi, 18), almost in the same breath he declares: "Whosoever putteth away his wife, and marries another, committeth adultery; and whosoever marrieth her that is put away from her husband committeth adultery." Thus Jesus modifies the Torah by prohibiting divorce and remarriage for the divorce, which the Torah permits.

Even while he proclaims his intention not to abrogate a single iota of the Torah, Jesus says: "Again, ye have heard that it hath been said by them of old time, Thou shall not forswear thyself, but shalt perform unto the Lord thine oaths. But I say unto you, swear not at all" (Matthew v, 33-4). Once more Jesus forbids a procedure allowed by the Torah. We find that in every case where seemingly complete loyalty to the Torah is expressed, there is an immediate negation of some particular law of the Torah.

The favorite formula is, "Ye have heard that it has been said ... but I say unto you. ..." With this formula Jesus abrogates many laws of Torah and Talmud, including the dietary laws, Sabbath prohibitions, divorce, oaths, and washing the hands before eating.

In using this formula, Jesus never obliges his listeners by explaining where it was told and who told it. Of course, he was referring to the Torah. The Torah is always explicit on this point, it was God who spoke it. Thus Jesus plainly sets himself up above God and his own words above the words of God as set forth in the Torah. And who can miss the air of haughty disdain in the expression, made even more emphatic by numerous repetitions: You have heard it said thus and so, but I say otherwise.

What, then, did Jesus mean when he said that he came not to destroy, but to fulfill the Law? The true attitude of Jesus toward the Torah is revealed in the following declaration: "The law and the prophets lasted until John v (Matt. xi, 13), with John the Baptist as prophet of the new dispensation." This is a clear, unmistakeable proclamation that with John the Baptist's foretelling of Jesus' coming there came an end to the ministry of the Torah, and there came complete fulfillment of all prophetic utterance.

Elsewhere Jesus declares that not an iota of the Torah would pass "until it is all in force," meaning that the Torah itself contains indications of its invalidation at his coming, hence he came not to destroy but to fulfill the Torah. His emergence therefore was the ultimate fulfilment and realization of both Torah and Prophets.

The Gospels abound with evidence that after revealing himself Jesus ceased to regard the Torah as *his* Torah. In a dispute with the Pharisees (John viii, 17) he says: "It is also written in *your* Law, that the testimony of two men is true." Again (John x, 34) Jesus speaks, "Is it not written in *your* Law, 'I said, Ye are gods?'" Another passage (John xv, 25), reads: "That the word might be fulfilled that is written in *their* Law (Psalms xxxv, 19) 'They hated me without a cause.'" It is always, *your* Law, *their* Law, but never *my* Law.

He explicitly substituted himself for the Law of Moses: "Moses gave you not that bread from heaven, manna; but my Father giveth you the true bread from heaven. . . . I am the bread which came down from heaven" (John vi, 32).

By indirection the Nazarene even denied that Moses knew God, thus denying the Torah. "Not that any man hath seen the Father, save he which is of God, he hath seen the Father" (John vi, 46). Also, (Matthew vi, 27): "All things are delivered unto me of my father; and no one knoweth the Son, save the Father; neither knoweth any man the Father, save the Son, and he to whomsoever the Son will reveal him." Yet we find in the Torah (Exodus xxxiii, 11): "And the Lord spoke unto Moses face to face, as a man speaketh unto his friend."

Jesus belittled not only Moses and his Law but in an angry moment he denounced everyone—everyone who came before him. In the parable of the sheep (John x, 7-8) he says:

"Verily, verily, I say unto you, I am the door of the sheep. All that ever came before me are thieves and robbers but the sheep did not hear them."

The Torah of Moses is of value to Jesus only insofar as he makes it serve as a witness to him and his advent. For he says (John v, 39): "Search the Scriptures; for in them ye think ye have eternal life: and they are they which testify of me." Which means —you believe that in the holy writings you have eternal life, but you are in error; the scriptures testify that not in them, but in me is there eternal life.

The Nazarene seems to have had no hesitancy in supplementing the words of the Torah, adding ideas not there at all in order to disparage it and detract from its dignity. In the Sermon on the Mount he said (Matthew v, 43): "Ye have heard that it hath been said, Thou shalt love thy neighbor, and hate thine enemy. But I say unto you, Love your enemies."

Now, just where does the Torah make it incumbent upon one to hate his enemy? What chapter and verse? Insomuch as all introductory clauses, "Ye have heard that it hath been said," refer to the Torah, it would seem that this allusion too is to the Torah. But such a command is not to be found there. Nor is it in the Prophets or Hagiographa. Nor is it in fact in the entire realm of Jewish lore. It is evident that in this statement we are confronted with one of the earliest libels against the Jewish people and Judaism.

Such utterances as "The Pharisees sit in the seat of Moses; obey what they command you" were probably intended for those Jews who were not yet followers of Jesus, or to be temporarily operative since "his hour has not yet come"—that is, the hour when Jesus would be revealed as the Messiah. Or the passage may be ironical in aim, its intent being to split the ranks of all antagonists. For immediately thereafter it is said, "But according to their deeds shall ye not act."

"For had ye believed Moses," spoke Jesus to his opponents, "ye would have believed me; for he wrote of me" (John v, 46). Again we find him making use of the Torah to his own advantage.

But again: Just where did Moses write of Jesus: Can one name the chapter and verse? Is it conceivable that in all the disputes between him and his opponents, no one but no one has ever thought of raising the query, "Where did Moses mention you? Point out the place!"

Had Sholem Asch shown the slightest consideration for the Jewish argument in the eternal Jewish-Christian disputation, he would never have passed over these New Testament declarations in silence. For they are the essential point of the Jewish argument. The Gospels record many recondite and mystic declarations made by the Nazarene concerning Old Testament mention of him. But in this particular instance no source at all is given; not a word quoted of what Moses had presumably written about him.

However, since the Church Fathers of later days could not leave the dicta of their redeemer unsupported they searched the Torah for corroboration. They claim to have uncovered Jesus in a number of passages of the Torah.

One of the verses chosen for such exegesis is from Genesis (iii, 15). In the Douhay Bible (Catholic), in what is by the way a faulty translation, the verse reads:

"And I will put enmity between thee and the woman, and between thy seed and her seed; she shall crush thy head, and thou shalt lie in wait for her heel." A trip to the moon would be less fantastic than the scholastic convolutions offered in the interpretation of the event between Eve and the serpent as a prophecy of the Nazarene's advent. The seed is made to stand for Jesus Christ, "she," which by the way is "he" in the original Hebrew, for Mary, and the Serpent for Satan.

A second passage similarly misconstrued is: "And in thy seed shall all the nations of the earth be blessed" (Ge. xxii, 18).

Genesis xlix, 10 is a third: "The sceptre shall not depart from Judah, nor the ruler's staff from between his feet, as long as men come to Shiloh; and unto him shall the obedience of the peoples be."

The fourth verse distorted by Christian apologists is: "A prophet will the Lord thy God raise up unto thee, from the midst of thee, of thy brethren, like unto me; unto him shall ye hearken" (Deuteronomy xviii, 15).

What reasonable certainty is there that such passages refer to the Nazarene? Baffled by these tortured interpretations, the Jew asks, Why should the Torah, to the Christian mind, always try to say something through the device of saying something else, always relying on reversal of meaning, where "black" is supposed to indicate "white" and vice-versa? Was Moses the inventor of "Aesopian language?" Allegory and symbolism have their place and function, in the Bible as elsewhere, but they can never take primacy over the plain and direct meaning of words.

Such, then, is the irreconcilable opposition and unbridgeable cleavage between the two faiths. Had Asch preserved any sense of loyalty to the Jewish side, he could not have written as he did. Having written, he placed himself outside the fold of Judaism.

Asch's offense was not only against his people and their faith, but against the principles of his very art. From a purely artistic standpoint it was a serious error to blur the very sharp distinction between the two viewpoints. His work would have gained considerably in stature and significance had he dared speak up for Judaism with boldness, meeting the Christian issue squarely. His pages should have been flaming with warfare—with the clash of

64

ideas, concepts, biblical passages, even of single verses. Verse should have been pitted against verse, chapter against chapter until they struck fire. But he stood weak-kneed before Christianity and the Church and sacrificed art and the truth upon the altar of expediency.

The Gospels themselves avoid mention of their opponents' basic arguments. They neither refer to nor attempt to answer the passages in question, but confine themselves instead to a statement of their own side. They are content merely to abuse their opponents, without meeting them in battle, or trying to demolish their arguments. But Sholem Asch, writing primarily in Yiddish and for Jews, had no license to pass over these matters in silence; he was under a moral obligation to his readers which he did not fulfill. In the days of the Nazarene, on the streets of Jerusalem and everywhere else in Judea, there must have been Jews who raised points of dispute concerning the biblical passages, demanding Jesus' explanation. What were his answers? He had none. There could not be any. But Asch carefully avoids mention of these crucial matters.

The disputes in the New Testament are vague and onesided. The pages of the Gospels expatiate on Jesus' differences with the Pharisees, but never does one come upon a single true-to-life, outstanding, learned Pharisee. The Gospels mention one, Nicodemus, whom they call Pharisee, and of whom Sholem Asch makes more use than they do. But Nicodemus is devoid of learning, a mere fellow traveler, caught up in the prevailing propaganda; in no book of Judaism, in no list of Jewish sages, will one find his name. There is a certain Nicodemon in the Talmud, but he is merely a dignitary, a man of wealth who provided the inhabitants of Jerusalem with food during the siege, and who is not numbered with the scholars and sages. In no manner does the Nicodemus of the Gospels represent the ideas of the Pharisees, the true exponents of authentic Judaism, who are diligently abused in the New Testament but never answered.

Although the Gospels mention only one of them, Asch introduces into "The Nazarene" at least two very authentic and very famous Pharisees, two of the greatest and most learned among them. (By the same token he could, of course, have introduced many more.) He gives some space to Rabban Gamliel (briefly mentioned in the New Testament, in the Acts of the Apostles), and considerable mention to Rabbi Johanan ben Zaccai. Using poetic license Asch could well have arranged a meeting, a debate, or at least an encounter between the Nazarene and Rabbi Johanan, and would then have had something worth writing about! Johanan could fittingly have been presented as chief antagonist of the Nazarene. For each aimed at exactly opposite ends from the other. Jesus (and much later, Paul) came forward to end the dispensation of the Torah and eventually bring about its extinction among the Jews, while Rabbi Johanan, at the crossroads of history, was devoting himself to implanting the Torah so deep within the Jewish soul that no storm could ever uproot it. And whether chronologically justified or not, (which will not be questioned here), Asch has Rabbi Johanan ben Zaccai delivering sermons throughout the land at the same time that Jesus is wandering about preaching his new gospel. On one occasion he even shows us the Nazarene among the group hearkening to Rabbi Johanan. Yet neither ever refers to the other by a single word during their separate disquisitions, and, of course, Asch never brings them together in any direct conversation or open disputation.

If Rabbi Johanan was not to be in open debate with the Nazarene, Asch could have used some of the rabbi's disciples, of whom there were many of high distinction. The greatest of these numbered five, as recorded in the Mishnah:

"Rabban Johanan, the son of Zaccai, had five disciples, and these are they: Rabbi Eliezer, the son of Hyrcanus; Rabbi Joshua, the son of Hananiah; Rabbi Jose the Priest; Rabbi Simeon, the son of Nathaniel; and Rabbi Eleazar, the son of Arach. He used thus to recount their praise; Eliezer, the son of Hyrcanus, is a cemented cistern, which loses not a drop; Joshua, the son of Hananiah—happy is she that bore him; Jose the Priest is a pious man; Simeon, the son of Nathaniel, is a fearer of sin; Eleazar, the son of Arach, is like a spring flowing with ever-sustaining vigor. He (Johanan) used to say, If all the sages of Israel were in one scale of the balance, and Eliezer, the son of Hyrcanus, in the other, he would outweigh them all. Abba Saul said in his name: If all the sages of Israel were in one scale of the balance, and Eliezer, the son of Hyrcanus, also with them, and Eleazar, the son of Arach, in the other scale, he would outweigh them all" (Aboth ii, 10-12).

From these men one could have heard the true opinion of the Pharisees concerning the Nazarene's onslaught on Judaism, but they are never mentioned, either in the Gospels or by Sholem

Asch. If Jesus came to overturn the world—as, according to the Gospels and to Asch, he did—and to make a complete revolution in the land of Israel, why do we not hear a single word about this revolution from the true representatives and spiritual leaders of the day?

Let us overlook the Gospels at this point, as our quarrel is not with them at all. But why did Sholem Asch so carefully omit these great men? Since he allowed his fancy free rein in similar matters, here was an excellent opportunity to go full sweep. And yet, for a reason we must seek, he let the opportunity pass. Why? Because he did not dare attempt to give voice to men of such stature. The field of their learning is forbidden territory to him. Their great wisdom and teaching is a closed book to him. He does not even possess its vocabulary. He, like the Gospels, realized the futility of engaging in a passage of arms with the true sages and leaders of Judaism.

In learned disputation Jesus could never measure up to these giants, Matthew's assurances (ix, 4; xii, 25) that he could read what the Pharisees were thinking notwithstanding. Of this he was fully conscious, as were the Gospels, and as was, alas! Sholem Asch. Jesus preferred to rely on supernatural manifestations. The Gospels teem with so-called miracles—the sick become well, the lame are made to walk, evil spirits are exorcised, and the dead are brought to life. This is the path trodden by Asch, too. But all this made no impression at all on the Jews, as the Gospels admit; for did not Jesus complain, I show miracles unto them and still they do not believe?

Quite properly did the Jews refuse to be taken in by these so-called miracles. Listen to the words of the Torah:

"If there arise in the midst of thee a prophet, or a dreamer of dreams—and he give thee a sign or a wonder, and the sign or wonder come to pass, whereof he spoke unto thee saying: Let us go after other gods, which thou hast not known, and let us serve them; thou shalt not hearken unto the words of that prophet, or unto that dreamer of dreams; for the Lord your God putteth you to proof, to know whether ye do love the Lord your God with all your heart and with all your soul. After the Lord your God shall ye walk, and Him shall ye fear, and His commandments shall ye keep, and unto His voice shall ye hearken, and Him shall ye serve, and unto Him shall ye cleave." (Deut. ii, 5).

The final test is this: What is the true purpose of this so-called prophet in working his wonders and miracles? If his aim be to turn the Jews even by a hairbreadth from the Torah of Moses, he is a false prophet.

8

Incendiary of the Temple

The Temple and the Sanhedrin are two of the most sacred entities in Israel; so have they ever been and so will they ever remain. In *The Nazarene* Sholem Asch desecrates them both, following in the footsteps of the Gospels, which sought to cast aspersion upon the Jews by means of vicious tales concerning these most venerated of Jewish institutions. As always, Asch made his own strictures even more severe, painting the Jew with blacker colors than the Gospels paint him.

Take the story of the "money-changers in the Temple." The Gospels tell of the Nazarene's coming to Jerusalem and discovering in the very Temple dealers in oxen, sheep, and doves, carrying on their business on the premises of the Temple and turning the house of God into a cattle market. He also found there a company of money-changers sitting by their tables and plying their banker's trade. Jesus' ire was aroused to the boiling point. Whereupon he seized a rope, fashioned a lash out of it and used it upon the backs of the disgraceful offenders. He succeeded in driving the traders out with all their live stock, chasing the money-changers out as well, overturning their tables and scattering their coin.

This is one of the best known parts of the Christian Bible. The story has always served as smear material for anti-Semites and maligners of Jewry—proof of their alleged materialism, which allows the Jew to introduce the vulgar meannesses of business even into the Holy of Holies of mankind. "Money-changers in the Temple" has become a synonym for "Jewish bankers" and "international financiers." It is a stock phrase of anti-Semitism. It has laid the basis for such dangerous calumnies of the Jews as "money is their God" and "their cash book is their fatherland."

Sholem Asch did not undertake to correct this slander, which has not the remotest basis in historical reality. On the contrary,

68

while the Gospels are satisfied to restrict the libel to a few lines, Asch spattered the muddy scene over a vast canvas.

The authors of the Gospels were admittedly far from proficient in Jewish learning, and when they discussed the Temple and its service, or the Sanhedrin and its procedure, they groped in the dark. Their errors in such matters are a measure of their lack of authenticity.

It is not even remotely conceivable that dealers in livestock and money-changers could sit on the Temple grounds and ply their trade within its sacred precincts. Not only an explicit law concerning the Temple, but also plain common sense, tells us that this is impossible. The law explicitly states: "One is not permitted to ascend the Temple Mount with a stick, with shoes, or with a moneybelt" (Berakhot 54a), "moneybelt" being the special feature of the merchant. If it was absolutely forbidden to carry money when coming up the Temple Mount, how then could trade have been carried on in the holy precincts? The "Temple Mount" is a term including the mountain upon which stood the Temple, all its buildings and the entire area surrounding them. This is the legal aspect of the matter.

Nor, as was noted above, does it comport with logic to assume that the priests would allow the domain of their patrimony, the source of their wealth and power, to deteriorate into a cattle market with all the unpleasant features that the term connotes. Would it be to their interest to sully the glory of one of the most beautiful structures of the ancient world, constituting the pride of the nation before all the peoples? True, the priesthood of that day had become low and corrupt, due to the alien, corrupting influence of Roman rule. As the high priesthood had become a negotiable commodity to be sold to the highest bidder, there was a new high priest almost every year. But this was only an inner contingency. It stands to reason that the priests would rather exert every effort to maintain at least the outward dignity of the Temple, since the Temple, properly honored and maintained, was the source both of their livelihood and their honorific status. Nothing could so readily damage the glory and dignity of the holy place as the opening of a market for cattle, sheep, and fowl on the premises.

All this accords completely with Jewish sources, which tell us that trading in sacrificial animals and the changing of coins were carried on not in the confines of the Temple, but outside the sacred precincts. In the Jerusalem Talmud, Taanit 5, we read: "There were two cedars on the Mount of Olives, under which there were shops selling doves and pigeons." Note the designation of the mount as the *Mount of Olives*. The Temple stood on *Mount Moriah*. It is also to be noted that even here, outside the Temple precincts, the Talmud speaks of pigeons, and not of sheep or cattle.

Similarly, the Gospels misconstrue the matter of the money-changers. There were money-changers but not inside the Temple. They served a twofold purpose: one, to change money for the second tithe, which the Jews had to take to Jerusalem for consumption in the Holy City; two, to exchange for Jewish currency foreign coins bearing the engraved images of rulers, which the many Jewish pilgrims from afar brought with them and which were outlawed within the sacred confines. The pilgrims would have to exchange their currency for Jewish money before they could donate their shekel to the Temple, and offer contributions to charity. For these reasons changers were permitted, but always outside the Temple, never within its bounds.

The Nazarene, coming from the provinces, strange to the Holy City, naturally had little acquaintance with the Temple as well as its procedures. He could have no clear knowledge of where the Temple, with its many structures, began and ended. And sure enough the Gospels themselves bear clear testimony to this. We read in Matthew (xxiv, 1): "So Jesus left the Temple and went on his way. His disciples came forward to point out to him the Temple buildings. . . ." Now we are in a position to evaluate the situation as it probably occurred. When Jesus came upon the money-changers and their tables, he knew neither what these were for nor whether or not they were within the holy confines. He had no way of ascertaining that these were there not for business but for ritual purposes. He did not know that the money being changed was foreign, money which could not be brought into the Temple itself because of the prohibition, "Thou shalt not make unto thee a graven image."

This prohibition was respected even by the Roman conquerors, who were generally tolerant toward the beliefs of subject peoples. The Romans had no desire to offer insult to the Jews and indulge in unnecessary provocation. For this reason the Roman legionaries never entered with banners unfurled into Jerusalem

70

or into other long hallowed cities of the Jewish people. Banners were folded outside the city to conceal the imperial eagle on the flags. For the same reason, Rome coined special specie without the customary engraved heads of the Caesars for use in Judea.

It thus becomes clear beyond doubt that the tables of the money-changers, whose primary purpose was to keep Gentile coins of forbidden aspect out of the Temple, could not themselves have been set up within the sacred structure.

When King Herod, to ingratiate himself with the Roman rulers, put up a sculptured Roman eagle atop one of the gates of the Temple, the infuriated populace of Jerusalem rioted and destroyed the symbol.

It is true we read in one place: "From the twenty-fifth of Adar tables were set up in the Mikdash" (the temple was called Beth Hamikdash). But Maimonides explains that here "Mikdash" means not the sacred structure itself, but the city of Jerusalem, which has been called by seventy names, one of which is "Mikdash" or "sanctuary."

That the Nazarene did create a disturbance before these shops and tables outside the Temple precincts is conceivable, but in the Gospels the incident is proliferated and applied to the Temple itself, either through error or with the intent of casting a shadow upon the House and upon the religious emotions of the Jews.

Sholem Asch did not take the trouble of going to the heart of the matter to dissipate such ignominious accusations. Instead he belabored the tale to make it even more effective than the version which appears in the Gospels. Still, Asch's account of the Temple is mild and harmless compared with the treatment of the Sanhedrin.

The Great Sanhedrin is the most revered name to come down from Jewish antiquity, second only to the Sanctuary itself. It has no equivalent in any people, ancient or modern. To gain some idea of its nature one would have to think of the United States Supreme Court and the Sacred College of the Church rolled into one. And a parliament to boot. To the Jewish mind it conveys the embodiment of the noblest strivings of man after justice on earth.

The Sanhedrin exercised some of the highest functions of the state. The King, the High Priest, and the judges were subject to its approval. War could not be undertaken without its sanction.

71

Trials of a false prophet, of a town that yielded to idolatry, or of a whole tribe could be held only by the Sanhedrin. The Sanhedrin was court and jury in one.

It supervised public worship and regulated the religious life. The high place the Sanhedrin held in the life of the nation can be gleaned from pronouncements such as these throughout the centuries: Maimonides says (Hilkoth Mamrim I.1) : "The Great Court in Jerusalem is the source of the oral tradition. Out of it goes forth right and law for the whole of Israel." Nahmanides writes: "The precept is given us in the Scriptures to abide by the sentence of the High Court sitting before God in His chosen place and by all they say in interpreting the Scriptures; no matter whether they received the interpretation by tradition or whether they give it according to their own conception of the Scriptures. For in reliance on their opinions-to-be God gave us the Torah" (Commentary, Deut. xvii, 11) .

Only men of genuine piety, attested probity and great scholarship could qualify for the Sanhedrin. Absolutely without parallel are the provisions of Jewish law to insure the emotional and psychological equilibrium of a member of the Sanhedrin. He must not be over-old, or a bachelor, or a married man without children, or a eunuch, or physically defective. For these conditions incline a man to misanthropy and do not permit him to enter fully into the psychology of other men. Nor must he be the father of an illegitimate child or a gambler, or a slave dealer, or of a cruel disposition. His family background was also carefully scrutinized.

No less unique was the trial procedure. Non-capital cases could open either with arguments for acquittal or for conviction, but capital cases must begin with reasons for acquittal and never with reasons for conviction. For a verdict of acquittal in a capital case a majority of one was sufficient, but for a verdict of conviction a majority of no less than two was required. In non-capital cases Sanhedrin could reverse a verdict either from acquittal to conviction or from conviction to acquittal; but in capital cases only from conviction to acquittal. In non-capital cases he that had argued in favor of acquittal could afterward argue in favor of conviction; in capital cases he that had argued in favor of conviction could change his argument in favor of acquittal, but he could not change his argument from acquittal in favor of conviction. In non-capital cases the verdict, whether of acquittal or conviction, could be reached the same day; in capital cases a verdict of acquittal could

72

be rendered on the same day, but a verdict of conviction not until the following day. Therefore trial could not be held on the eve of a Sabbath or on the eve of a Festival day. In cases where the sentence was left over until the morrow, the judges went together in pairs, they ate a little (but they used to drink no wine the whole day), and they discussed the matter all night, they fasted and prayed, and early on the morrow they came to the court. The youngest members of the Sanhedrin were polled first, in order that they might not be influenced by the example of their seniors. If the entire Sanhedrin was unanimous for conviction, the accused was acquitted.

The reader will have noted several remarkable differences between the ancient Hebrew court procedure and the American jury system. A unanimous jury is required for conviction in an American court, while a unanimous Sanhedrin in favor of conviction worked in the reverse direction and set a man free. A Sanhedrin where not a single voice was raised in favor of a man facing the death penalty became suspect itself. It was decried as derelict of duty and faith and tending to excessive cruelty.

Then again, an American jury sometimes consumes hours and even days in an effort to argue a juror into changing his vote from acquittal to conviction, to make it unanimous, while in the Sanhedrin a member could only change from death to life and not from life to death.

Then there was an awe inspiring scene of admonishing the witnesses in order to drive fear into their hearts and arouse them to the seriousness of the situation. They were exhorted in the following manner: "Know ye that capital cases are not as non-capital cases: in non-capital cases a man may pay money and so make atonement, but in capital cases the witness is answerable for the blood of him that is wrongfully condemned, and the blood of his posterity that should have been born to him to the end of the world. For so we have found with Cain that slew his brother, for it is written, *The bloods of thy brother cry.* It says not the *blood of thy brother,* but the *bloods of thy brother*—his blood and the blood of his posterity. Therefore but a single man was created in the world, to teach that any man who has caused a single soul to perish Scripture imputes it to him as though he had caused a whole world to perish; and if any man saves alive a single soul Scripture imputes it to him as though he had saved alive a whole world." And more in the same vein.

When sentence had been passed the convicted was led out immediately to be executed. The place of execution was at a considerable distance from the court. One man stood at the door of the court with a towel in his hand, and another, mounted on a horse, at a distance, but near enough to see him. If in the court one bethought himself of a new argument and said, "I have somewhat to argue in favor of his acquittal," the man waved the towel and the horseman galloped forward and stopped the prisoner convict. If the culprit himself said, "I have somewhat to argue in favor of my acquittal," they took him back, even four or five times, provided that there was substance in his words. There were Rabbis escorting him for that purpose. The culprit was given a death draught that rendered him unconscious and insensible to the agonies of death.

Such was the composition, mode of procedure and positive orientation in the direction of leniency and mercy of the highest Jewish tribunal. The death penalty was very rare in ancient Israel. A court that passed the death sentence once in seven years was called a murderous court.

The two-millennial and perennial conflict between Judaism and Christianity stems from the role presumably played by the Sanhedrin in trying and sentencing the Nazarene. But a distinction must first be made between the sentence and the crucifixion itself. All four Gospels admit that the crucifixion was executed by the Romans. The Jews are blamed only for the trial of Jesus and the sentence of death they imposed and for insisting that the Procurator, Pontius Pilate, carry out the verdict. The Gospels go to some length to spare the tyrannical Procurator, relating that he really wished to offer Jesus the pardon which custom provided for one convict every Passover season, but that the Jews loudly demanded that the pardon be granted a common felon. When the Jews denounced Jesus, crying: "Crucify him! Crucify him," Pontius Pilate publicly washed his hands before the assembled throngs, as a symbol that he was innocent of the blood of the Nazarene; whereupon the Jews shouted, "His blood be upon us and our children!"

It was this account in the Gospels which led to the Jews being branded deicides, murderers of God, "Christ-killers," which to the Jew has always raised the dread spectre of dire persecution. But in the curse of the blood of Jesus, which the Jews, with so much haughtiness and insolence, allegedly called upon themselves

74

and their posterity, the Christians find justification for the rivers of Jewish blood which they have spilled in the course of the generations.

We are here unquestionably treading on most sensitive ground, ground saturated with Jewish blood and tears. It is the central point of the tragic tension between Christian and Jew throughout history. It is, therefore, the sacred duty of every righteous man, particularly of the Jewish writer, to hold the trembling scales with extreme solicitude and care when weighing that terrible accusation against Israel. This judgment of Christendom on Jewry is fraught with greater destiny than the judgment of the Nazarene by the Jews (if there ever was such a trial and judgment).

In this latter point we reach the very core of the problem from the Jewish standpoint. The traditional Jewish view is that a Jewish trial of Jesus never took place. If there ever was such a person as Jesus, he could have been tried and executed only by the Romans.

We need not here venture upon an extensive analysis of a subject on which many scholarly works have been written. Our chief concern here is not the problem as such, but the way it has been dealt with by Sholem Asch. We shall, therefore, touch only briefly upon several points requisite to an understanding of the way Asch handled the fateful story and its problem.

As to the Jewish evidence that there could never have been a Jewish trial of the Nazarene there is first the testimony of the great Roman historian, Tacitus, who writes: "Christus, the founder of the name, had undergone the penalty of death, in the reign of Tiberius; by sentence of the Procurator, Pontius Pilate" (Annals 44, 15). The sentencing is here plainly and unequivocally attributed to the Roman. No part in it whatsoever is ascribed to the Jews.

This testimony is entirely sufficient as far as the Jews are concerned. The leading Roman historian plainly lays the onus for the trial upon others, not upon the Jews. Although we could quite contentedly rest our case here, we shall offer some further considerations.

There is first the authenticated record that forty years before the destruction of the second Temple the Roman power divested the Sanhedrin of all right to judge capital cases and to pass a judgment of death (Sabbath 15a). That would make it from three to four years prior to the reputed crucifixion of Jesus. Then the details of the trial of Jesus, as transmitted by the Gospels, are so far in contravention of the basic Jewish law and of the established procedure of the Sanhedrin that no connection or relationship whatever can be discerned between them. The Gospels betray no knowledge whatsoever of the principles and procedure that governed this high court. In other words, a trial such as reported by the Gospels could not possibly have been carried out by the Sanhedrin.

It was definitely contrary to Jewish law to apprehend and try a person for a capital crime by night; but the Nazarene, according to the Gospel story, was arrested after nightfall and summarily tried in the same night.

It was contrary to the statutes of the law to pronounce sentence on the same day as the trial was held. Only on the following day the members of the court would meet to complete the sentencing. But Jesus was sentenced that same night.

On Sabbaths and festivals and eves of those days, the Sanhedrin was interdicted from holding sessions. Jesus' trial took place on the first night of Passover, according to Matthew, Mark, and Luke, and on the eve of the Passover, according to John.

There are other similar contradictions of Jewish legal procedure which justify the Jewish claim that such a trial never took place or could never have taken place in ancient Judea at the hands of the Sanhedrin. By no stretch of facts or imagination could or would the ancient Sanhedrin have carried out any judicial process after the manner described.

Under these circumstances the imposition of guilt on Jewry for the death of Jesus is nothing but an unmitigated libel and an historic injustice of fearsome magnitude.

However, presumably in deference to the Gospels, there has arisen a school which seeks to find a compromise between Jewish criminal procedure and the Gospel story. These men have suggested a theory based on the works of Josephus Flavius that under the commonwealth there was a second Sanhedrin, a body that served as the political tool of Pontius Pilate; a sort of Quisling-Sanhedrin dominated by the Romans. If this theory could be proved true and accepted, it would still tend to support the view that the Jews were not responsible for the penalty imposed on Jesus. The Romans would bear the guilt for having created an illegal court composed of irresponsible politicians, and having used it to condemn Jesus, whom they suspected of instigating a revolt against Roman rule in the Jewish land and trying to set himself up as king.

Numerous non-Jewish scholars have probed and established Jewish guiltlessness in the matter of Jesus' trial and condemnation, and consequently in his death. The Gospels, however, place the entire blame on the Jews and exonerate the Romans. The reason is not hard to discern. At the time of the writing of the Gospels, the end of the first century, Christians had already grown aware that their new faith would muster very few followers among the Jews. They therefore directed their ministry toward the Gentile world and sought to obtain for their religion the status of legality in the Roman Empire. Thus they could not write in such a manner as to present the Romans as the murderers of their god and redeemer. It was much safer to court the Roman rulers and render the lowly Jew the scapegoat.

We now turn to Sholem Asch. How does the author of *The Nazarene* resolve this tremendous problem? What contribution does he make to the solution upon which, in the past, more than once the very life of Jewry hung in the balance, and of which the ultimate effect is beyond human calculation?

Asch ignores all scholarly opinion, Jewish and Gentile, and faithfully follows the Gospels in proclaiming against the Jews. Nor is he aware of any political Quisling-Sanhedrin; for his purposes the trial court was the duly constituted Sanhedrin. He has taken his stand with Israel's enemies. He had stretched forth his hands in solemn benediction upon the source of eternal hatred for the eternal people.

He affixed his signature to a document that meant the death sentence to Jews without number across the generations. He placed a wreath on Pontius Pilate and a fagot at the stake that consumed countless Jewish martyrs.

And he makes bold and goes even beyond the Gospels. He dares to name names. He mentions as members of the Sanhedrin two of the greatest sages in Judaism, Raban Gamliel and Rabbi Johanan ben Zaccai, who do not figure in the New Testament in connection with the trial at all. There is no source material whatever to warrant that Rabbi Johanan even served in the Sanhedrin. Thus, purely out of his imagination, without even the biased evidence of the Gospels as basis, Asch involved the two great men in the fateful story. He has lightly employed the belletristic license of fictionalizing what purports to be a concrete historical situation of frightful significance.

And what did these sages, these luminaries of the faith, say and do on that night, at the illegal, impossible trial of Jesus, the Nazarene?

It would be more to the point to ask—what *would* they have said, and what *would* they have done, had they actually been there. For, though he proclaims them members of the Sanhedrin, Asch does not present them at the trial of Jesus. By an "ingenious" contrivance he has them be absent from the court. One is puzzled. Why? Why did he introduce them with one hand and exclude them with the other just where their presence was of supreme importance? There is only one plausible explanation: Asch would not know *what* to have them say and do, what words to put in their mouths, and what actions to have them perform had he included them in that awe-inspiring situation at the crossways of peoples and ages. Before the majesty of their minds, even the imaginative resourcefulness of Asch was numbed into silence.

To explain their absence Asch resorts to an awkward literary device: As the trial took place at night, he simply puts them to sleep. Thus, it came to pass, according to Asch that on a night when the fate of heaven and earth was weighed in the balance, when the shape of the future world was being fashioned for countless generations and the entire future course of Jewish history was being channeled into a new direction, Rabbi Gamliel and Rabbi Johanan peacefully slumbered in their beds. This clumsy and obvious trick is proffered without the slightest degree of plausibility, as if all artistic sense had suddenly abandoned our author. After his disciples have approached the alleged Pharisee, Nicodemus, to bring him the horrible news that Jesus has been arrested and taken for trial, Asch tries to persuade us:

"He (Nicodemus) wanted to send them to awaken and assemble the members of the Sanhedrin. He wanted us to run to Rabbi Johanan ben Zaccai and Raban Gamliel ben Simon and the other leading Pharisees. Then he mastered himself and became calm. He sat down and meditated audibly, 'To begin with, they (who apprehended Jesus—L.) cannot sit in trial in the night. In the second place, even if they dared to try him in the night, they cannot pass sentence on him. Thirdly, in matters of this kind they must have at least the complete attendance of the small Sanhedrin, which is impossible without our presence. Fourth, they

78

cannot under any circumstances try him on the eve of a festival. . . No. Morning will be time enough. I need not alarm the sages'" (p. 629).

At best this is a literary trick, betraying the author's inability to dispose of Gamliel and Johanan on that fatal evening except by having them go to sleep, and by depriving his hero, Nicodemus, of common sense enough to have them awakened. But this whole scheme must be rejected on still other grounds—it is simply inconceivable that they should have gone to bed at all on that particular night.

For it was the night of Passover, the night of the paschal sacrifice, the night of the seder, the watch night, which since time immemorial has traditionally been a night when Jews, young and old, stay up late, keep a joyous and protracted session at the table and merrily recite the story of the Exodus from Egypt—even as commanded in the Haggadah—"Whoever dwells long on the story of the departure from Egypt is praiseworthy" . . . on this night of Passover.

In New York today Jews often remain awake through the seder night until dawn. Is it possible to believe that in Jerusalem, in the days of the Temple, the people would have retired early; and even if they had, that Rabbi Gamliel and Rabbi Johanan would have done likewise?

We have clear testimony to the contrary. Josephus (Antiquities, ii, 18) writes that on Passover night, after midnight (following the eating of the paschal sacrifice, which must be concluded by that time) the priests threw open the Temple gates. It is not difficult to picture the animation of Passover night in Jerusalem, with all the populace wending its way to the Temple. Yet on that night Rabban Gamliel and Rabbi Johanan ben Zaccai are supposed to have lain peaceful and carefree on their couches, dreaming sweet dreams, when they should have been most awake.

Such an artifice is too simple even for Asch. Helpless to cope with these giants he must have Gamliel and Johanan asleep and thus away from the trial. But to lend the first deception some plausibility, Asch introduces a second hardly more credible than the one it seeks to conceal, namely, that that night, which was Passover to Jesus, was not yet Passover to Rabban Gamliel and Rabbi Johanan!

In the twentieth chapter of Part III of *The Nazarene* Asch portrays Jesus conducting the seder, which was later to be known

79

as the Lord's Supper. There is the paschal offering to be eaten, the unleavened bread and bitter herbs, the wine and its sanctification, and the singing of the Psalms of Praise—all as prescribed, indicating that Passover has arrived. After this account follow four chapters recounting the arrest and trial of Jesus, and his condemnation. But in chapter twenty-five, timed the next morning, with the description of Nicodemus hurrying to the two rabbis to enlist them in the effort to save Jesus, Asch reveals to the surprised reader that that morning—"the morning after the night before"—is only Passover eve to Gamliel and Johanan!

How was it possible among one section of Jews in Jerusalem for Passover to take place a day earlier than among another? Asch sets forth an extraordinary explanation. In that year, he says, because of the Sabbath, the priests had decreed that the paschal offering be sacrificed on the thirteenth of Nissan, while the sages insisted that the sacrifice be offered according to law, on the fourteenth day of the month. Part of the populace followed the priests and the rest joined the sages. Jesus, surprisingly enough, joined with his mortal enemies, the corrupt priests, rather than with a savant like Rabban Gamliel, for whom even the Gospels have a kind word.

Asch writes: "The Rabbis of the Pharisees were assembled to take counsel against the Priesthood, which had chosen this year to carry out their Sadducean interpretation of the law of the Passover Sacrifice and to refrain from giving it precedence over the Sabbath. The Pharisees planned to bring their sacrifice according to the law of the Torah, to wit, on the fourteenth day of the month, toward the evening, that is, when the Sabbath had already set in." (p. 663)

The complication here offered by Asch with regard to the paschal sacrifice is nothing but a clumsy fabrication. The situation here reported flies in the teeth of every known fact of the clear teachings of the Torah and the Pharisees, the old established practice of the priests, as well as the teachings of Jesus himself.

The Torah clearly commands the offering of "two he-lambs *on the Sabbath,* as the burnt-offering of every Sabbath" (Numbers xxviii, 9-10). This precept had been observed in all the days of the Temple.

As to the paschal offering the Torah commands: "Let the children of Israel keep the Passover in its appointed season" (Numbers ix, 2), which the sages interpreted to mean that the

80

Passover offering took precedence of the Sabbath (Pessachim 77), and there is no record of any rift between the Priests and the Pharisees on that score.

When rebuked by the Pharisees for having permitted his disciples to profane the Sabbath by plucking the heads of wheat in the field, Jesus replied:

"Have you not read in the Law, how that on the Sabbath days the priests in the Temple profane the Sabbath, and are blameless"? (Matthew xii, 5).

Thus, sacrifices on the Sabbath were an ancient practice. Why then should the priests have balked at offering the sacrifice on that particular Sabbath?

This supposed cleavage over the paschal lamb is unheard of in the annals of Judaism. No such problem concerning the paschal sacrifice ever rose to mar the festival of Passover. No savant, Jewish or Gentile, ever encountered this problem or ever grappled with it; it is sheer nonsense. It is a lie out of whole cloth, a monstrous concoction sweated out by Asch's warped inventiveness to conceal a literary swindle, an awkward predicament he got himself into, a predicament impossible of solution—that of keeping the two sages in the story, yet keeping them out of the trial.

Asch here makes himself guilty on at least two counts, the one political-historical, the other literary. What a fearful price to pay in historical veracity, in artistic integrity, not to speak of loyalty and fairness to the Jewish people and to Judaism.

This is a turn in the story which comes with utter unexpectedness, and Asch is never able to redress the balance lost. Things have come full circle. The story at this point is plainly coming apart at the seams, a penalty for his muddle and venality.

The "inspiration" for this bit of fraud undoubtedly came to Asch from the contradictions in the Gospels concerning the exact night of the trial: three of the Gospels place the episode on the night of Passover, and one on the night before. This contradiction has always been employed as proof of the unlikelihood of the entire trial having taken place, but it served Asch as a new lead in the old puzzle. Perhaps he thereby intended to resolve the contradiction in the Gospels and win for himself the title of Christian theologian on top of the title of "Hebrew scholar."

To return to the trial by the Sanhedrin.

The Gospels are very sparing in their recital of the trial. They confine themselves to the barest statement of the essential points. But Asch offers a full length description of the proceeding —long, invented arguments, imaginary wranglings, all purporting to show the allegedly criminal perversion of justice by the prosecutors and the presiding high priest, the miserable witnesses appearing against the Nazarene, up to the ultimate judgment— conveying the impression of loyal reporting and producing, for the uninitiated, the effect of documentation: he takes the awful liberty of composing pure fiction about a matter fraught with staggering implications and scarcely apprehended dangers, as past history has amply demonstrated.

Ancient historians were wont of inventing discourses which they imagined their heroes might have delivered or should have delivered on some special occasion. This kind of historiography, which has long been discredited and discarded, has been revived by Sholem Asch in the trial of Jesus. Asch pictures the complete trial, constructing his story out of thin air, presenting matters about which nothing is known as if they had positively taken place. Such methods might perhaps be permissible in an ordinary historical novel but they are hardly to be condoned in this tale, which, real or imaginary, towers above all other tragedies known to history; in which every available fact, expression, or word has been investigated, probed and microscopically analysed a thousand times over; and into which a careless syllable may fall as a spark to kindle new fire in an ancient conflagration which has already consumed millions of Jews. It has been said, "Wise men, be wary of your words;" to this should be added: "Fools, be wary of your words!"

Even though Asch wished to give support to the libel that the Jews alone sentenced Jesus to death, still there was a way whereby he could do it with some semblance of honor and self-respect. It was his option, if not his duty, to present the Sanhedrin granting the Nazarene a proper and fair trial in terms of its own law, so that it would appear that at least in accordance with their own idea of justice the Jews had acted fairly. He could have pictured the Sanhedrin as fallen into error (to err is human) and not as consciously perverting the judicial process. Instead he chose to make the Sanhedrin naught but a band of rogues, knaves and rascals, low, vile, fallen and corrupt, and the trial a regular lynching party after a night brawl, so that the Jew emerges from the trial devoid of any sense of justice, fairness, kindness, and mercy. It has not the faintest dignity of a trial; it is a mock-trial, a bur-

82

lesque, a travesty, a caricature. Asch offends Jewish dignity and wounds Jewish pride in the one field, in which above all others a nation usually reveals its true beauty and greatness, in the field of justice. He brings disgrace to the Jewish people in a department in which it most deserves to be honored.

Asch had a rare opportunity of picturing the Sanhedrin in all its exalted dignity, and to exemplify Jewish concepts of justice in their full enlightened sanctity. All this is writ large in Jewish lore and is readily available in the talmudic tractate, "Sanhedrin," which, next to the Bible itself, is possibly the noblest book on earth: out of its pages peers the inspired face of a nation bright with justice and truth. Asch could have shown the scrupulousness of Jewish law concerning the sanctity of human life, the many safeguards with which the law surrounded a defendant in a capital case, so as to render the death penalty virtually nonexistent. One Sanhedrin which passed a single sentence of death in seventy years was called the "murderous" Sanhedrin. Whereas Christian nations many centuries after Christ inflicted the death penalty for stealing a horse or even lesser offences, the Jews many centuries before the Christian era were withholding the death penalty even in cases of premeditated murder. While most nations of Christendom have practiced the crude and cruel method of trial by ordeal, in the "Sanhedrin" and other legal works of the Jews centuries upon centuries before, we find the procedure of examining witnesses and weighing evidence firmly elaborated and established on the most profound bases of logic, psychology and justice.

All this lay ready at hand for Asch to relate and enlighten an ignorant and prejudiced world. But he never availed himself of that privilege. Instead he persuaded himself, and tried to befuddle others, in the belief that he had performed a feat by describing the Sanhedrin of that day as controlled not by the Pharisees, but by the Sadducees. But the difference is meaningless to non-Jewish readers. The only thing that matters to them in either case is that *Jews* are blamable for the crime against their Redeemer. So much for the trial.

On the morning after the trial Asch finds much work for Rabban Gamliel and Rabbi Johanan ben Zaccai. They rush about Jerusalem, knocking on countless doors, seeking to rescind the evil decree— but to no avail. Their tardy action obviates nothing.

But strangely enough, as we arrive at this point there finally emerges the hidden and real purpose Asch must have had in mind in introducing the two savants into his story in the first place. In making the rounds of the great and near-great on behalf of the condemned Nazarene, the two distinguished Rabbis are made to say things which they could not, by any extent of the imagination, have said, and which never should have been uttered in their name. Falsifying history, Asch tries to identify them with the ideas and aims of Jesus, obscuring the fact that he stood ranged against everything they represented. Violating the truth Asch makes them idealize a man, whom they could not but reject every step of the way, though this need not have interfered with their efforts to save his life. How could they unqualifiedly extol one, who set himself up above the Torah, above the prophets, above the Sabbath, and claimed an equal place and authority with the Deity? Compounding the injury, and as a final act of betrayal, two of the most glorious luminaries of Judaism of all times are made to join, with Asch, in a heresy which they would have scorned. To sum up:

Christian historiography looks upon the advent of Christianity as the climax of Judaism, and considers the Nazarene the highest point to which Judaism was destined by Providence to climb. It was this idea which fashioned the Gospels, and which governed the writing of *The Nazarene*. To Asch, too, Judaism was but the rotting and discarded hull from which was to emerge the ripe fruit of Christianity.

By what right does a Jewish writer dare to accept such an interpretation of Jewish history and still regard himself a Jewish writer? What swayed or attracted him to so vicious a negation of Judaism and everything pertaining to the Jewish people? A Jewish writer in search of elevated themes, need not go far afield. He can discover material aplenty in his people's real history. There is substance enough not only for a book but for a whole literature in every line of Jewish history. Beginning with the patriarchs, through the story of Egypt and Moses, the giving of the Law, the early prophets, David and Solomon, the first Temple, Isaiah, Jeremiah, Ezekiel, the Babylonian exile and return, the second Temple, the period of the first talmudic teachers—Shemayah, Abtalion, Hillel and Shammai, Rabban Gamliel and Johanan ben Zaccai, and Rabbi Akiba, this real martyr at the hands of the Romans of whom it was said that he deserved that the Torah be given through him, had not Moses preceded him—in all this there exists a story of unequalled glory and splendor of spirit. There is no more magnificent panorama of spiritual elevation and beauty in the entire history of mankind. How could a Jewish

84

writer bring himself to relate this story through the mouth of a non-Jew, a Pole, a boor and the vilest of anti-Semites?

Such a Jewish writer may indeed gain the whole world, but what of his soul?

After the trial by the Sanhedrin Asch proceeds to depict the crucifixion of Jesus. Fire and brimstone, flood, plague and doom have been called down upon the heads of the Jewish people since the time of these alleged occurrences. Thus, to the incitement of the Gospels Sholem Asch had added a "refresher," in some respects with even more harmful invention; by having Jews deliberately break all their precepts and statutes in turning the man-god over to the Romans, he renders the ancient libel even stronger and more incriminating than the Gospel story itself.

In *The Nazarene*, just as in the Gospels, when Pontius Pilate leads Jesus before the populace and asks what they wish done with him, priests and Jews incited by them are made to shout, "Crucify him! Crucify him!" The inference is the same as that evident in the Gospels; if the Jews had so desired, even the cruel and autocratic Pilate would have had to liberate the Nazarene. Where is the favor Asch boasts of having performed in behalf of his people through his book?

The entire scene, with the ensuing procession to the place of the crucifixion and the crucifixion itself (which comprises a goodly portion of the book) Asch portrays in such bloody hues, with such gruesome detail and horrendous fantasy, with such agony for Jesus and such beastly derision of his persecutors, as to make a perfect exercise in terror. A dog sniffing the pages would turn mad with blood lust. Certain passages are downright unbearable with their cruel ferocity. The depictions of the Gospels themselves are sweet music compared to the horrible pages of the Asch opus.

Even the Jew will rise from these pages of horror with bitter resentment against his own kind, and demand acidly: How could they do it? Why indeed did our ancestors so cruelly torture a "zaddick," a prophet, God's greatest gift to man?

It is this that makes this book a dangerous, sinful tome, a crime against Jews and Judaism. This is a work of apostasy; it may lure away ignorant Jewish children into worshipping foreign gods. Let the Christians crown Asch as a new apostle. To Jews he is but a desecrator, a misleader and seducer, a traitor to all that is most precious and holy, a corrupter of the house of Israel, an incendiary of the Holy Temple.

CHAPTER II

The Apostle

The sequel to *The Nazarene* is *The Apostle,* a work about the Nazarene's chief preacher and emissary to the gentiles, whose Jewish name was Saul and who was to be canonized as Saint Paul.

It is an ancient custom of pious Jewish writers to append to their books praise and thanks to Him above, for the strength and merit granted them to compose their works. This reverent custom of humble piety is adopted by the bottomlessly cynical Asch for his apostatic novel about Paul. At the conclusion of the book the author appends the following legend:

"I thank Thee and praise Thee, Lord of the World, that Thou has given me the strength to withstand all temptations and overcome all obstacles, those of my own making and those made by others, and to complete these two works, 'The Nazarene' and 'The Apostle', which are one work; so that I might set forth in them the merit of Israel, whom Thou hast elected to bring the light of the faith to the nations of the world, for Thy glory and out of Thy love of mankind."

This is reminiscent of the anecdote of two Jews meeting, and one inquiring, "And how is your son?"

"Too bad," was the reply. "He's become a writer!"

"What's wrong with that?"

"Waste of time. He'll never sell anything."

"And why not?"

"Atheistic stuff; against God, you know."

"I wouldn't worry," comforted the first. "With the help of God he'll succeed."

Which is exactly what happened to Sholem Asch. Having writ-

86

ten against God, he "succeeded," and he takes time out to thank God for his help.

There would be more appropriateness in his prayer, addressed to heaven, at the end of the book, had Asch not prefixed a more mundane request at the beginning: "Copyright by Sholem Asch . . . all rights reserved . . . must not be reproduced." Payment is expected for any use of Asch's pious words.

Which reminds one of another story—about a Cohen who was asked what his thoughts were while he was standing before the Ark unshod, prayer shawl over his head, in the solemn act of offering the priestly benediction to the congregation.

"I am thinking," said the descendant and heir of the priesthood, "lest someone steal my shoes."

Let us linger a while longer in this mood of innocent humor. Once, Berl, passing a synagogue, saw Shmerl there begging alms. The next day he found him begging in front of a church.

"How come?" demanded Berl, in amazement.

"It's like this," answered Shmerl. "In these hard times a man can't make a living from only one God."

Acording to his prayer at the end of *The Apostle,* Asch wrote his books to portray the merit of Israel and its election. But Paul was the first who sought to deprive Jews of their place as a chosen people and to transfer that glory to the gentiles. He disparaged and abolished God's Torah; he supplanted God, enthroning his son in his place; and he uttered curses against the Jewish people.

In his "First Epistle to the Thessalonians," presumed to be the very first of his messages as apostle, he starts out with a series of charges and denunciations against the Jews, with curses and recriminations, announcing God's eternal judgment against them. He writes of the Jews (iii, 15-16) "Who both killed the Lord Jesus, and their own prophets, and have persecuted us; and they please not God, and are contrary to all men: forbidding us to speak to the gentiles that they might be saved, to fill up their sins always: for the wrath is come upon them to the uttermost."

Asch holds to his heart the man who was the first enemy of the Jews among the Christians, the first Jewish informer among the gentiles, the first falsifier of Judaism to the gentile world, the foe of Israel, and the foe of the Torah. When among Christians everywhere in the world one hears or reads that Jews are a materialistic people devoid of spirit, a practical people devoid of soul, the source is Paul. When in evil times Christians drag forth our

87

Scrolls of the Law, dishonor them, rend them and burn them, it is owing to Paul, who taught them that the Torah is the quintessence of sin, the apotheosis of death.

Sholem Asch attempts to insinuate Paul into the house of Israel through the backdoor of the English language, and at a time when in more enlightened and discriminating Christian circles Paul is being politely but firmly bowed out of house, church and faith. It is one of the remarkable paradoxes of all history that in one sense Paul is Christianity entire, and in another sense he is so clearly Christianity's angel of death, that the demand has risen to dethrone him from the high place in which for many centuries he has ruled the Christian Church. There has long been a movement afoot with the slogan, "Away from Paul! Back to Jesus!" The problem of Paul which confronts Christianity arises from the fact that Paul from the start caused the ethical teachings of Jesus and the first apostles to be relegated to the background, pushing to the fore theological notions which originated in Greek mythology and idolatry. What little warmth Christianity, as a legacy from Judaism, was able to give man's heart, Paul dissipated, and the Christian faith became a repository of hair splitting disquisitions and empty conjectures on desiccated dogmas.

Ernest Renan, the great French historian, writing of Paul, says:

"The writings of Paul became a peril and a hidden rock. They are the reason for the outstanding faults of Christian theology. What gives life to Christianity is what little we know of the utterances and personality of Jesus." Paul's theology, he describes in the same treatise as "the acme of transcendental nonsense." And Renan prophecizes that "Paul's dominance in Christianity is approaching its end."

There are many in Christendom who detest Paul with a violent hatred. They detest him because he took hold of what they believe to have been a religion of a meek and humble ethic and transformed it into a dry and dizzying theology.

None has written with a more burning hatred and greater contempt of Paul than Thomas Jefferson, author of the Declaration of Independence and third president of the United States. Jefferson writes:

"There were other rogueries, absurdities, and untruths perpetrated upon the teachings of Jesus by a large band of 'dupes and impostors' led by *Paul, the great Coryphaeus, the first cor-*

88

rupter of the doctrines of Jesus." Elsewhere Jefferson referred to the dross in the writings ascribed to Jesus, accrediting them to the stupidity of some, and the roguery of others of his disciples; and then Jefferson says: "Of this band of dupes and impostors, Paul was the great Coryphaeus and great corrupter of the doctrines of Jesus" (The Mississippi Valley Historical Review, Vol. xxx, No. 2, Sept. 1943).

Jefferson was a figure of the eighteenth and early nineteenth centuries, Renan of the nineteenth. We now skip a half century and proceed to a work which appeared in the early twentieth century (1911), called "St. Paul in the Light of Modern Research," by an English priest and theologian, J. R. Cohu. The aim of Rev. Cohu is to defend Paul in the "Back to Jesus" dispute. Nevertheless he, too, justifies the objections raised by Paul's critics: "If Paul were alive today," writes Rev. Cohu, "he would have been the first to demand a revision of his own theology . . . for the good of religion." He adds the comments of other Christian thinkers, who maintain that had it not been for Paul, the Christian religion would long before have been spread all over the world. Cohu presents the views on Paul by another theologian, Jewett, who describes the apostle in the following unflattering terms:

"A man whose appearance and discourse made an impression of feebleness . . . out of harmony with life and nature . . . a confused thinker, uttering himself in broken words and hesitating forms of speech, with no beauty or comeliness of style; so undecided in his Christian belief that he was preaching fourteen years after his conversion a gospel which he, four years later, confessed to have been carnal" (Cohu, p. 25).

To leap deeper into the twentieth century, we turn to a book by an American—Ernest P. Scott's "Varieties of New Testament Religion" (1944):

"Countless efforts have been made," writes Dr. Scott, "to discover in it (Paul's system) some kind of logical cohesion, but it is now generally admitted that this cannot be done. Paul's ideas continually intersect, and frequently contradict each other. He lays hold of any idea that immediately suits his purpose, careless of how it may harmonize with what he had said elsewhere" (p. 99).

These destructive descriptions of Paul and his dogmas are not limited to a few individuals, but represent vast currents of Christian thought. Interesting in this connection is the statement

89

by Herbert Hewitt Stroup in his book, "Jehovah's Witnesses," which discusses that widely scattered sect:

"The Witnesses commonly believe that Christianity was begun by a noble, divine leader. But the pristine teachings of Jesus were polluted early in the history of the religion by Paul, who weakened Christianity, systematizing and churchifying it until the resulting form was unsanctioned by God and was against the truest interests of man. In the opinion of the Witnesses, the Roman Catholic Church may not have been founded by Jesus and St. Peter, but certainly it was by Satan and Paul. Thus, Paul is made the scapegoat for all the misinterpretations of the original Christian message" (pp. 132-133).

In the most ancient beginnings of Christianity Paul was looked upon as the black sheep of the new religion. The eleven apostles who were Jesus' first disciples had no love for him, and when Paul changed from a persecutor of the new faith to its protagonist, they at first refused to accept him as one of their own; they did not believe his story that Jesus had revealed himself to him, and when ultimately they accepted him, it was with much reluctance. Then, when he joined their circle and became a full-fledged member, there were many bitter contentions. But Paul triumphed over them all. For while the other apostles (as is frankly admitted in the Gospels) were egregious ingoramuses, Paul was possessor of a modicum of Greek and Hebraic learning.

Ernest P. Scott says that Paul's associates had little affection for him: "They regarded him as one who was all things to all men, who had no settled opinions but kept veering from one side to another with the one object of attaining his own ends" (p. 99).

The phrase "all things to all men" deserves closer examination. In American politics the phrase is used to refer to an unprincipled politician, who varies with his audiences. It is a powerful term of reproach. It is strange, therefore, to recall that the expression comes from Paul's description of himself. He uses it to symbolize his own labors in propagating the new religion. Writing in I Corinthian (ix, 19-23) he says:

"For though I be free from all men, yet have I made myself servant unto all, that I might gain the more. And unto the Jews I became as a Jew, that I might gain the Jews; to them that are under the law, as under the law, that I might gain them that are under the law. To them that are without law, as without law, (being not without law to God, but under the law to Christ,) that

90

I might gain them that are without law. To the weak became I as weak, that I might gain the weak: I am made all things to all men, that I might by all means save some. And this I do for the gospel's sake, that I might be partaker thereof with you."

Such is the appearance of the most important apostle of Christianity to the eyes of a great sector of Christendom. How then should that visage appear in the mirror of Judaism? Nevertheless, Sholem Asch finds it possible to present this half-repudiated, half-castout figure as the man who knew God best. To the Jews, this great traducer and destroyer of the Jewish religion is presented as a faithful and pious Jew. Even as "the greatest Jewish patriot" (Christian Herald, Jan. 1944). Jewish patriot indeed! When the Jews rejected his obscure and gloomy doctrines, Paul shook his raiment and said unto them, "Your blood be upon your own heads; I am clear. From henceforth I will go unto the Gentiles" (Acts xviii, 4-7). Elsewhere he dubbed them "Vessels of wrath, fitted for destruction," while the Gentiles he called "Vessels of mercy, which he (God) had prepared for glory" (ibid.).

2

"The Devil's Masterwork"

Paul was not one of the first apostles, the immediate disciples of Jesus. He joined the new sect long after the crucifixion. At the outset he was a bitter enemy and an active persecutor of the growing heresy; but suddenly, in a flash, he was converted. As often happens with converts, he became a more ardent and flaming Christian than the original apostles. Indeed, he considered himself superior to them. He called Peter "hypocrite" to his face.

Being shrewder than the others, Paul early came to the realization that Christianity had no future among the Jews, and therefore decided to take the new teaching to the world at large, where there was a great spiritual void to be filled. He proclaimed himself — "apostle to the gentiles." He was eminently fit for this mission, for he hailed from the gentile world, having been born not in Judea but in the Hellenic town of Tarshish or Tarsus. He was thus a Greek Jew of Roman citizenship. He was well versed in the Hellenistic culture of the era, but knew little of Jewish lore, despite the claim that he sat at the feet of Raban Gamliel, a claim which Asch, to extol his hero, exploits to the utmost. There is every indication that he did not know the Bible in the original Hebrew, but relied on Greek translation. He nowhere betrays the slightest familiarity with post-biblical learning, such as had flourished for generations and was later to emerge as the Mishnah and Talmud.

The gentile world of that time was receptive to Jewish preaching, as its own beliefs had grown rotten and hollow, and it was searching for a new faith. Among the intellectuals and upper strata there was widespread interest in Judaism and there were many converts to the Jewish faith.

The most noted of these was the convert Onkelos, immortal translator of the Torah into Aramaic, known as "Targum Onkelos," whose work has been held in all generations in such reverent esteem that it is printed side by side with the original Hebrew and is recited together with the weekly portion of the Torah on the Sabbath. Onkelos was a student of Rabban Gamliel. It is said that he was more observant of Jewish precepts and practices than his great master, and that he was most strict in observing the laws of food and of ritual cleanliness.

Another distinguished convert of the epoch was Aquila, who, after turning to Judaism, translated the Bible into Greek, of which work only fragments have come down to us. As a Greek pagan he had served as a priest in a temple of idolatry. Married to the sister of Emperor Hadrian, he was appointed by the Emperor supervisor of construction in Jerusalem. There, having made the acquaintance of the early Christians, he accepted their faith, only to turn from them in a short while to become a Jew. The Midrash relates that when Hadrian was informed by Aquila of his desire to convert to Judaism, the Emperor strongly objected and said: "You want to join that people? See how I have humiliated them, how many of them I have slaughtered. Would you become fused with the most debased of peoples? What do you see in them that so impresses you?"

To this Aquila rejoined: "The least among them knows how God created the world."

Said the Emperor: "Go then and study their Torah, but do not permit yourself to be circumcised."

To which Aquila with profound perspicacity replied: "Not

92

even the greatest sage in your empire, even if he lived a hundred years, would be able to understand their Torah if he were not circumcised."

For a literary artist with true Jewish sentiment and approach, the converts Onkelos and Aquila, who forsook the ranks of the powerful of the world to join the feeble clan of Jews, offer a far richer theme than Saul the deserter, who forsook his weak and oppressed people to join the "world." The historic progress of the heathen spirit to the Judaic is the very process by which mankind has advanced; and it is of a higher order and reaches to loftier peaks than are possible for a spirit traveling from Judaism to paganism. But Asch took the way of Paul and the theme of anti-Judaism.

When Paul first started out upon his journeys into the world to preach the "good news," his teaching was not so violently opposed to Judaism as it later came to be. He was still close to the views of the original eleven apostles, who held that the Nazarene came primarily to the Jews, and who further held that a gentile who sought to become a Christian needed first to become a Jew. Paul caused the first gentile whom he converted to Christianity to undergo circumcision. When he reached a non-Jewish town, his first act was to search out the Jewish group there, and to preach in their synagogue—if they had one. Like Jesus himself, Paul did not tire of reiterating that Jesus came to the Jews first and foremost; and only because the Jews had rejected Jesus was he, Paul, constrained to take his message to the gentiles. His new slogan was that the gentiles were to gain what the Jews had lost.

However, Paul perceived more clearly than the others that the new religion would never take root among Jews, even those of the Diaspora. For the Nazarene made his advent not merely as a messiah, but as the Son of God, and an equal authority with God, thus contravening the very essence of the Jewish concept of divine unity. He also laid his hand upon and demolished several fundamentals of the Torah, disparaging its eternity. As a messiah he failed completely, for the true Messiah was to bring not only spiritual redemption, but liberation from foreign oppression; Jesus did not free the Jews from the yoke of Rome.

So Paul carried the teaching of the Nazarene to the gentiles, and at the same time to Jews living outside of Judea. But among the Jews in the diaspora he encountered the same opposition he had suffered from those in the Holy Land; and he met many obstacles even among the pagans.

In one respect it was easy at that time to obtain recruits among the pagans for the emerging Christian faith. The entire known world, most of which was under Roman rule, was then in great turmoil; the Roman Empire was already well on its way to disintegration; it was devoured by corruption, reeling under revolt and barbarian attack; it was decadent in art and literature, as well as in religion and morals. The people felt premonitions that their world was on the verge of catastrophic collapse. Early Christianity offered the proper amelioration for their state of mind, for it, too, prophesied the end of the world. A sense of doom haunted the minds of men in all of the then civilized world, and the Christians fully shared the state of mind. Indeed, they helped create it. Everywhere the Christians raised the alarm that the world was about to perish and the destruction of the planet was imminent. But, what was most important, they had a definite "recipe" for the day after the catastrophe: the crucified messiah would make his second appearance and pass judgment on all men; the sinners would be hurled for all eternity into Gehinnom, and only the righteous, those truly prepared for the cataclysm, would be saved to enter into eternal life in the "Kingdom of God." And who would be considered righteous enough to partake of the promised redemption? Only he who believed in Jesus the Nazarene.

Ernest Renan maintains that without the worked up terror of the "end of the world," and without the great reward offered for the mere promise of belief, the heathen would never have so readily accepted Christianity.

But the heathen's compulsion to Christianity was but one half of a complex matter. The canon of the apostles which held that the way to Christianity lay through Judaism was then still operative, and conversion to Judaism was therefore a prerequisite. But conversion meant, first of all, circumcision, and not many were eager to submit to the necessary operation.

And there were other commands of the Torah that raised serious difficulties for heathens. For instance, the laws against bondage and slavery. The heathen world rested entirely on the foundation of involuntary servitude, but the enslavement of Jews by Jews is forbidden by the Torah. Other precepts of the Torah

94

were too profoundly Jewish-nationalistic to attract outsiders. The festival of Passover, for example, which is based upon the exodus from Egypt. Why should a Roman celebrate the fact that Jews had once been delivered from Egyptian bondage? Even the Sabbath bears a national temporal flavor: though its basic principle is universal sanctifying creation (and time)—it, too, is a "memorial to the exodus from Egypt."

But Paul was not one to be deterred by obstacles. With the flexibility of his principles, and with his talent for being "all things to all men," he found an "easy" solution: if it proves difficult for the gentile to accept the covenant of circumcision, simply abolish it! Following the hardy experiences of his tour of the heathen lands, Paul returned to the apostles in Jerusalem with the following immediate agendum: Is it a must for a gentile to be circumcised before becoming a follower of the Nazarene? The other apostles declared that it was a duty, but Paul insisted that it was not. This disagreement developed into the first great dispute in Christendom.

Paul won. But his proof was woven out of thin air. God, said he, had revealed Himself to Abraham before the patriarch was circumcised—solely out of recognition of Abraham's faith. It followed, therefore that circumcision was of minor importance; the primary thing was faith.

The absurdity becomes apparent at once when the argument is presented in reverse: God revealed Himself to Abraham before the circumcision, entirely because of his faith; yet thereafter He commanded Abraham concerning circumcision. Consequently faith alone is not enough.

There is no need here to discuss at length the significance of circumcision in Judaism. It is only necessary to show on what tenuous ground the final and absolute break between Judaism and Christianity was based. For this was indeed the crucial moment, the time of the parting of the ways. Here began what is known as Paulinism; here is rooted Pauline theology which, with all its dire consequences to Judaism and Christianity, quickly came to comprise Christianity entire.

Annulment of the commandment concerning circumcision was but the beginning. Driven by the same compulsion, and finding justification in the same logic, Paul proceeded to abrogate other precepts of the Torah, until finally he pronounced the entire Torah null and void. But Paul was faced with the dilemma

95

of breaking the cask, while preserving the wine: even while abrogating the Torah he was compelled to acknowledge its divinity and sanctity. For here the Christians sought authority for the new faith. On the Torah and the Prophets Christians from the beginning had laid the basis for their own religion. Jesus had said, "Moses wrote about me." But if the Torah had been handed down by God Himself, how could Paul venture to declare it void? This required exposition. Furthermore, discarding the Torah as binding upon Christianity, Paul was confronted with the task of offering something new to take the place of the old.

Paul provided his elucidations and offered his substitutions in what has come to be called the "Pauline theology" which we shall examine later. Suffice it to say here that in the entire history of the human mind there has never been a graver assault upon man's intelligence than the reasoning employed by Paul in repudiating the Torah and its commandments.

Let us pause here briefly to inquire in what manner Asch, in *The Apostle,* treats of Paul's assault upon the Torah in general and of the matter of circumcision in particular, which caused strife and contention within the ranks of the early Christians, and which in the end became the one mark that above all others sets off Judaism from Christianity.

There is not a vestige in his work of what the experience of nineteen centuries of Jewish history, from Paul to Asch, had taught concerning that mystic ritual of the Jewish faith. There was no power in history that could tear Israel away from it, neither the preachments of Paul nor the persecution by later Christians nor the pagans that preceded them. More than once the oppressors of Israel decreed the death penalty for observance of the rite, and more than one Jew paid for its performance with his life; but always, beginning with the reign of the wicked Antiochus in the Greek period, through Hadrian and the hegemony of the Roman imperium, through the Inquisition instituted by Christendom, to the communist dictatorship in Russia, Jews have persevered. The precept of circumcision has been observed with a devotion surpassing that accorded all other commands and ceremonials. Even free-thinking Jews have not been able to free themselves of its mystic power. The estranged and excommunicated Jewish heretic, Benedict Spinoza, said: "In the sign of the covenant I see such great significance that I am convinced that this command alone is sufficient to maintain eternally the existence of the Jews as a separate people." At the beginning of the twentieth century, when radicalism among the Jews reached its apogee, there were some radical Jews who avoided circumcising their children. The results often proved tragic, however, for regret in later years caused the error to be corrected when the children were already full grown. Often the children themselves made up for the omission of their parents when they reached adulthood. There is one case of the son of a radical father raising an unusual complaint: "By what right," asked the son of the sire, "did you *rob* me of my *right* to be circumcised? There are certain paternal rights, which one may employ as he sees fit, but circumcision is not a right within the purview of the father. It is a duty and a privilege that the child receives not from his parents, but from his people."

Something of this unique phenomenon should be reflected in Asch's novel of Paul, in order to give it a smattering of truth as well as greater artistic integrity. Nineteen centuries of history cannot lightly be dismissed, nor the light they cast backward upon the early dispute between Paul and the Jews ignored. But Asch neither includes, nor indeed is able to include the truth, for he too has been known to oppose the rite of the covenant of Abraham. In his early years of authorship he once caused a minor furor when he spoke out against this basic observance of Judaism, calling it a "barbarism."

To return to Paul's theology: what positive content did he give to Christianity once he had dissociated it from the Torah?

Let us here remind ourselves of the gentile who once approached Hillel the Elder with the demand that the sage expound the entire Torah to him while standing on one foot. To which the distinguished scholar placidly replied, "That which is hateful unto you, do it not unto thy neighbor. This is the entire Torah; the rest is commentary. Go forth and study it."

In imitation, the Gospels offer a similar episode, which is reputed to have taken place not while the speaker stood on one foot, but while he was shaking in an earthquake. Once, amidst the consternation of a great earthquake, Paul was asked to name the central point of his teaching. His answer was:

"Believe on the Lord Jesus Christ, and thou shalt be saved" (Acts xvi, 31).

This is what is crucial to Christianity: Not Torah, not good works, not divine commandments, but solely belief in Jesus.

97

We have already seen that Paul attempted an elucidation of the story of Abraham, to prove that faith alone is fundamental. This he made the entire basis of his religion, but at the same time transferring Abraham's faith in God to belief and faith in Jesus.

So firmly has this tenet of belief in Jesus been established as the core and basis of Christianity that it is not unnatural for a Christian theologian to write:

"There is only one sin which can damn the sinner forever. It is not murder or stealing or lying or immorality. All these are forgiven the moment the sinner trusts Christ. The one and only sin which will condemn you is unbelief, failure to believe the record that God gave His Son" (Dr. M. R. DeHaan: The Unpardonable Sin).

We shall have occasion to see that where a basic principle is involved, Judaism almost always presents a complete antithesis to Christianity; this first tenet of Pauline Christianity is a case in point.

Faith is unquestionably a basic factor in every religion, and therefore in Judaism. Nevertheless, as between faith and deeds, Judaism gives primacy to the latter. Concerning the divine charge in Jeremiah (xvi, iii)—"and they forsook Me and kept not My law"—the talmudic sages interpret it to mean: Would that they had forsaken Me, but kept My law. In other words: Great is faith, but greater still is the keeping of the Torah and its divine commands—practical faith. The believing act is held a more potent power for redemption than the believing abstraction.

However, one must not assume the mistaken notion that belief as such is disparaged or minimized in Judaism. Nothing is farther from the truth. Faith is an integral part of the Jewish religion. Israel has not been redeemed from Egyptian bondage except through faith, says one Midrash.

What exactly did Paul mean when he said, "Believe on the Lord Jesus Christ"? What must the Christian believe about Jesus? What content did Paul give to that belief? Having invalidated the Jewish Torah, he drew upon another source—Greek mythology.

Among the Greeks there were cults that believed in gods who died and were resurrected—symbolizing the agricultural changes of winter and summer. They further believed that men who practiced the mysteries of these gods and ate of the flesh and bathed in the blood of animals dedicated to them were invested with their divine attributes, their power and immortality. This

98

was later to emerge in the consecrated elements of the Eucharist.

Such is the essence of Paul's doctrine of "believing on the Lord Jesus Christ."

In place of the Torah, he built into the basis of Christianity the chief elements of Greco-Roman idolatry. He adopted the prime motifs of the Greek mystery cults, and clothed them in a Jewish garment. It was chiefly this that facilitated the spread of Christianity among the idolators and polytheists. These converts felt perfectly at home in the religion taught by Paul. It was their old home, newly decorated. "It can be shown," says Dr. Scott, "that in the most literal sense he was 'debtor to the Greeks and the barbarians, to the wise and the unwise.'"

Some of the mystic cults had man-gods who came down to earth, suffered there, and through their sufferings found their way back to heaven. They died and returned to life, again attaining their place among the gods, leaving their secrets to mankind, which—if man observed certain rituals—would assure his attainment of the celestial life of the gods. It was this esoteric teaching which Paul transferred to the Nazarene. To become a Christian, one must undergo the ritual immersion in water. This immersion signified going down into the grave with Christ, and then being reborn as a new man. As Christianity grew and spread it picked up more and more from pagan religion and absorbed it into its own body.

From the earliest days Christian apologetes have struggled to explain away this similarity between their religion and ancient idolatry, but with no success. Justin Martyr offers a very ingenious explanation indeed of this strange similarity. It was, he says, but a trick of the devil and the evil spirits. These spirits, he writes, having read the Bible, divined from Holy Writ that which was destined to come—the Christian religion. A great fear beset them, since this meant the end of their power. So in order to confuse mankind, they thought up and devised rites and ceremonies similar to those which they foresaw in Christianity. Thus they hoped that when the Nazarene made his advent and established his service, men would assume that Christians had borrowed their ritual from the ancient idolworshippers.

In the spirit of Justin, Tertullian adds, "We see how diligently the devil imitates the acts of God and also advocates baptism . . ." ("Christian Beginnings," Morton Scott Eslin, pp. 190-4).

The comments of these early Church Fathers find their echo

in the twentieth century, though of course in a slightly altered manner. Dr. Garr, Bishop of Worcester, England, says: "We find in heathenism, together with much that is false, superstitious, and horrible, anticipations of Christianity" ("The Churches and Modern Thought," Vivian Phelips, p. 111).

The active and widespread Christian sect, Jehovah's Witnesses, preaches that Catholicism is only a synthesis of Christianity and ancient paganism, a synthesis which was accomplished by the devil. In fact, they call it his greatest achievement. They therefore term Catholic Christianity "the devil's masterpiece."

In attempting to recapitulate the reasonings and dialectics employed by Paul to disannul the Torah, one discovers himself in a labyrinth of logical processes so twisted and eccentric as to make him ask in wonderment: Is this the fundament upon which rests a world religion, a universal church, an international civilization? The thought is frightening, intolerable.

By contrast, one stands in awe before the majestic grandeur and illumination of historic Judaism.

Yet Sholem Asch, nineteen centuries later, has adopted what Renan has termed Paul's "transcendental nonsense," rendering it even more nonsensical, and has come forth to propagate it to the Jews as "divine wisdom" by the man who "knew God best."

3

The Pauline Theology

In order to understand the full measure of sacrilege which Asch directs at the Jews and all that is most sacred to them in his book *The Apostle,* we must dip further into the confused murkiness of Paul's thought.

But to penetrate the mind of Paul is easier said than done. Not a single scholar but has despaired of discovering any logical coherence in the ideas of Paul. It should be remembered that even in the Gospels Paul is called "mad" (Acts xxvi, 24-5). In a second, more friendly description in the Gospels, Paul's epistles are described as containing "some things hard to be understood, which they that are unlearned and unstable wrest. . . . unto their own destruction" (II Peter, iii, 16).

100

Paul's entire stream of thought consists of one twisted idea enmeshed in another, usually based on a verse from the Torah or the prophets, which in its turn is twisted, distorted and wrenched from its true sense and meaning.

It can be said with perfect justice that Christians believe, but know not what they believe. What, asks Renan, does Paul mean by "justification" or "salvation" or "redemption"? It is no use denying, writes Rev. J. R. Cohu, that Paul's theology, nearly two thousand years old, is old-fashioned and often very involved even for the professional theologian. Involved indeed! So much so that two thousand years have not been enough to unravel the involutions. If such is the case with professional theologians, what of ordinary folks? Paul is so full of contradictions that scholars have been forced to the conclusion that not all thirteen epistles ascribed to him are actually his. The ultimate judgment, writes E. P. Scott, is that "Paul's Christianity has never been accepted by the whole Church, and in the nature of things it can never be." (Varieties of New Testament Religion, pp. 116-7).

But Sholem Asch had no scruples in accepting him *in toto,* and in presenting him to the Jews with the adjuration, "This is thy teacher, O Israel."

We now come to Paul's ideas of the Torah. The essence of his thought can be condensed into the following simple propositions:

1. The Jews believe the Torah was given to be valid eternally. No, says Paul; it was a temporary gift, operative only until the advent of Jesus. "It was added, because of transgressions, till the seed should come" (Galatians iii, 19).

2. The Jews believe that the Torah was handed down in order to serve as a guide to righteousness and virtuous living. No, says Paul; the exact opposite is true; it was transmitted to make sinners of men. "For by the law is the knowledge of sin" (Romans iii, 20).

3. The Jews believe the Torah conduces to life. By no means, declares Paul; it is the source of death. "The motions of sins, which were by the law, did work in our members to bring forth fruit unto death" (Romans vii, 5).

Lest anyone imagine that I, a Jewish partisan, show partiality in detailing the thoughts of Paul, let me quote from a Christian scholar, a Paulist and an apologete of Paul, the Reverend J. Cohu, previously cited here. Cohu characterizes Paul's ideas on the Torah as follows:

"Paul wants to do away with the Law altogether, and he hits on a peculiar method of cancelling it. He makes out that it is of no moral or spiritual value whatever in the religious education of mankind, except to convict men of sin and show them how bad they are. This is its only object. Therefore, says he, God intended it only for a season by way of a temporary makeshift till Christ came" (p. 50).

To quote further from Cohu:

"Not content with branding it as worthless for righteousness, he deliberately adds that the Law was given 'for the sake of transgressions'—i.e., merely to convict man of guilt in his own eyes and to provoke the latent power of sin to put forth its whole energy. In other words, Paul's whole contention is: The Law is revealed by God for a good purpose, only it is the exact opposite of what the Jews fancy. It is not given to make us good—that is utterly beyond its power—it is given only to make us see how bad we are . . . to bring us to the verge of despair which forces us to cry, 'Lord, have mercy on me, a miserable sinner.' Beyond this it cannot go one inch" (p. 51).

This is an informed statement of Paul's attitude toward the Torah. Or, as Paul himself states the case, in his unique fashion: "The sting of death is sin; and the power of sin is the Law" (I Corinthians, xv, 56).

The Torah or Law is then responsible for all sin! For, insists Paul, before the Torah was given no one knew what sin was; and when there was no knowledge of sin there was no sin.

"Because the law worketh wrath," says Paul, "for where no law is, there is no transgression" (Romans iv, 15). "Nay, I had not known sin, but by the law: for I had not known lust, except the law had said, Thou shalt not covet. But sin, taking occasion by the commandment, wrought in me all manner of concupiscence. For without the law sin was dead. . . . For sin, taking occasion by the commandment, deceived me, and by it slew me" (Romans vii, 7, 8, 11).

The Jew asks in amazement: Is this the language of one in his full senses?

Even the Ten Commandments are corrupters in the eyes of Paul. Instead of their conducing mankind to goodness and morality, he sees in them the actual origin of crime and cor-

102

ruption. This in spite of the fact that the Nazarene himself pronounced the Ten Commandments the very core and foundation of his teaching.

The theme of the Torah as the source of sin is repeated again and again by Paul, in numberless variations, like the theme of a symphony. The passages cited are not isolated and exceptional; they comprise his basic premise, though we have as yet only entered the antechamber of his doctrine. But enough has been seen to give us an idea of the inside of the mansion. It is a house with trick mirrors on every wall, where the mind is turned upside down and inside out, where common sense emerges to stare at you with the face of an atrocious looking gargoyle. It is a strange world indeed into which we are led by Paul—almost a pathological world. In this milieu it is not the corrupting lust of the flesh that is harmful; harmful and dangerous instead is the divine commandment, "Thou shalt not covet." It is not stealing that corrodes the social structure, but the command against stealing. Men apparently could go about happily cutting one another's throats, were it not for the tragedy of the Torah which impudently intruded itself upon man with the injunction, "Thou shalt not kill!"

From all this it would appear that until the giving of the Law man lived in blessed innocence. No one had any awareness of sin or transgression, of evil desires and wicked thoughts until the Torah was given to the Jews, and through the Jews to the world. It was the Torah that released all forces of evil. The Torah was like the serpent—may heaven protect us—which destroyed the happiness prevailing in the Garden of Eden. Or perhaps it was itself the tree of knowledge which brought death to the world.

And there rises again the old query—is this the way of the world? Does humanity live in accord with the notion that without laws there would be no crimes, and that it is only after a parliament or legislature promulgated laws that transgressions and criminal acts emerge?

Elsewhere Paul says: "For until the law sin was in the world: but sin is not imputed when there is no law" (Romans v, 13). "But sin, taking occasion by the commandment, (sin being provoked to action by the law) wrought in me all manner of concupiscence. For without the law sin was dead" (Romans vii, 7-8).

103

This is sometimes explained as follows: Before the Civil War it was perfectly legal to own slaves in the United States. One could buy them, sell them, pay for them, much or little or nothing. It was no transgression of any law on the books. But then the law came and made it illegal, and it was made punishable severely, but slavery is no more nor less morally wrong now than before the law was made, but where there is no law there is no transgression (Dr. M. R. DeHaan).

From this it would logically follow that the law should be maintained and upheld at all cost. But in the twisted logic of Paulinism the reverse is true: the law is voided. For "the law entered, that the offence might abound" (Romans v, 20). The law created the offence!

A quite appropriate illustration of Paul's teaching would be the case of the British scientist and the native African. A British scientist on an expedition in Africa saw a native eat a strange dried fruit. Curious to learn the nature of the fruit, he began examining it through a magnifying glass, where upon he discovered swarms of minute creatures upon it, invisible to the naked eye. He made the native look through the magnifying glass and admonished him not to eat the fruit. The native soon made the discovery that when he applied the glass the vermin were there, and when he removed it they ceased to exist. He decided that the glass was the cause of the vermin and he smashed it.

Paul provides neither enlightened analysis nor illuminating criticism of the Torah. His is merely the perverse hatred of a perverted mentality which has developed a fanatic animosity toward something it previously adored with fanatic devotion, and developed a most fantastic line of argumentation to bring about its destruction.

His detestation of the Torah extends to every single precept thereof. He makes light of the divine commands and abolishes them, declaring them incapable of making man just and righteous. In all his epistles he fulminates against the rules of living prescribed by the Torah. The precepts and works, he declares, are only outward things that do not touch the heart. They are of the "flesh" and not of the "spirit." They are the mere "letters," purely materialistic.

"Therefore by the deeds of the law there shall no flesh be justified in his sight: for by the law is the knowledge of sin"

104

(Romans iii, 20). The commands of the Torah, according to Paul, are a cumulative burden which mankind cannot endure; they are too difficult to perform, and when one does not perform them he is punished and thus he comes to "death." "For as many as are under the works of the law are under the curse" (Galatians iii, 10); this is a reference to Deuteronomy xxvii, 26: "Cursed be he that confirmeth not the words of this law to do them."

This interpretation is a good example of the barbaric methods employed by Paul to rend the Torah apart and trample upon its fragments. He is the father of the base and despicable method of using the Torah against itself. His modus is most simple: quote a passage and omit its companion piece. Better than this—omit the second half of a passage. For in a long chapter immediately following the curses in Deuteronomy are recounted the blessings to be visited upon all who do observe the Torah: "Blessed shalt thou be in the city, and blessed shalt thou be in the field. Blessed shall be the fruit of thy body, and the fruit of thy land. ..." (xxviii, 3-4).

The dark abyss of Paul's thought appears even more dim and frightening when one further peruses that portion of the Torah and notes the commands which Paul would frighten men into believing are incapable of fulfilment. We note that it is the non-observance of these laws which bring men into the purviews of the biblical curse. We read:

"Cursed be the man that maketh a graven or molten image. ... Cursed be he that dishonoreth his father or his mother. ... Cursed be he that removeth his neighbor's landmark. ... Cursed be he that maketh the blind to go astray in his way. ... Cursed be he that perverteth the justice due to the stranger, fatherless, and widow. ... Cursed be he that lieth with his father's wife. ... Cursed be he that lieth with any manner of beast. ... Cursed be he that lieth with his sister. ... Cursed be he that smiteth his neighbor in secret. ... Cursed be he that taketh a bribe to slay an innocent person" (xxvii, 15-25).

Is it maintained that these prime principles of justice and morality are also incapable of fulfilment by man? Was it by such commands that the Torah brought about concupiscence and transgression? Are these the restraints which Paul wishes mankind to discard on penalty of death?

In the law, according to Paul's theology, God demands something that sinful man cannot do. But what about the Sermon on the Mount, this piece of ingrained passivity and inadequacy in the face of life?

All this, however, Sholem Asch would make us believe, inspired and exalted the Jews listening to Paul: "Flames of hope shone in the eyes of the Jews; fountains of joy opened within their hearts" (The Apostle, p. 446).

At no time does Asch raise a voice of protest, objection or contradiction to any of these perversions of the Torah, nor are any of his Jewish characters permitted to do so. Can Paul be right?

God forbid my posing such a question! It need never cross the lips of a Jew! But Cohu, in the book already cited, does question Paul and dispute his declarations. He shows that Paul is not right in his evaluation of the Torah, nor of the "ill" effects of the laws and statutes therein. Well do we know, he writes, that under the influence of the Torah there developed many wonderful Jews; Jesus and the apostles themselves were products of the Law. "Paul's wholesale condemnation of the Law is too sweeping and, indeed, unbiblical," says Rev. Cohu (p. 50).

Here is a Christian minister, born and reared in the Christian faith, undertaking the defense of the Torah's honor against the apostle to the gentiles. But Sholem Asch does no such thing! Asch travels with Paul through a long literary production, accompanies him through life, on all his journeys and through all the vicissitudes of his soul. He delineates his character by means of Paul's own words as recorded in the Gospels and in words of his own devising; yet never a syllable is ventured against the apostle when he abuses the Torah and treads its honor in the dust.

4

Man: Corrupt or Divine?

One should ask of Paul: if it be true that the Torah and all its statutes lack the power to lead mankind to God, why should it have been given to man in the first place?

We discover the answer emblazoned on the crooked walls of another weird chamber of the bizarre edifice of Paul's thought. It is premised on his singular views on the nature of man. Paul's

106

prime thesis concerning man is that he is naturally a sinner, maculate, unclean, corrupt. He bears an inherited sin, the original sin of Adam. Adam's malefaction in rebelling against God is transmitted like a kind of mystical "substance" to all Adam's descendants, from generation to generation, polluting every soul. Every man is therefore corrupted at birth, every soul sullied with evil at its very origin. "Each man then is born an enemy of God," in the language of Catholic theology. And there is nothing that man can do to change this condition. It lies not within his will or power to redeem himself from this dark heritage. Neither righteousness, prayer, nor acts of charity are of any avail. As the leopard is unable to remove his spots, man cannot erase the stain from his soul. No matter what he does, no matter how virtuous and pious he may be, no amount of good deeds and noble striving can liberate him from the stigma of original sin. The punishment therefore is death from everlasting to everlasting.

Only God could rescue man from this awful doom. And, thank God, He did: such is the solution proffered by Paul in a dogma accepted by all sects, shades and ramifications of the Christian religion. It is the central creed and tenet of Christianity. The substance of it is as follows:

Insomuch as man had not the power, nor indeed the will, to save himself from that fatal sin and its consequences, God, in His infinite mercy and love, took pity on man and laid out the course whereby he might be forgiven for the terrible crime of the first Adam, as follows:

Original sin, like every other sin, could be atoned for only through a sacrifice with shedding of blood, according to Pauline theology. But man could never command a sacrifice so precious as to be commensurate with the enormity of the crime of original sin and conciliate the Lord in his divine justice. God alone could provide a suitable sacrifice to conciliate himself. And he did, says Paul.

He sent His son, Jesus, down to earth. The son, as the lamb of God, was the perfect sacrifice. He suffered, was tortured, and was finally crucified. He died to wipe out the sin that since Adam polluted the nature of man. God thereupon wiped out the guilt of Adam. This was done by the Lord not because of the merit of man, in the way of reward for good deeds, but as a voluntary gift, a present, an act of grace. This grace consists in eternal life after death. However, that grace is granted only those who believe on

Jesus and are baptized in his name. All those who refuse to accept belief in Jesus go to hell and there suffer excruciating torments everlastingly.

Pauline theology thus turned heaven into a strictly Christian reserve with signs nailed everywhere on its well guarded gates bearing the legend: "For Christians only." At the very point where God is supposed to have displayed his greatest mercy and love, Pauline theology has planted the seeds of rejection and bigotry.

At the risk of digression let me here point out that Dante, good Christian that he was, in his Divine Comedy dismisses his pagan guide Virgil as they reach the gates of Paradise. Virgil took him through purgatory and hell, but as a non-Christian he could not set foot in heaven. He is left behind in a neutral zone between heaven and hell, where dwell in eternal twilight the great spirits of antiquity, like Socrates, Aristotle and Plato, who have been spared hell in virtue of the fact that they walked the earth prior to the appearance of Jesus.

Compare with this the teaching of Judaism: "The righteous of all nations have a share in the world to come" (Toselta Sanhedrin, 13). Now, which is the broader outlook, the greater basis for mutual understanding, the stronger bulwark for democratic civilization?

To return to our discussion of Christian grace. Paul makes the Torah, or Law, a forerunner of grace, but all in a negative sense. The core of the Pauline doctrine is that grace was in the mind of God from the very beginning. It was pre-existent with God. Then the Law of Moses "was added" (Galatians iii, 19), i.e., placed alongside of grace. Why? "Because of transgression" (ibid) —whatever that may mean. Christian theology has interpreted it to mean that the Law was promulgated to show that it was impossible of fulfillment and therefore it was ineffective as a means of attaining righteousness. And there being no righteousness there could be no redemption. At the same time the Torah was designed to show and reveal the true character and awfulness of sin, to the point where man will realize his utter dependence on the grace of God. This was granted in the death of Jesus.

This is as clear a simplification as one may hope to get out of the serpentine course of Paul's writings. No less singular than the doctrine itself is Paul's proof thereof. "For if righteousness come by the law, he argues, then Christ is dead in vain" (Galatians ii, 21).

In the wake of this doctrine Christian theology saw its main task in abusing, reviling and disparaging the law of Moses: "The law," argues one preacher-theologian, "could not save, justify or sanctify the sinner. It cannot make the sinner a saint, it cannot forgive sin, it cannot change the heart, it cannot teach us to live better, it cannot help us out of our predicament in any way whatsoever. God knew when he gave the law it would never save a single sinner, never make a single man better . . . the law was a slave driver, an executioner, seeking to kill us because of our sins. The law condemns, curses and accuses the transgressor, but it cannot forgive, justify or save the sinner, it cannot redeem nor make one holy."

That the Torah stood up under this universal deluge of abuse is further proof of its indestructibility.

The doctrine of grace is focal in Christianity. It is responsible for the Christian God being called the "God of Love" while the Jewish God is called a "God of vengeance." For one cannot *earn* the grace of Christianity. It can only be attained as a free gift, from on high, granted out of pure love, whereas the Jew must work hard at attaining the world to come. He must observe the 613 divine precepts and live a life of righteousness, charity and good deeds. For this reason, too, the Christians call Judaism a "legalistic" faith, a sort of give-and-take religion—no reward without services rendered. The Christian gets everything for nothing.

In brief, in Pauline theology the Torah was transmitted to the Jews not that they might thereby attain perfection and show the way to perfection to all men; it is not at all suited to the task. The divine intent in regard to the giving of the Law was precisely to prove this impossibility, and to prepare humanity for the understanding and acceptance of divine grace.

But when Jesus came down to complete that divine idea, the plan miscarried, because the Jews threw a monkey wrench into the scheme. They failed to comprehend the divine design. They refused to recognize the redeemer. They flew in the very face of Providence. They remained halfway on the road to fulfilment; they saw only the negative side of redemption; they wilfully shut themselves off from the complete fulfilment of redemption in Jesus. This came about because the Jews were so obstinate about the Torah. God had never intended the Torah to remain eternal; only the Jews labored under that misapprehension. Thus the Jews, chosen only to demonstrate that the Torah does not save, became victims of their own election. "They remained bound up in their Torah," writes Jacques Maritain, "as though in God's trap." ("St. Paul" p. 71) To put it somewhat vulgarly: the Torah was meant to be only God's grand jest, but the Jews, fools that they were, accepted it in all seriousness.

Thus in Paulinism the Torah, with the divinely directed Jewish destiny therein, is turned into a heavenly farce, where heaven and earth are the stage, mankind the audience, God the chief actor, and the Jew "he who gets slapped."

It was this theology which Jefferson termed "great corrupter of the doctrines of Jesus"; and Renan—"the acme of transcendental nonsense."

And Sholem Asch?

Asch testifies: "The thoughts of Saul were clear and fresh, the wheels of his mind spun smoothly, like wheels of a mill driven by a steady stream. His senses, his heart, the intuition of his spirit, were alert, working vigorously, driving forward ceaselessly toward the ultimate truth" (196).

In the eight hundred pages of *The Apostle* he finds no occasion for a single favorable word in behalf of the Torah and its commandments nor does he anywhere offer at least a neutral presentation of the Jewish viewpoint vis-a-vis the Paulinist, as his integrity as a literary artist, if not also, his integrity as a Jew demanded that he do, regardless of whether or not he was competent to have any say in such matters at all.

From Asch's book one would hardly surmise that there is such a thing as a Jewish viewpoint in opposition to Paul's Christianity. Asch seeks to create the illusion that when Paul traveled among the Jewish communities in the diaspora the Jews fell before him like wheat before the reaper. Judaism just melted away in the breath from his lips. There was but minor resistance here and there, but no ideological opposition to speak of.

But the case was not as simple as all that.

Not out of obduracy or blindness or entanglement in "God's trap" did the Jews arise in opposition to Christianity, but for fundamental reasons great and glorious. We may take as an example the matter of "sin." Judaism offers a totally different concept of human nature from that offered by Paul. Paul's idea of mankind is pessimistic, fatalistic. Man is subject to a fatal sin, and he can do nothing on his own to extricate himself from his fate. Such a thought is alien to Judaism. It is a legacy Paul inherited

110

from his Greco-Roman background. "Fate" is Greek. To the Greeks man is nothing but a plaything of the gods and he can do nothing whatever to influence his destiny.

Judaism rejects with all its energy and might Paul's basic dogma of original sin, or of the essential corruption of man. Judaism holds firmly to the principle of free will. To the Jew sin is of the world which man enters when he is born; one does not come into the world with pre-natal sin. "Thy coming into the world is without sin" (Baba Mezia 107a), says the Talmud with a directness that is symbolical of the fundamental gulf between two essentially opposed systems of thought. "Know you that the Holy One is pure, his angels are pure, and the soul which He gave you is pure" (Niddah 30b), is the basic teaching of Judaism.

"O my God," daily prays the observant Jew, "the soul which Thou gavest me is pure; Thou didst create it, Thou didst form it, Thou didst breathe it into me."

"As God is pure, so is the soul pure," the Talmud says elsewhere (Berakhot 11). Can there be a higher concept than this?

Sin is man-made and entirely of this world. "Behold, this only have I found, that God made man upright; but they have sought out many inventions (Ecclesiastes vii, 29).

And in Proverbs we read: "The foolishness of man perverteth his way; and his heart fretteth against the Lord" (Proverbs xix, 3).

In the middle ages Saadia Gaon wrote: "We say that in the whole body of the human being there is nothing that is morally impure; he is pure" (Emunot Vedeot vi, 17).

A contemporary Jewish writer, Martin Buber, adds, "According to the Jewish concept, the human personality is in the same status of inner freedom as was the first Adam."

Judaism, generally speaking, has no propensity for abstract theology. Where other religions express themselves through theological speculation, Judaism speaks by way of parable. And so we find the idea of man and sin conveyed in the following Midrash:

"Thus will it be in the Time to Come. The soul and the body will be standing for judgment. What will the Holy One, blessed be He, do? He will let the body alone, and take the soul to task. The latter will say before Him: 'O Lord of the universe, we have sinned both of us as one; why dost Thou let the body alone, and take me to task?' He will answer her: 'The body is from the lower (earthly) regions, from a place where they sin, but thou art from the upper (celestial) regions, from a place where they do not sin.

111

Therefore do I let the body alone, and take you to task'" (Leviticus Rabbah iv 5).

Man enters the world, not with sin, but with God. Instead of original sin Judaism believes in the original divinity of man. The psalmist pours out his heart before his Maker: "Thou art my God from my mother's womb" (Psalms xxii, 11).

Christian insistence for support of its view on Psalms li, 7, "Behold, I was brought forth in iniquity, and in sin did my mother conceive me"—is negated by the Midrash (Leviticus Rabbah xiv, 5), which holds that the passage bears on the process leading to birth, not on the emergence of the soul.

Judaism holds a far more exalted opinion of man than Paul introduced into Christian doctrine. One might add that it is one of the most remarkable phenomena of history that the Jew, who has suffered most from the evildoing of men, has greater faith in the inherent goodness and purity of mankind than the mighty Christians who rule the earth.

Man comes into the world with grace, which if he loses it is through his own sin. Sin is not given, it is taken. "A man does not commit a transgression except the spirit of madness enter into him" (Sot. 3b). It is something external. It is not a contamination of the soul, but a product of the will. However, man is a free agent and he may by his own effort regain his grace, by turning away from his evil ways. He may *repent*.

Repentance has sometimes been called "the Jewish doctrine of salvation." Where Paul places grace as pre-existent with God, Judaism places repentance. Our sages taught: "When the Lord God conceived the idea of creating the world, he thought: how will it stand up in the face of the sins of man? Whereupon he created repentance first and then proceeded to create the world." (Beth Hamidrash) Elsewhere (Pes. 54a): seven things were created before the world was made: the Law, repentance etc. Paul may well have borrowed his notion from here.

Repentance is thus revealed as one of the Divine things that formed part of God's plan for man even prior to creation. The Jewish teaching concerning sin, repentance and forgiveness forms a rich man-redeeming message. Yet the same malignant perversion apparent in Pauline theology with reference to the Torah, emerges here too, as will appear from the following quotation:

"Paul asserts that any man who at any time or in any measure has ever broken one of the laws of God only once, is under the

112

curse of the law and is lost, condemned and hopeless as far as the penalty of the law is concerned. If you have not kept the entire law in every detail all of your life without a single interruption, then according to these (Paul's) unmistakable words, you are under the curse of God and must suffer the penalty of the law which is eternal death and separation from the presence of your Creator." The law "could not save or pardon or redeem or improve or fix up or help or assist, forgive or change the heart of the sinner (M. R. DeHaan)."

There can be no grosser misrepresentation and violation of the truth than this. Opposed to grace, the central principle of Judaism is that man is perfectible through his own powers.

The key to the understanding of Judaism is the doctrine of repentance. Judaism knows the human heart inside out, not missing a single beat. It is fully aware of human weakness, of man's inclination to evil—the "yetzer hara," which lives in every human heart. Unlike Christianity, Judaism does not strive at uprooting the "yetzer," but at gaining mastery over it. It subjects inclination to will. And where he yields to weakness man's heart is a battlefield—he can always regain his equilibrium by repenting. It is here where his real humanity lies, in the exercise of his free will. He has freedom of choice and moral responsibility. Man, like his Maker, is himself Creator who lends dignity to life. The Jewish doctrine of repentance is infinitely simple. To Paul, and to all Christianity, a person who does not believe in Jesus as intermediary is completely cut off from God. In Judaism the bond between God and man—be the man Jew or Gentile—is never completely severed. The way for God and man to meet again is always open. Judaism has accorded the penitent a most exalted position. "How great is the virtue of repentance!" exclaims Maimonides with ecstasy. "But yesterday he was loathsome and repulsive before God, and today he is beloved and accepted before God" (Hilchot Teshuvah). And there is that outstanding dictum of the Jewish sages: "In the place where repentant sinners stand, the perfectly righteous are not permitted to stand" (Ber. 34b).

From all the foregoing it follows as a corollary that, insomuch as Jews did not believe in original sin, they could not accept the belief that the sin was wiped out by the sacrifice of "God's only begotten son."

The legend of Jesus coming as a vicarious sacrifice for mankind raises more questions to the Jew than it offers answers for the Christian. In the first place, what of the prophet who orates: "And the word of the Lord came to me, saying: What is the meaning that you use among you this parable as a proverb in the land of Israel saying: The fathers have eaten sour grapes and the teeth of the children are set on edge. As I live, saith the Lord God this parable shall be no more to you a proverb in Israel . . . the soul that sinneth, it shall die" (Ezekiel xviii, 1-4) . Does not this argue powerfully against the doctrine of vicarious sacrifice and settle the question as far as the Jew is concerned, once and for all?

Then, if God did in truth send down His son with the express intent that he suffer a martyred death, then the Jews—assuming that they were in fact responsible for the death sentence—were merely the good messengers of the Lord, loyally carrying out His behest. They were the instrument whereby Christian humanity was blessed with its greatest good. The Scriptures are replete with reproaches against the Jews because of their rebelliousness to God; but if the Jews had again remained faithful to this "tradition," God's plan for humanity would never have been executed, and the Christians would have remained eternally deprived of redemption. "But by their offence, salvation is come unto the Gentiles" (Romans ii, 11) . Properly speaking, the Jews should have been gratefully embraced by the Christians for their stand. Instead, Israel has forever smarted under showers of Christian blows.

If, on the other hand, what the Jews did to Jesus—if, it must again be added, they ever really did anything but reject him—was the most outrageous of all crimes, deicide, then, we cannot avoid the conclusion that mankind was redeemed through commission of a crime. Does this offer a very exalted concept of redemption? God, appearing to atone for all sin, could accomplish His own will only through commission of the gravest sin of all! In terms of theology, is this not a contradiction within the Deity itself?

These are some Jewish queries which Asch could have posed about Paul, had he not in writing his opus forgotten that he was a Jew. But there are other more general questions.

There is one that is at once very simple and very disturbing: To whom, in the last analysis, was God's son offered as a sacrifice?

Sacrifices are offered to God. In this case it would appear to have been God's demand that His own son be sacrificed to Himself. But had not God long before, in the binding of Isaac by Abraham, revealed His will and desire for the pure heart, humble obedience, and not the sacrifice of humans?

114

Again, what is the aim of sacrifice? It is offered as remuneration, compensation, fine, or redemption price, to satisfy God's justice and appease His anger. Then according to Paul God must have spoken thus in His heart: I shall send My son down to earth, so that men shall torture him and in the end slay him. In that manner My anger will be stilled and My justice satisfied. Because of this I shall forgive all men's sins and redeem them from death.

This is a strange kind of divine economy, indeed. Could not the Almighty restrain and mitigate His own anger without subjecting his only Son to the torments of death? Here were God's son and God's moral order: wasn't the placating of His own grievances by sacrificing His own son like taking something out of one pocket of the celestial trousers and placing it in another?

As a Jew, Sholem Asch should have been troubled by these questions. They have greatly disturbed even Christians, who to this day have vainly sought for answers that would satisfy human reason or the religious conscience.

The theology of the early Christian centuries maintained that the martyred death of Jesus was a redemption or a fine paid to the devil; which meant that men were under the control of Satan, and that the only way for God to win them back was to appease Satan through the greatest imaginable sacrifice. The chief exponents of this teaching were three of the most distinguished Church Fathers —Irenae, Origen and Augustine.

Obviously such a doctrine could not be satisfactorily maintained, despite the high authority of its proponents. The theory apparently solved the difficult problem of the need of a sacrifice, but it made God subservient or inferior to Satan, God being compelled to buy off the devil.

This solution was favored until the eleventh century, when Anselm of Canterbury proposed an alternative answer: he taught that the death of Jesus was to be understood as damages or quitclaim paid to God because of the injury done God's honor through humanity's sinning. But since humanity itself did not possess a fully satisfactory sacrifice God Himself became human in Jesus to make proper payment feasible in the form of the death which He then voluntarily chose for Himself instead of His creatures. Thus the devil was disposed of, but the inference was that God offered Himself up to Himself, and the confusion was by no means allayed.

Innumerable other interpretations followed. It is not the

115

task of this work to enumerate them all, but one recent highly original solution should be cited: It has been suggested that Jesus was not a sacrifice to God or devil at all, but of all things an offering from God to man, God offering His son as a redemption of the sin He had Himself committed against mankind in having created men sinners!

With this umbrageous web of thought and puzzlement of heart, contrast the genial simplicity wherewith Judaism solves the God-man problem. On the passage: "The heavens are the heavens of the Lord; but the earth hath He given to the children of men" (Psalms cxv, 16) the ancient sages comment: "Before the Torah was given the heavens were the heavens of the Lord and the earth was given to the sons of man; but when the Torah was given, Moses ascended to God and God descended to Mount Sinai" (Yalkut Shimeoni 273).

It is thus that the vital contact between heaven and earth has been established: God and man met in the Torah.

They were first united in the Image of God. They were again united at Mount Sinai. They are forever face to face in the Torah.

"Said God to man: Thy lamp is in My hand and My lamp is in thine hand. . . . If thou lightest My lamp I shall light thine." (Vayikra Rabbah, xxxi, 4). Thus man is made dependent upon God, and God is made dependent upon man, and they meet in the light of the Torah.

The same idea, here symbolically expressed, is expounded in philosophical terms by Maimonides: "Thought is the intellect, whose influence is spread over us, and which is the vinculum between man and God. And just as we grasp godliness through the light of the intellect, just so are we perceived by God through the same light, and through that illumination He is ever with us and envelops us in His glance."

The idea of an intermediary between God and man is completely alien to the Jew. The true intermediaries, says the Zohar, are repentance, prayer, and charity: "Just as the flame clothes the black coal in a garment of fire, and liberates the heat sealed within, so does prayer clothe a man in a garment of holiness, and evokes that light and fire the Creator placed within; and it illuminates his entire being, and unites the lower and upper worlds."

Such, then, are some of the problems raised by Paulinism, which more than once have perturbed the Christian Church and which are the terror of every thinking Christian who seeks clarity

116

and warmth in his religion. They show themselves even more glaringly to the inquiring Jew.

In *The Apostle,* however, Sholem Asch never touches on these profound issues and points in dispute, which form the polarity of cleavage between Judaism and Christianity.

5

Torah and Works

When Asch wrote *The Apostle* and gave new utterance to Paul's aberrant teaching that the Torah and commandments are capable only of creating sinners and wicked men, not righteous humans, how could he keep a straight face before Jewish people, before Jewish history, before the heroes and heroines of his own works? The numberless Torah—true Jews in his own *A Town, Kiddush Hashem,* and *The Psalms-Jew* (Salvation), the men of righteousness and love and kindness, the pious, the pundits and the worshippers, the upright and pure in heart, Jews and Jewesses not only of his own writings but of all Jewish literature are a living denial of the perverted idea that "By the deeds of the Law there shall be no flesh justified in His sight; for by the Law is the knowledge of sin" (Romans iii, 20).

Forty centuries of Jewish history look down upon Sholem Asch, and cry into his face, "Shame!"

And twenty centuries of Christian history also cry in his face, "Shame!"

For what is the verdict of history?

That by its fruit you shall know the tree is a principle set up by Christianity itself. The German people, with its Auschwitz and Maidanek, is the fruit of the Christian tree, twenty centuries later.

What is the Jewish retort to this brutal assault upon the Holy of Holies of the Jewish people, and to the Christian contention that belief in the Torah leads to moral death and decay? Even a birds-eye view of the historic landscape will reveal marvelous things.

There is not, nor has there ever been, in all the world, greater courage and greater pride than the courage and pride of the Jew, who, despite the violent condemnation of the Torah implanted by

117

Paul among the nations, has cherished and exalted it above all else on earth and has held it up in the face of all the peoples. There is not another faith or place of worship under the sun that knows so impressive a ceremony, a ritual inspiring such lofty dignity, as that constituting the reading of the Torah in the synagogue, from the moment when the Scroll with pious trepidation is removed from the Holy Ark until the time when with pious challenge it is lifted, unrolled, above the heads of the congregants, and its face is turned in all directions, with the entire congregation proclaiming in ever new affirmation and reassertion: "And this is the Torah which Moses set before the children of Israel, according to the commandment of the Lord by the hand of Moses!"

One of the most dulcet prayers in the Jewish prayerbook is uttered in the sweetness of the first morning hours, when dew still rests on the fields and slumber on many an eyelid:

"Make pleasant, therefore, we beseech Thee, O Lord our God, the words of Thy Torah in our mouth and in the mouth of Thy people, the house of Israel, so that we with our offspring and the offspring of Thy people, the house of Israel, may all know Thy name and learn Thy Law. Blessed art Thou, O Lord, who teachest the Law to Thy People Israel."

God is a "melamed," a pedagogue, teacher of Torah to His people Israel!

The Torah is a curse, says Paul. What matters it to us what Paul says? Let us relearn the words of Hananiah ben Akashiah:

"God wished to give worth and virtue to the people of Israel; for this reason he gave them a plenitude of Torah and commandments." The more the merrier.

The 613 divine commands of the Torah were not sufficient to satisfy the soul in its craving for fulfillment. The sages labored in the Torah and exerted themselves to the utmost to derive and extract more and more laws and principles out of the text of Holy Writ. The Gaon of Vilno taught:

"The 613 commands are but the roots. These develop into many branches. In truth it is concealed from us which are the roots and which the branches. And it is not at all necessary that we know this. For in every separate precept and every single word of the Torah are contained the entire Torah and all its commands, with all their details and particulars. That is why the Torah is compared to a tree. Just as in a tree the single root grows to expand into many branches, and every branch into many twigs, and

118

every twig bears many fruits, and each fruit has numerous seeds, and every seed has the power to bring forth an entire tree with the roots and branches and fruits and seeds, and the extended power to create more trees, without end—such is the Torah, and its commandments." (Maalot Hatorah) The Gaon also taught that man is accounted above the angels, for the Torah was entrusted to man not to angels.

Sholem Asch's Apostle has no better designation for the Torah than "death," whereas our sages have no other name for it but "Torah of life." It is "thy life and the length of thy days" not only for Jews but for all the world. The world can endure only through the Torah, says the Midrash; God made this condition at the time of the Creation to apply to all He created: if the Jews accept the Torah, all will be well; and if they do not, all things will revert to a primordial chaos.

Asch's hero preaches that the commands of the Torah create sin and sinners, but our holy sages teach us that through the Torah man ascends to the level of holiness, is joined with the Holy One, and that nothing is so capable of breaking man's evil inclination as study of the Law. The sages speak for God: "I have created the evil inclination, and I have created the Torah for which it is the seasoning." The sages have added: "If you are beset by that ugly creature, the evil inclination, drag him into the House of Study." The Torah tears man away from sin, purifies of sin, and gives a remedy for sin. The sages declare that he who is zealously occupied with Torah is not required to present burnt offerings, meal offerings, or guilt offerings; for the Torah purifies of all sin. The Torah is likened to water and fire: Just as water cleanses of impurity, so does the Torah provide cleansing; and just as fire burns thorns so does the Torah consume sin, which is likened to thorns. The Torah even possesses the power of physical healing. If your head aches, says the Talmud, study Torah. If you apprehend agonies approaching you, turn to the Torah, and the agonies will flee from you.

Asch's hero, Paul, proclaims that the Jews' clinging to their Torah and commandments and their repudiation of Jesus have caused God to repudiate them. As if in direct reply, the Midrash (Echah Rabah) says, in the name of Ben Azzai, that Israel was exiled because the people denied the one and only God of the universe, rejecting the rite of circumcision, the Ten Commandments, and the five books of the Torah.

119

By instrumentality of the Torah, at Mount Sinai, did the Jews become a nation; and through the Torah did they remain a people in exile. The secret of the preservation of the Jewish people in foreign lands, and the perpetuation of its historic national life under the rule, and the oppression, of powerful and frequently hostile governments, have occupied the minds not only of Jews but of wise men everywhere. After the breach of the walls of Zion and the fall of the fortress of Bethar, when Rome's mighty sword hacked down our national existence, the people were uprooted from fatherland, state, soil; and the world thought assuredly that Jewish history had come to an end. In particular Christianity had thus assumed. But events did not follow that pattern. The Roman imperium could lay low all bulwarks and ramparts, but one bulwark it could not overcome—the yeshivah, the academy of Torah. There were Jabneh and its offshoots, Tiberias, Nahardea, Pumpeditha, up to Telz and Mir and Wolozhin and New York. The Divine Presence in the form of the Torah accompanied the Jews in all lands of exile, preserving the body and soul of Israel from disintegration.

But the Torah was given not only to the Jews. Through the Jews it was transmitted to all humankind. All men have been exalted through it. "A gentile studying Torah is equal to the high priest," says the Talmud.

Numbers xix, 14 begins with the words, "This is the law: when a man. . . ." The sages expounded the juxtaposition of these words by asserting: He is called a man only by virtue of the Torah. Referring to Genesis v, 1, "This is the book of the generations of Adam," the comment is that this is the Book in which *man* has his birth. Again, in connection with "Thou makest men as the fishes of the sea," the sages explain that, just as the fishes of the sea die as soon as they are removed from their element of water, so it is with men; once they remove themselves from the Torah, they are doomed to death.

A man lacking Torah, assert the sages, is defective, even when apparently sound in every limb; and he is poor even though his apparent affluence be equal to that of Korah.

Thus the Jews from of old elevated study of the Law as the highest aim of mankind. One estimated a man's worth by his knowledge of the Torah. In the cradle the babe heard lullabies that Torah was "the best of all wares." The most exalted occupation was zeal and devotion to Torah day and night. There

120

have been Jews who have reputedly studied the Torah in their sleep and in their death-throes.

That "Torah is the best of all wares," was no idle phrase. Torah was commingled with one's daily occupation. While arranging a sale, seller and buyer would discuss Torah. Men gave up their businesses or turned them over to their wives in order to give themselves entirely to Torah, contemptuously relegating economic welfare to a minor role. On journeys to the fairs men would take huge tomes of the Talmud with them.

It is related that once in the city of Minsk, during the high holidays, a Jew approached the Holy Ark with the prayer:

"Master of the universe, if Thou hast inscribed me for the coming year with success in my business affairs, I beg you to take it back and give it me instead in the study of Torah."

Jewish love of the Torah is a unique phenomenon. This singular devotion has a character all its own. Among the loves of which the human heart is capable, the love of Torah is of a distinct content. Like all love it is difficult of definition, but it remains actual and of amazing potency. The Torah has taken an entire people under its wing, and has extended its power over them for thousands of years. This eternal rapture has been the theme of innumerable parables, glorified in prose and sung in poetry. An example of prose glorification of Torah study is to be found in Pesach Marcus' "Der Vilner Gaon," a novel of the era of the Gaon of Vilno; and its poetic counterpart is the magnificent "Hamathmid" by Bialik. The love animating the Marcus novel into an exciting tale is the love of Torah. One of the characters says: "There is no greater pleasure in the world than gazing into a devout book, even when one does not understand what is written therein." And these are some of the lines of Bialik's poem:

"O God, I pray Thee, take me as I am,
Take all Thou wilt, my body and its blood,
For I am vowed to Thee and to Thy Torah . . .
For her my body knows no rest, for her
These eyes shall ask in vain for sleep, until
The thirst that burns my soul is satisfied.
With earliest dawn I will awake, keep vigil
Through half the night till I have conquered all,
Till I am master of the sacred lore."

(Maurice Samuel's translation)
For centuries upon centuries, Torah study has been the prime

interest, ambition, ideal, pride, glory, pleasure, raison d'etre, and divine service of the Jewish people.

The love for the Torah is a consuming passion, which even pain in achievement has failed to mitigate. Numbers xix, 14, says, "This is the law: when a man dies. . . ." The proximity of the words, "law" and "die," makes the sages interpret the partial sentence to mean: The Torah may be achieved only if one is willing to die for it. Jewish students of all generations have been aware of the bitter truth: "A morsel of bread with salt thou must eat, and water by measure must thou drink; thou must sleep upon the ground, and live a life of trouble, the while thou toilest in the Torah" (Aboth vi, 4). However, "If thou doest this, happy shalt thou be and it shall be well with thee (Psalms cxviii, 2): happy shalt thou be in this world, and it shall be well with thee in the world to come" (ibidem). The implications of another world are also derived from Torah study.

There is the story of the sage who pondered much over the idea of the world to come and longed to gain an insight into the meaning of Paradise. Then one day this insight was granted him. He dreamt he was in the other world, and was being conducted by an angel to behold Eden. He was led to a plain, humble structure, in appearance much like the ordinary, homely beth-medresh or House of Study. The angel opened the door, and pointing inside, said, "This is Paradise!"

The visitor beheld a group of Jews seated around a table, deeply engaged in the study of Torah, just as in the Houses of Study he had known on earth.

"Is that it?" he asked in amazement.

"Yes, that is it," replied the angel.

"Is that all there is?" he plumbed further. "Yes, that is all there is," said the angel, explaining: "It is not that the righteous are in Paradise, but that paradise is in the righteous."

Thus all there is to the world to come is preoccupation with the Torah: in studying it in this world man has a taste of the world to come.

The same idea, somewhat differently slanted, is contained in a popular Yeshivah-song, the first lines of which run something like this in English translation:

After-life, in Heaven, is a vision grand and sweet;
But the study of our Torah is a greater treat.
Therefore, put aside your every burden, yoke and chore

122

And devote yourself to Torah studies ever more.

Studying the Law or learning Torah is different from every other kind of learning. The relationship between child and teacher in the "Talmud Torah" or "kheder" is entirely different from that between teacher and child in the schools of the nations. The relationship of the yeshivah student and his teacher of Talmud differs from that of student and professor over ordinary books; and no outsider can really appreciate the distinction. Torah is studied not for utility, but for perfection of the soul. The Jew does not study Torah to prepare himself for the world, but to redeem the world; his study of Torah is a prop upholding the universe, and is the reason and justification of its existence. The Kingdom of God on earth is brought nearer. The Jew ponders the Torah to gain a taste of the world to come in the world here below and to glorify God's name. He studies not merely to know; but goes a hundred times over matter he already knows, sounding the depths anew. He studies Torah, for in it he perceives the secrets of creation; in it the heavens stand open before him; in it he speaks to God, and God speaks to him.

The story is told of a certain rabbi who used to speed through his prayers in order to hasten back to his studies. While the congregation was still reciting the prayers, he was already back over his tomes. When questioned about this practice, he answered: "When we pray, we talk to God; when we study the Torah, God talks to us. Which is preferable?"

As has been said, one studies Torah not for the purpose of amassing knowledge, nor for utility or enjoyment, but as divine service. It is the pathway to God. A student of the historic yeshivah at Mir has described the mode and spirit of learning in that noted center of Torah as follows:

"It was a kind of workshop, which took apart all the screws of the spiritual apparatus of a man. Took apart and cleaned and polished, and put together again into the essence of a greater personality, with a high mind, a sound strong heart, and a pure soul . . . . After the students finished at the yeshivah and journeyed home, many returned with their wives to resume their studies there, for after leaving the yeshivah it was not easy to adjust one's self to the sinful world without. When away the soul had no rest; the return had to be made even from a foreign country, and even with an entire family." . . . On the night of Simchath Torah (the Rejoicing of the Law) they used to dance all through the dark hours, singing stentoriously, 'Moses is true, and his Torah is true!' and 'the heavens joined the dance and were doubtlessly envious of the small plot of earth on which stood the Mir yeshivah'" (Rabbi A. J. Hertzman, "The Mir Yeshivah in Exile") . This description applies equally to all similar institutions.

The thoughts expressed by Jews on the Torah and its study in the Torah itself, in the Talmud, in the Midrash, in philosophical volumes, and in every branch of Jewish lore, are as numerous as the particles in the Milky Way, as numerous and as bright and beautiful. And if a Jewish writer has no knowledge of them, has he the right to function as a writer among Jews? And if he knows but wilfully ignores them, and instead he comes to advance teachings alien and even antagonistic to the Torah and its statutes, what should be said of him?

The first thing a Jew says after arising and washing his hands so that he may begin to pray is a proclamation before heaven and earth that "the Torah which Moses commanded us is the inheritance of the congregation of Jacob." Then follows the morning service full of prayers and supplications concerning the Torah, —that God may open our hearts with understanding of the Torah, enlighten our eyes in the Torah, and turn us again to the Torah. The entire Siddur (prayerbook) is replete with references to the Torah, as is the machasor (holiday prayerbook) , as are the schools, the yeshivot, and the homes. All of life is rendered sacred by Torah.

To all this Sholem Asch's own works bear testimony. He writes of a Jew standing in recital of the sacred prayer of the Eighteen Blessings. A messenger rushes up breathlessly and cries, "The stream has torn away the rafts and carried them off! All your fortune is in peril! Master, what shall be done?"

But the Jew does not move. He continues to recite the Eighteen Blessings. He does not speed nor hurry the recitation. He continues in his regular tempo.

How can Sholem Asch dare approach this Jew of his own creation with his Gospel-preaching that the Torah is causing moral death?

Another of Asch's beautiful stories tells of a boy lying at night on his bed. It is winter and the house is cold; he yearns to creep into his mother's bed, cuddle up to her and warm himself. He cannot restrain himself from finally going over to her. While he rests there, he begins to think perhaps it is not proper for a boy

124

already going to kheder to sleep in bed with his mother. Upon which he devises a penalty for himself: he sticks his little foot out from under the featherbed and into the cold room, as atonement for his transgression.

Is it to this lad grown old that Asch presents *The Apostle* with its message that the Torah corrupts?

Who can truly describe the attachment of the Jew to the Torah, the inseparability of the Torah and Israel, and the manner in which each glorifies and beautifies the other?

There is a story of the famed Rabbis Akiba Eiger and Jacob Lisser arriving in Warsaw. At the station they boarded a cart and were riding to their lodgings. When the news of their coming was heard, all Warsaw Jewry rushed out to greet the two distinguished scholars. In their enthusiasm the townfolk removed the horses from the harness and themselves drew the cart. But the thought came to Rabbi Eiger that their actions were in honor of Rabbi Lisser. So he managed to crawl out of the vehicle and put his shoulder to the wheel. In the excitement no one remarked the change.

The Lisser Gaon, for his part, was equally sure that the honor was being accorded to Rabbi Akiba Eiger. So he, too, unnoticed, descended and helped push the conveyance.

Thus it came about that a congregation of Jews in devout exaltation pulled and pushed a wagon load that carried nothing— except the honor and glory of the Torah.

That is what Torah means to the Jew.

O Paul, where is thy sting?

6

"Flesh" and "Spirit"

Having done away with the Torah what does Christianity hold in place of the laws and precepts in Judaism?

With that involved dialectic which Renan termed "the acme of nonsense" Paul concocted the idea that the Christian requires no commandments and no guides to conduct. Faith alone is sufficient and itself achieves morality. When the "sinner" is "baptized in Jesus," the "holy ghost" enters to dwell within him, providing light and guidance in his thoughts and actions. The Christian, at least in theory, can do no wrong, since the Nazarene lives in him and he in the Nazarene. He finds himself always carried by the stream of loving kindness. He is clothed with the perfect, sinless righteousness of Jesus himself.

"The Christian needs no outer signs of external deeds as the Jew does," writes Professor Maritain, in his work on Paul: "The soul of the Christian is turned inward, and not commandments observed or deeds performed, only faith and love and inner purity make the Christian, who is the true Israel of the spirit, replacing the Israel of the flesh."

This is the basic difference, defined and bequeathed to the Christians by Paul, between Judaism and Christianity. And if Paul has been termed the first corrupter of Christianity, this is the point where he must also be termed the greatest falsifier of Judaism. For there can be no viler falsehood than to say that Judaism is a faith only of outer deeds, which do not touch the heart and soul. In the prime principles of the Jewish faith, recited in the Shema while the worshipper is clothed with the prayer-shawl and phylacteries, there is the adjuration, "And thou shalt love the Lord thy God with all thy heart and with all thy soul and with all thy might." Every line from the Prophets cries to high heaven for heart and soul in man's religion. Let one but read the first chapter of Isaiah, or the sages of the Talmud, who said: "God demands the heart," or any of the later Jewish writers. The heart's devotion is the life and spirit of chassidism.

Nevertheless, on this utterly false assumption Paul deprives us of the name of Israel, and the Christians with it. Judaism, which requires true circumcision in the flesh, to him becomes a religion of the outer flesh and one of the dead letter, not a true faith. The Jew is only an Israelite by the mark in his flesh; only through circumcision is he still a descendant of Abraham. But the Christian is the heir of Abraham's *spirit,* and is the true Israel. In fact, throughout the centuries the Catholic Church has designated itself the true Israel.

Judaism is not an abstract doctrine, not merely a collection of fine phrases, but a doctrine of lofty concepts, striving to find realization in deeds: "Not the word is the thing but the deed." The strength of Judaism is in its direction of practical life, in the rites and ceremonies, laws and customs wherein its philosophy is embodied. In Judaism man is not left to grope alone in the dark or to have to decide for himself the wrongness or rightness of

126

everything he does; he is educated and enlightened as to what is right conduct and the proper course of life.

The sages have taught that "a man's mind is governed by his deeds." Man is what he does. He makes himself in and through relating himself to God, to his world and to his fellow men. Deeds become habit. Habit becomes nature, and nature is character. This is the basic idea underlying all Jewish commandments and precepts. This is why it has been said that commands performed without intent are still considered meritorious; for even though a man does not set out to do good for the sake of the good, he will ultimately do so for the sake of the virtue therein. For this reason the Jewish sages encompassed all Jewish life, weekday as well as festival, by day, hour and minute, with divine precepts and prescribed deeds of goodness. Both the Written Law (Torah) and the Oral Law (Talmud) have been transmuted into one law of the heart.

Judaism is first and foremost a code of behavior, with none of the chill, however, that informs the legal codes. Rather is it the passion of belief translated into the reality of concrete life. Its commandments are not commands or orders, but rather in the nature of instructions, directions, recommendations, advice, counsel, promptings, pleas. The pursuit of happiness is the pursuit of the good deed. The Jew is taught to pursue the good deed, to seek it out, not only do it when it comes to hand. The first duty is to make others happy, then your own happiness will follow, as a matter of course. Voluntary effort on behalf of one's fellow men is the core of this code. Under the influence of this inspiring teaching the Jewish community during the ages has become so strong in common virtues that they seemed highly uncommon.

The extraneous non-Jewish world has not had the remotest conception of the lofty heights often attained by Jews in the realization here and now of the ideal of "a kingdom of priests of a holy people." In the midst of a corrupt world the Jewish people, small, weak, and often dwelling apart, off the main highways of humanity, through long stretches of time actually touched the very heavens with its head. There were great and blessed moments when Israel became in the truest sense of the word "God's people," not in any borrowed or rhetorical sense, but in full actuality. This is a vast and fascinating subject which can here receive only passing mention. However, he who is thirsty for the knowledge need only dip up the pure well of Judaism and taste. Lying on the open road of history, three such clear, sparkling springs can here, in passing, be pointed out. There is a Hebrew book, "Yeven Metzulah," by Rabbi Nathan Hanover of the seventeenth century, the last chapter of which should be read by every seeker after such knowledge. This offers an account of life among the Jews of the Ukraine on the eve of their extermination by Khmielnicki in the massacre of 1648, one of the most atrocious in history. And there is A. J. Heschel's "The Earth Is the Lord's," recounting the mode and mood of Jewish life in East Europe before Hitler destroyed it. Or one may read Rabbi J. D. Soloveitchik's "Ish Hahalachah" —"Man of Law," published in "Talpioth," 1944—a spiritual portrait of the Talmudic Jew, really the Pharisee, shamefully and unjustly maligned by the Christians as "hypocrite."

In all the three essays of small format, the searcher will realize the mystery of Israel's survival unto eternity. There he will clearly perceive the actual and living union of the Israel of God with the God of Israel.

In the chapter mentioned of *Yeven Metzulah* the reader will note how the Polish Jew lived in piety of body and mind, ever alive to his duty to God and to his fellow-man, whether Jew or Gentile. He studied the Torah and gave to the poor. He studied his Torah and provided succor for the widow, the orphan, and the dowerless bride. He studied the Torah and extended hospitality to the wayfarer. He studied the Torah and clothed the naked. He studied the Torah and piously watched his weights and measures. He studied the Torah and supported the study of the Torah. Such was the effect of the Torah.

The small work by Heschel shows us the Jew poor in possessions but magnificently rich in spirit. Heschel shows the very matter transformed into the spirit. The Jew is revealed in his perpetual impulsion towards the heavens. His feet never leave the ground —he takes the earth with him on his lofty journey.

And in the *Ish Hahalachah* we see the realization in flesh and blood of that paean to man. "And Thou hast made him only a little less than God." Godly man in his purest essence—this is what the "Ish Hahalachah" has been throughout the generations. He is the pious scholar who has been purified in the divine fire of the Torah and whose mind has been refined in the workshop of the Jewish law and jurisprudence, where the Jewish spirit attains the lofty heights, where dwells absolute justice.

128

And the "Ish Hahalachah" is none other than the great-great-great etc. grandson of the "Pharisee."

Life such as this described in the works cited above are not isolated phenomena, but characteristic of communities and epochs. Men of great piety and holiness abounded everywhere one turned. There was no place, no street, no family, which lacked its exceptional ethical personality, the wonder of the vicinage, and even beyond, exercising that beneficent influence, which was to endear him to countless generations. The Jews were not alone in finding blessing from these men; gentiles did also. But we are not dealing here with individuals. We are concerned with large communities, the entirety of Israel. "Yeven Metzulah" speaks of Polish Jewry during a specific epoch. "The Earth Is the Lord's" covers centuries of the Jews of East Europe. "Man of Law" presents the Jewish spiritual character through all the generations under the Talmud.

Sholem Asch was well familiar with all this. In his own works he more than once pictured this kind of Jewish life. But when he entered the Christian literary field he adopted the Christological outlook, that Judaism, with its elaborate system of divine commands, was naught but a yoke. "There were also Jews," he says, "who were weary of the heavy burden of the laws, which were increased from day to day by the Rabbis—Jews who, lapsing from observance, always felt sinful and trembled at the thought of Judgment Day. Here suddenly by their faith in the Messiah preached by the messengers, they were freed from the yoke; not only was their future free but the sins which they had committed in the past . . . were wiped out" (The Apostle, p. 334). The same tune was sung in *The Nazarene* and was to be repeated in *Mary*: "caught between two millstones—the government on the one hand and, on the other, the learned scribes and doctors who brandished the Law over their heads, and kept them pent in a prison which held their souls together with their bodies captive" (Mary, p. 63).

There were two views of the works of the Torah and the Rabbis held by the apostles. One, the yoke-view, was held by Peter, who said: "Now therefore, why tempt ye God, to put a yoke upon the neck of the disciples, which neither our fathers nor we were able to bear" (Acts x, 15); and there was the view of the more subtle Paul that they were useless for salvation. Sholem Asch accepts both views and hammers away at them throughout

129

all his Christological effort. Nowhere does he make an attempt for a just appraisal of their significance in the light of Jewish history.

What Peter and Asch call a yoke is strength in the Jewish estimate. On the other hand, the basic weakness of Christianity, in the Jewish view, is its failure to provide clear precepts and rules of observance for its votaries. No, the commands are not a yoke that oppresses, but rather wings that elevate. "A wild Ass's colt is born a man" (Job xi, 12) —he must be educated and enlightened. "The commandments were given only to purify mankind" (Genesis Rabbah lxiv). To perform them is to exercise in sanctity, virtue, and beauty. The man who knows how to conduct his days in sanctity, virtue, and beauty, is truly the free man. It is in this sense that the sages declared, "No one is free except he that deals in the Torah."

Far from being a yoke, the commands are the source of freedom. The ultimate aim of the liberation from Egypt was the Giving of the Law. True liberty is in the Law.

The view that the biblical statutes are an oppressive yoke is one of the most foul perversions of truth in the history of human thought. What has been the noblest and most successful experiment in the education of man has been smothered under a fog of misunderstanding, denial, prejudice and hostility. Christian doctrine considers the human soul utterly corrupt, never redeemable by any man's good deeds. In Judaism the soul is looked upon as bearing both good and evil within it; through good deeds and religious observances the good is aided in gaining ascendancy over the evil. The very life and nature of the Jew have justified these ways of God to man. But Christians have been blinded by a Pauline dogma. And Asch has come to carry forward this blindness.

Jewish biblical precepts are by no means of the nature of stern orders of a king to his subjects, or a master to his servants, but the gestures of a good father to his children, of a preceptor to his pupils. They are not the blind fiats of a capricious God, but the concretizations of divine goodness and the wisdom of the ages. They are blessed imperatives, duties that become benedictions in performance.

Fear of God, knowledge of God, faith in God, and consummation of religious acts are the fulfillment of Judaism. But action is basic. Neither learning nor belief is sufficient, nor both together; they must be upheld with good deeds. Not what a man be-

130

lieves but what he does is his true measure. As to mere faith in God—some of the world's most wicked individuals have professed such faith.

The Jew's modes of conduct are minutely prescribed, or rather described; and he knows exactly what he must do to render his life proper and acceptable before God and man. Through the unity of faith and deeds the religious Jew becomes inwardly and outwardly unified. There is nothing secular in his life. Every move he makes reflects a sense of the Divine Presence. But one must be taught and enlightened as to what is the good life, worthy of pursuit. "Thine eyes shall see thy Teachers; and thine ears shall hear a word behind thee, saying: 'This is the way, walk ye in it, when ye turn to the right, and when ye turn to the left'" (Isaiah xxx, 20 —21).

Except for the strictly religious rites, Christianity prescribes no specific pattern for living. The Christian is enjoined to a vague "be nice, do good," but is offered no advice on just what constitutes goodness and how it is attained. Says Protestant Martin Luther: "Just as the New Testament can provide the physician with no prescription for the healing of physical man, so can no man derive from the book any rules of conduct." The same is admitted by St. Thomas Aquinas on behalf of Catholicism. Aquinas does not undertake to establish a social system from the New Testament, and he is compelled to take recourse in the ethics of "natural law." Although Judaism trusts in the essential goodness of the heart of man, it has nevertheless set markers and milestones all along life's road to guide man to the good, the true and the beautiful. But Christianity, which teaches that man's heart is inherently corrupt, still leaves him largely to his own devices, blindly to tap a cane in the dark. Christian theology is well aware of this weakness and it seeks to make a virtue of its fault by appealing to free will. It acknowledges that the Nazarene never established any economic system, or definite rules of social justice or of righteousness. These matters were to be left to one's choice and device as a free agent.

Judaism rejects this conception of free will. "Greater is he who is commanded and acts than he who acts without being commanded" (Kiddushin 31a). There is a profound theological-philosophical principle reflected in this dictum. He who performs a good deed because he is bidden to must often overcome the evil inclination which bids him not to perform it. There is a struggle in the soul. And even if he stops short of performance, he still

131

agrees that God's will should be his. But he who performs the good deed on his own account often does so as a natural act, neither invested with spiritual values nor elevated by God's holiness. In evil deeds there has long been recognized a distinction between an intended and an unintentional crime.

Only he can be truly religious who has the choice of being non-religious. In the eyes of Christians the Jew, with his prepared roster of commandments, appears a mere legalist, or, what is worse, an automaton. But Judaism sees in its commandments the greatest liberty and the highest creativeness. "He who fulfills the Torah and carries out its precepts in truth, is even as though he himself had decreed it and handed it down from Mount Sinai" (Tanhuma, Ki Tavo), said the sages.

No finer tribute to man can be imagined.

Judaism has long known the psychological truth of what William James said that if one acts a part one presently develops the feelings that implement the action.

The practical precepts, in the view of the Rabbis, are best calculated to awaken the intellectual love of God and the inward emotions of the heart. It is written, "The divine commandment is the candle, the Torah is the light." When can the light be seen? When the candle is illuminated. And as Saadiah Gaon put it: "A fire cannot be made visible except it be attached to some tangible thing."

Passion alone quickly spends itself and perishes.

"He whose wisdom exceeds his deeds, to what is he like? To a tree whose branches are many, but whose roots are few; and the wind comes and plucks it up and overturns it upon its face" (Aboth iii, 22).

By his deeds man, in Judaism, gains his standing before God through his own efforts. He is co-creative with God of his own destiny. Christianity is a redemption from evil; Judaism is a pilgrimage toward the good. In Christianity salvation is a gift, in Judaism salvation is a prize.

7

A Tragic Cleavage

In Christianity God is limited to the sphere of faith or theology, as is attested by Jesus' dictum, "Render unto Caesar what is Caesar's, and to God what is God's." This is one of the most fateful utterances ever made. It drives a wedge between heaven and earth, between creed and life. It leaves Caesar without God and God without concern for Caesar's doings. It is of a piece with "my kingdom is not of this world," bespeaking a recoiling and revulsion from the world. It was this concept that led to the tragic cleavage between the divine and the secular in the life of the Christian nations. It is otherwise with Caesar in Judaism. Here he is sternly subjected to the laws of God, like any ordinary mortal. It is written of him, "And it shall be, when he sitteth upon the throne of his kingdom, that he shall make him a copy of this law in a book . . . and it shall be with him, and he shall read therein all the days of his life; that he may learn to fear the Lord his God, to keep all the words of this law and these statutes to do them . . . and that he turn not aside from the commandment to the right hand or to the left" (Deut. xvii, 18, 19). Judaism is not weighted down by the oppressive dichotomy which cuts the heart of Christianity in two.

This dichotomy takes on an even more frightening meaning as it is further developed by the founder of Protestantism, Martin Luther: "There are two kingdoms," he wrote, "one the kingdom of God, the other the kingdom of earth. God's kingdom is of kindness and mercy; but that of the earth is marked by wrath and horror. Those who wish to mingle both realms, as is the case with certain fanatics of error, would transfer the wrath to the kingdom of God, and mercy to the kingdom of earth—but this would be tantamount to removing the devil to paradise and God to hell."

An excellent illustration of the workings of the God-Caesar principle is offered in a humorous piece that is supposed to emanate from turbulent Colombia.

A priest was sent on a religious mission to a section of Colombia where the Conservatives and the Liberals were particularly violent in their opposition. When he arrived, one of the Conservatives approached him for a confession. "I accuse myself, father," he began. "I have killed many Liberal men and children, I have raped their women, burned their homes, destroyed their crops, and . . ."

"Let's not talk politics, my dear son," quickly interrupted the priest. "Just tell me your sins." (Pathfinder, March, 1952; *Awake,* June 22, 1952).

And of course the sins have been forgiven, too. This easy forgiving of sin is one of the chief allurements of Christianity.

133

Gloating over this, Sholem Asch writes: "Most assuredly this was something which imparted a special attraction to the words of the messengers" (p. 334). It constitutes a great attraction to this day and is preached with even greater fervor by the messengers of today than by the first messengers. Thus we read: "You may be the meanest, lowest, despicable, iniquity-smitten, sin-ridden, devil-deluded, liquor sodden, law-breaking, blaspheming, hell-bent and hell-deserving sinner in the world and feel that you are the worst creature in the universe, yet the moment you believe on the Lord Jesus Christ and receive him as your Saviour you are instantaneously transformed into a child of God, justified in his sight, saved for time and eternity, and all your past record blotted out forever and forever" (Dr. M. K. DeHaan: "Tetelestai," p. 28).

The Jew recoils in dismay at such a conception of sin and forgiveness. Voicing Pauline sentiments, Asch deprecates Judaism beacuse its votaries "always felt sinful and trembled at the thought of the Judgment Day." Assuming this to be a fair representation of Jewish doctrine, it is far better that the sinner always tremble at the thought of Judgment Day than that he spend a lifetime in spreading corruption and misery in the world, and in the end, at a mere signing of himself with the cross find himself "immediately seated in the heavenliness" with Christ.

It is a misreading or misrepresentation of the spirit of Judaism to say that the Jew must always be oppressed by a sense of guilt, with no priest, no grace and no saviour to relieve him. Repentance is always his and forgiveness ever within reach. We read in a beautiful Midrash: Wisdom was asked, what is the punishment of the sinner? And she replied: Sinners are pursued by (their) evil. Prophecy replied: The soul that sinneth, the same shall die. The Torah replied: Let him bring a sacrifice. But God replied: Let him repent and it shall be forgiven him (Jerushalmi Makos, 2).

But here is a significant consideration: it is the sinner that is forgiven by repentance, not the sins. There must be utmost endeavor to undo the guilty action and to conciliate him who has been wronged. Rabbi Elazar ben Azaryah is the author of a saying which has become a part of Jewish parlance in all ages: "For transgressions against God, the Day of Atonement atones; but for transgressions against a fellow-man, the Day of Atonement does not atone, so long as the sinner has not redressed the wrong done, and conciliated the man he has sinned against." Of such repentance the

134

Rabbis said: "Great is repentance for it brings healing to the world"—to the world, not just to the penitent.

Thus in Judaism sin is sweated out and worked off, while in Christianity it is washed away into the cesspool of time, which is growing and swelling with the growth of time and is today engulfing mankind and sapping the foundations of civilizations.

It was Jewish teaching as here outlined that made possible an episode like the following:

Rabbi Ezekiel Trentschiner, eighteenth century rabbi of Unzdorf, who served important congregations in Hungary and Slovakia, once addressed his congregation in this manner on the eve of Yom Kippur (Kol Nidre night):

"It is well known, my brethren, that every rabbi is required to offer admonition to his worshippers on Yom Kippur. He must open their eyes to their errors, so that they may repent and avoid similar transgressions in the future. But tonight I shall be silent; I have nothing to say to you, nor do I know what to say. You are all good, devoted, and pious; you study the Law and perform good deeds. There is not a home in Unzdorf from which there does not resound the voice of Torah. Therefore, brethren, instead of rebuking you, I give you my blessing. May the All-highest grant you all a happy new year" (J. Greenwald, "A Thousand Years of Jewish Life in Hungary.").

It was under the divine light shining out of the pages of the Torah that this blessed fruit blossomed forth, the Torah that is supposed to corrupt.

Let us summon up from ancient days two Jewish spirits as witness to the effect of the Torah upon those who ponder it and walk in its ways:

"Said Rabbi Phineas ben Jair: Torah leads to precision, precision leads to zeal, zeal leads to cleanliness, cleanliness leads to restraint, restraint leads to purity, purity leads to saintliness, saintliness leads to meekness, meekness leads to fear of sin, fear of sin leads to holiness, holiness leads to (the possession of) the Holy Spirit" (Abodah Zarah 20b).

Subtly and profoundly are here depicted the psychological stages and degrees through which the Torah guides man, step by step, to the highest rung on the ladder, Jacob's ladder, which rises from the earth and reaches unto heaven.

A second deposition: "Rabbi Meir said: Whosoever labors in the Torah for its own sake merits many things; and not only so,

135

but the whole world is indebted to him; he is called friend, beloved, a lover of the All-present, a lover of mankind; it clothes him in meekness and reverence; it fits him to become just, pious, upright, and faithful; it keeps him far from sin, and draws him near to virtue; through him the world enjoys counsel and sound knowledge . . . and it gives him sovereignty and dominion and discerning judgment; to him the secrets of the Torah are revealed; he is made like a never-failing fountain, and like a river that flows on with ever-sustained vigor; he becomes modest, long-suffering, and forgiving of insults; and it magnifies and exalts him above all things" (Aboth vi, 1).

Nevertheless Paul passed us off as "Israel of the flesh," labeling Christians the "True Israel of the spirit." Witness:

"For they that are after the flesh do mind the things of the flesh; but they that are after the spirit, the things of the spirit. For to be carnally minded is death; but to be spiritually minded is life and peace. Because the carnal mind is enmity against God. . . . So then they that are in the flesh cannot please God" (Romans viii, 5-8).

Consider the horrifying picture of the Jew painted in these few verses of Paul. The Jew is sunk in things of the flesh; he is a carrier of death, an enemy of life and peace, an enemy to God himself.

It is this view by the most powerful figure in Christianity that misled and forever blinded the Christian world to the true face of Judaism.

"To begin with," writes Dr. Cohu, "Judaism does not fall into line with our idea of a true religion. Our idea of a religion is that it should work from within outwards. The heart is the mainspring of all our actions; the driving power must be there, and no religion will quicken and leaven our daily life which does not first appeal to the heart. It should, therefore, lay stress upon the spirit rather than the letter of its commands, upon the motive rather than the deed, upon being rather than doing.

"Now the Jewish Law seems to do just the very opposite. The bulk of it consists of precepts to be literally obeyed, rites and ceremonies to be punctiliously observed, while its moral and spiritual elements seem infinitesimal. It orders us to do this and refrain from that for the sake of our own weal or woe. We obey from selfish fear of punishment or hope of reward. Morally and

136

spiritually this compliance does us little or no good. It does not touch our heart or will, and leaves us in character as we were.

"Again, the God of the Law may be a just Judge, but He does not appeal to us as a Father, neither do we feel the love of children towards Him. Under the Law, the relationship between God and man becomes a kind of legal contract between master and servant. So much work and so much pay.

"In other words, Judaism is avowedly a legal religion, and our modern contention is that all legalism in religion, with its endless inelastic rules, must soon degenerate into a mere hollow routine" (Cohu, St. Paul, pp. 52-53).

It grieves one no end to hearken to such sacrilegious nonsense!

Of such it is said (Aboth vi, 2): "Every day a heavenly voice goes forth from Mount Sinai, proclaiming these words, 'Woe to mankind for contempt of the Torah!' "

One can only feel pity for Reverend Cohu and the like-minded in Christendom, but it is hard to forgive them. For through two thousand years a people has lived among them with its Torah, and they have wilfully remained ignorant of both, knowing not what the people accomplished with the Torah, and what the Torah did for the people. Unfortunately this is the generally prevailing picture of Judaism in all of Christendom. For millennia Paul has kept mankind blind to the true spirit of the Torah and Judaism, the blind spot in the Christian view being that Judaism is a religion of give-and-take.

In truth it is Christianity that exists on promise of reward granted in advance, whereas Judaism is an entirely free transaction. "Elect for Christ and escape damnation" is Christianity in a nutshell. For mere believing in Jesus, man is granted God's grace, forgiveness of all sin, eternal life, and the resurrection. No other faith offers such extraordinary bargains. "Behold, I come quickly and my reward is with me," said Jesus (Revelations xxii, 12). And Peter spoke to his master and said: "See, we have given up all and followed thee. What shall we have therefor?" "A hundred-fold," answered Jesus (Matt. xix, 27-29).

Judaism teaches, "Be not like servants who serve the master for the sake of receiving a reward (Aboth 1, 3); also, the reward of a good deed is the good deed" (ibid iv, 2). It is written further: "If you chance to say, I am studying Torah in order to amass

137

riches thereby, or that I may be called rabbi, or that I may be rewarded in the world to come, it is written (Deuteronomy xi, 23) 'to love'; everything you do in this regard must be done out of love only." The Midrash says: "Said the Lord, If the nations should open their treasuries and offer my people all the money in the world for a single word of the Torah, they would never succeed" (Shir Hashirim Rabbah vi, 7).

It is told that the Gaon of Vilno dreamt one night that for some reason he had lost all future life in the world to come. When he awoke he was unusually gay and happy. Queried by his associates, he told them of the dream, and said:

"I rejoice because from now on I can serve God without any thought or prospect of reward."

The Rabbi of Ladi, addressing himself to the Lord, said: "I fear not Thy hell, I care not for Thy heaven, I only love Thee alone." "For God I will even go to hell," said another Rabbi.

Mr. S. B. Shragai, first Jewish Mayor of reclaimed Jerusalem and a religious writer of note, says: "We cling to the Torah and its precepts not for reward, nor for fear of punishment, but because of their truth."

The Torah is the mighty stream of spirituality, flowing since ancient times through Israel. It would have caused no useful fruits to grow, and would have produced no spiritual progress, no moral advancement, had the mitzvah not been there to lead its divine floods into the homes, the hearts and the minds of the individual members of the people by connecting practical life in all its variety and activities with the spiritual truths of religion. It is the greatest mistake, based on an entire misunderstanding of human nature to assume that men are capable of living in a world of ideas only, and can dispense with symbols that should embody these ideas and give them tangibility and visible form (M. Jung). The mitzvahs (commandments) in Judaism and the lack of them in Christianity are symbolical of the diametrical disagreement of the two faiths that is irreconcilable.

This is not to say that the concept of faith as such, or of pure grace, is not given due recognition in Judaism. All of the elements upon which Paul has erected the structure of Christianity are contained in the single verse from Hosea (ii, 21-22) included in the daily morning prayer:

"And I will espouse thee unto me for ever, I will espouse thee unto me in *righteousness,* and in Judgment, and in loving kindness

138

and in mercy: I will espouse thee unto me in *faith,* and thou shalt know the Lord." But Paul gave these new directions, into which the Jew could not follow him.

The doctrine of God made man in Jesus is only a projection of the teaching of man made in the image of God. All men.

As to faith, the Midrash says: "Israel has not been redeemed from the bondage of Egypt except through faith."

The doctrine of the indwelling presence of the Holy Spirit as guide to Christian conduct is only an extension of the Jewish teaching for all men, "In all thy ways acknowledge Him and He shall direct thy paths" (Proverbs iii, 6).

And whatever meaning Paul reads into the Cross—atonement and grace—is contained in the story of the deluge and the covenant of the rainbow. After the deluge which atoned for all the sins of mankind, God said:

"And I will establish my covenant with you; neither shall all flesh be cut off anymore by the waters of the flood; neither shall there any more be a flood to destroy the earth." I have set my bow in the cloud and it shall be as for a token of a covenant between me and the earth . . . between me and you and every living creature of all flesh . . . that I may remember the everlasting covenant between God and every living creature of all flesh that is upon the earth" (Gen. ix, 8-17). The meaning of this, according to the Hebrew sages, is that when strict justice demands that man shall be destroyed for his sins, this sign of the rainbow in the clouds shall save him.

Paul usurped the meaning and significance of the rainbow and substituted the cross for it. But the rainbow is still there.

All this is of the essence of the position of Judaism over against Christianity. It is the ultimate opposite of it. But nowhere in *The Apostle* is it treated with proper reverence and dignity. Asch piously restates Paul's views, but their counterweights in Judaism are omitted. No attempt is made to offer the Jewish side on any point in the controversy, to counterbalance arguments and to match logic. Judaism is here merely surrendered. It is betrayed.

8

Two Towns

Nineteen hundred years separate Paul and the book about him written by Sholem Asch. After close to two millennia it could not be the task of a writer merely to rehash a story that had been better told a thousand times before. A writer, especially a Jewish writer, should have kept in mind the need for appraising the work of the Apostle in the light of the experience of the past two millennia. How true did his doctrine and vision concerning Judaism prove themselves to be? Two thousand years is a long enough period for any experiment. In the final analysis, it is not a question of which side can present the more beautiful quotations and passages from its holy writings. It is a question of the shaping of souls, of the moulding of man. This problem is of interest not only from a religious, but also from a social and pedagogic viewpoint.

The Christians have frequently interested themselves in certain practical aspects of Jewish life, but neglected most others. The question of the humanity of ritual slaughter (shehitah), for instance, has often been raised in the Christian countries. Anti-Semites, the murderous Nazis among them, have frequently demanded suppression of shehitah on the ground of its cruelty to animals. Yet over five hundred Christian experts have in their times pronounced this the most humane method of slaughtering. One even expressed his hope that his own death might be as easy as that suffered by an animal put to death in accord with Jewish law.

Other scholars have investigated the Mosaic laws of hygiene in general and particularly in matters of food and sex, and have found that only through these laws has Jewry been able to muster the strength of body and soul to withstand the persecutions and oppressions of long and bitter exiles. It has been found that because of these laws Jews are less susceptible than others to certain illnesses, among them cancer. Concerning the latter, one international authority had this to say: "The Mosaic law again shows itself as an amazing example of divine wisdom and providence, and should doubly appeal to today's enlightened minds" (Lt. Col. P. E. Frimenthal, chairman, International Cancer Conference, London, July 1928).

But there has been no such searching judgment of Jewry's general way of life, also shaped by the power and influence of the Law of Moses, a way of life, every single facet of which, from the cradle to the grave, whether concerning the relationship of man and God or man and man, bears the reflection of the divine. The Jew has always been ruled by the consciousness that godly ideas manifest themselves not only in extraordinary events which rock

140

the world but also in the daily minutiae. The seemingly unimportant actions, when permeated with high ideals, add up to a life of true greatness.

All this has imparted to Jewish life a beauty and loftiness often provoking the Gentiles to envy—either friendly or bitter. In the same cities and towns of East Europe which the Germans so barbarously destroyed, Christians often went for legal judgment to the rabbinic in preference to the civil courts. They would go to Jews for counsel, and solicit the blessing of the saintly "good Jews." Non-Jews used to invite the famed "Hafetz Hayyim" to cross their fields in order to induce God's favor for a bountiful harvest.

But there were evil gentiles in whom the envy turned into a consuming fire of hate. They beheld Jews celebrating their Sabbaths and festivals in spiritual joy, while their own coreligionists were spending their festive days in low liquor dives, often winding up in the gutter.

A Town, or "A Shtetl" is one of Asch's earliest works. It was the first to bring him fame among the Jews. As is evident from the title, the protagonist is not an individual but the town itself, the Jewish community. This early work of Asch's remains to this day an epic song of Jewish life.

One could justly point at this epic and ask Sholem Asch: if this be true, can Paul be right? Could your "shtetl" ever be, if the Torah corrupts?

But Asch has since broken faith with his "shtetl." Unable to deny the superior beauty of Jewish life as it has been lived in the shtetl, he makes the extraordinary statement that the Jews were good only because the gentile peoples made it impossible for them to be bad! However, the shtetl has been celebrated in other books, among which "Life is With People" by Mr. Zborowsky and E. Herzog (1952) occupies a special place. This is a scientific study, and despite some errors and misinterpretations it is destined to become a classic in its field. In this fascinating volume one beholds the Jew on his work days and on the Sabbath, in his reality and in his dreams, in prayer and toil, in trade and charity, in love and in peace, in poverty and in prosperity, in his reverence to God, in his piety and meekness, and indeed, in his sins, such as they were. But the good deeds were great, the sins trifling. The pursuit of happiness was only understood in terms of the pursuit of "mizvahs" or good deeds. There was one term for both honesty

141

and piety: "Ehrlicher Yid." It was a life completely consecrated to the practical implementation of piety and kindness. To this type of observation and evaluation also belongs "Horeve Welten" ("Worlds in Ruins"), by A. S. Sachs. Also "A Shtetl in Poilen" by Itzchok Bloom and a host of others, all bearing witness to a life of high purpose and supreme beauty.

Now for a single, hurried glimpse at the shtetl in general Jewish literature. One unique characteristic of this literature is that murder as a motif is unknown. Although every other literature in the world exploits this theme, it is not strange that Yiddish and Hebrew literature fail to do so, because bloodshed is unknown in the "shtetl."

For another illuminating illustration, let us turn to the liturgy. During the Days of Awe, the High Holidays, a lengthy litany each line of which begins *al chet,* "for the sin" is recited. Here numerous transgressions, gleaned by the authors from the complete lexicon of sins and trespasses, such as may be committed by an individual, community or nation, are recounted. All possible weaknesses and foibles of the human heart are incorporated into this national confessional.

But one type of crime is lacking: that of violent assault and murder. The pious authors who composed this confessional and compiled this roster could not even imagine such crimes being committed by Jews.

The "Al Chet" is many centuries old. Yiddish (Jewish) literature is very modern. But they reach out over the centuries and unite in bearing witness to the unique character of the Jew, whose nature abhors the taking of life.

Gangsters and murderers only appeared among Jews since they adopted the ways of the world and grew away from Torah. Only when removed from the benign influence of the Law do Jews become "like unto all the people."

Yet, in spite of changed conditions, Jews continue to consider a murderer of their religion as a stigma on Jewish national character. Actually, it is the very integrity which compels Jews to shudder at murder which keeps Jewish national character inviolate.

There is a city wherein a Jewish criminal was sentenced to death. On the eve of the execution the entire Jewish community, men, women, and children, rose and left the city, deserting it as

142

if driven out by a plague. Their minds could not endure the repercussions arising from the execution of a Jew.

Jews all over the world viewed the first electrocution of a Jewish murderer in America as a calamity, a blot upon their entire nation. The case constitutes a remarkable study in the national psychology of the Jew.

And now for a glimpse of the same "Small-Town" transplanted to a world metropolis, London, and now dubbed The Ghetto:

"The tearing Sambatyon of life was at rest in the Ghetto; on thousands of squalid homes the light of Sinai shone.

"The Ghetto welcomed the Sabbath Bride with proud song and humble feast, and sped her parting with optimistic symbolisms of fire and wine, of spice and light and shadow. All around their neighbors sought distraction in the blazing public houses, and their tipsy bellowings resounded through the streets and mingled with the Hebrew hymns. Here and there the voice of a beaten woman rose in the air. But no son of the Covenant was among the revellers or the wife-beaters; the Jews remained a chosen race, a peculiar people, faulty enough, but redeemed at least from the grosser vices—a little human islet won from the waters of animalism by the genius of ancient engineers" (Israel Zangwill).

Such, then, was the "shtetl" Sholem Asch knew well and loved much.

We now turn to another small town. It is non-Jewish and is a sacred Christian site dedicated to the life and suffering of the Nazarene on earth. It is located in Bavaria, Germany, and is called Oberammergau.

Its history begins with a German legend, which relates that in 1634 under a severe pestilence which raged throughout Germany, Oberammergau suffered heavy losses. An unusual course of action occurred to the citizens of Oberammergau: they vowed that if the plague speedily lifted they would from then on honor their Lord with a decennial dramatic performance portraying the life and passion of Jesus. According to the legend the pestilence spent itself at once, and the citizens of Oberammergau piously carried out their vow. To this day, every tenth summer they therefore conduct a grandiose "Passion Play," the drama of "God's agony."

The Passion Play in itself was no novelty in Christendom, since for many years Passion Plays had been accepted popular entertainment in the Christian world, and in ancient days had been presented in churches, monasteries and schools. But Oberammergau was unique in that it was a case in which an entire community for all time dedicated its life and efforts to the making of the plays.

Those who take part in the Play today are not professional actors, but plain citizens of Oberammergau; and since the production requires several hundred performers, there is a part for almost every citizen with any degree of talent. Over a quarter of a million persons, from all parts of the world, make the pilgrimage to witness the performance. The Passion Play has become the chief source of the town's income, as about the decennial presentation there have developed a number of related industries. Most important of these is the production of carved wooden statuary of Christian historical significance. There are figures of Jesus, of the Virgin, and of the apostles and saints, and elaborate crucifixes of all kinds and manners. The wooden carvings of Oberammergau are in demand throughout the world.

Over six hundred persons take part in the drama, which is probably the greatest spectacle in theatrical history. Years of rehearsal are commonplace. From one performance to the next, trials and tests are made and the chief roles are taken by actors who have spent ten years in preparation. No outlanders may take part, and the citizens appear in their roles without mask or makeup. Since with the exception of a few Romans all the actors in the original story were Jews, the contemporary players are chosen for their Semitic appearance. The men chosen refrain from shaving, permitting their beards to grow out like those of traditional Jews.

1934 was the tercentenary of the Oberammergau Passion Play as a permanent institution, and the Germans celebrated the event with proper eclat. It was one year after Hitler's accession to power and the performance was given under the Nazi symbol. The pious Catholic town was completely nazified, with most of the actors members of the Nazi party. The irony of Jesus and Mary and the Apostles being members of Hitler's party was overwhelming, but neither the pious inhabitants, nor Germans and Catholics in general were aware of the contradiction.

As the war was being waged in 1944, the Passion Play was

not performed, and was not revived until 1950. In that year three hundred thousand visitors came to witness the spectacle. One of these was the Very Reverend Sturgis Lee Riddle, dean of the American Cathedral in Paris, and it is his reaction that commands our attention here.

To Pastor Riddle the Play was an overpowering experience of the magnitude of those which sometimes alter a man's whole life. His impressions appeared in the form of a letter in the New York Herald Tribune, of September 15, 1950. The letter might be called an Epistle to the Christians. It constitutes a significant Christian document, meriting more permanent form than publication in a daily newspaper, for its writer dips deeply into what may be termed the central and eternal problem of Christianity.

He saw the performance at Oberammergau, writes the prominent clergyman, and left with two profound impressions, one revealing, the other depressing. Although as a clergyman he knew the story of his Messiah well, he had never before beheld it so clearly and in such splendor as in the German production. The entire account, says he, became more understandable, and perhaps even more credible than the account in the New Testament itself. "I have read many books," runs his letter, "on the credibility of the Gospel story; but no historian or theologian has been nearly so convincing to me as the action of this play."

To him there had never been a performance to compare with that at Oberammergau; from Shakespeare to Eugene O'Neill there had never been a greater theatrical tour de force. During the eight hours which the play required the audience of five thousand sat amazed and entranced. "If," he says, "you don't believe Christ lived and died, and that his life and death have something definitely to do with the human scene, this Play's the thing for you."

This is part one of the cleric's letter. But what interests us most in his letter is the second part of his impression.

Sitting through the performance, he says, he could not for a moment forget that less than a hundred miles away stood Dachau —one of the most horrible of the Nazi concentration camps, where thousands upon thousands of innocent victims had been tortured, burnt, annihilated.

At the performance he attended, reports the writer, there were virtually no foreign tourists, and the audience was almost entirely German. It had assembled from all Germany to witness the agony and death of the Nazarene, and "not one eye remained dry" in the vast audience. "The appalling uneasiness overtook me," continues the American divine, "that perhaps among these very people weeping at the passion of Christ there were some who had a part in staging the passions at Dachau, that all the tears shed at Oberammergau would never wipe out the blood shed at Dachau."

In Dachau the clergyman felt there had also been a stage of suffering, but far more imposing than the one he had seen at Oberammergau. "Just over the hills from where we sat weeping at the sufferings and the death of Christ, is that infamous place where in our day the brutality and cruelty of the passion were reenacted a thousand times," he writes.

As he departed from the city, the bitter thoughts would not cease tormenting him—what connection was there between Dachau and Oberammergau? And between the Germans, who on the one hand showed their piety in presenting a pious Christian drama, and on the other, were capable of gassing and burning thousands of innocent people in cold blood?

Both acts are true, complains the cleric, Oberammergau and Dachau: the Germans weep and the Germans slaughter. What cohesion can there be between these two phenomena, these two realities?

Pastor Riddle goes farther and poses the same query concerning all Christian conduct. How can one reconcile the Christian reality of wars and murders and persecutions of man by man, with the Christian teachings of love and peace? The concluding part of the letter gives the impression that his faith was indeed shaken and a gnawing doubt had penetrated his heart. This is evident from the last paragraph:

"The reality of the Passion Play is beyond dispute, but to me the perplexity and contradiction of it in our modern scene and against the background of modern passions is just as real, profoundly disturbing, perplexing, and condemning. If this message cannot wipe out wars and Dachaus, there is no reason to give this play. It becomes a sentimental travesty of futile suffering. That is something the Germans must decide for themselves. That is something we must all decide. If we cannot overcome this horrible contradiction between the reality of Christ and the reality of our human society dramatized and brought to stinging inten-

146

sity by the play of Oberammergau and the vicinity of Dachau, then God have mercy upon us! It is the end."

The American cleric came away greatly perturbed. But actually the source of his pain is an ancient woe in Christianity. It is good Pauline doctrine, but its beginning goes even farther back. The New Testament tells that when Jesus was crucified, he was not alone that day on Golgotha. Two robbers were crucified with him, one on each side of him. One mocked Jesus, asking why, if he were in truth God, he could not save himself. But the other believed in him. And to him Jesus said, "Verily I say unto thee, Today shalt thou be with me in paradise" (Luke xxiii, 43).

The fact that the man had been a sinner, a criminal, a robber, did not matter much in the eyes of the founder of Christianity. His sins were no bar to paradise; the mere act of believing in Jesus wiped away all guilt. Paradise was handed over to the sinner for next to nothing.

It is here where we have to look for the heart of the problem. There is obviously a deep mystic relationship between Christianity and sin. They do not repel, but rather attract each other. This is to be learned in the New Testament itself, from the very mouth of Jesus. He announced that he was not come to call the righteous, but the sinners (Matt. ix, 13). He associated largely with denizens of the underworld. In all the Gospels it is the pious and virtuous Pharisees that are singled out for scorn and abuse. Fire and brimstone were the lot of the godly people of the time, who observed Torah and tradition, and remained loyal to their faith. Not a single word of praise did Jesus afford his righteous and saintly opponents. Addressing the chief priests and the elders of the people, Jesus said: "Verily I say unto you, that the publicans and the harlots go unto the Kingdom of God before you" (Matt. xxi, 31).

This has colored the mind of all Christian humanity. Perhaps one may look here for the source of the esthetic theory in European literature that the just and the righteous and the saintly are not suitable subjects for artistic endeavors; that stories of upright living and innocence are boring. The chief heroes of Europe's literature have virtually always been the sinner and the criminal, as is best exemplified by the works of Dostoyevsky. This giant of Russian literature pictures one of his heroes sneaking into the room of a sleeping friend to murder him, and crossing himself while preparing the knife. The true "Christian souls" among the

147

heroes of this great Russian novelist, are the criminals, the prostitutes, thieves and murderers—these always manage to wind up in heaven.

Not by its doctrine of love did Christianity move the world, but by its doctrine of sin as symbolized by the three crosses. It was on the basis of such doctrine as this that Martin Luther was able to formulate the dangerous dictum: "Pecca fortiter, crede fortius" —"Sin strongly, as long as you believe more strongly" (Quoted by Monsignor E. Roberts Moore in Roman Collar).

It is on this dramatic episode of the three crosses that theologians have based the doctrine embodied in the following:

"Many people have an idea that going to Hell or getting to Heaven is just a 'hit or miss' proposition, but such is not the case. Hell and Heaven are both prepared places. Those who don't definitely prepare for Heaven are unconsciously preparing for Hell. You don't have to be a gangster, a murderer or a 'person of the streets' to go to Hell. You can be a 'respectable' Atheist and go to Hell. You can give all your money away to the poor, and do only kind deeds and still go to Hell.

"Likewise, you can (though it isn't advisable) be the most terrible sinner there is, commit every sin on the calendar, and still in a death-bed conversion be prepared to go to Heaven." (Rev. Arthur D. Hamilton: Hell and Heaven, Hamilton Free Bible Tract Society, New York).

Here is more of the same:

"Works have nothing to do with the obtaining of salvation. Men are saved by faith, not by works. The greatest, the meanest, the lowest, the vilest, the blackest sinner is saved the moment he sincerely receives Christ and takes Him as Saviour, and all his sins are blotted out, while the most refined, dignified, religious, moral sinner is lost unless," etc. (Dr. R. W. DeHaan: The First Resurrection and Second Death).

Dachau and Oberammergau are a commentary to that kind of doctrine. In the light of such doctrine and such dicta it is not surprising that the Germans could find no contradiction between Dachau and Oberammergau. The one was for sinning, the other for believing and forgiving.

The Jew shudders at the thought that the atrocities committed by the Nazis in the extermination of six million Jews might be forgiven and the conscience of the perpetrators eased and cleared. We have heard of only one priest, Father Don Fra,

148

of Turin, Italy, who publicly announced that he will not render absolution to those guilty of handing over Jews to the Nazis or of having possessed themselves of the properties of Jewish victims, unless, where possible, such property be returned to the owner.

Such is the difference between the two small-towns. Asch would have us exchange one for the other. The fool!

Dachau and Oberammergau! Oh, Paul, where is thy sting, Maker of Gods, where is thy victory?

9

"Cursed Be The Man"

In his book on Paul, as well as in *The Nazarene,* Sholem Asch faithfully follows the Christian Bible. But the New Testament describes the journeys of Paul through Jewish communities in the lands of the Roman-ruled Hellenized world in brief strokes, while Asch paints the sweeping canvas of his imagination.

Paul's target was the gentiles and he was called "apostle to the gentiles." But whenever he reached a city, he first turned to Jews. In the synagogue he would request the opportunity of preaching at Sabbath services. As a traveler from the Holy Land and message-bearer from Jerusalem he was readily given that permission, for Jews were ever anxious to hear a word of sacred lore, as well as news from the Holy City.

The deceptive missionary method was established even then: the speaker would begin as a Jew, then suddenly depart into a Christological disquisition. Paul abused the hospitality of the synagogues to preach his particular brand of Christianity, announcing the arrival of the messiah, the annulment of the Torah and its laws, and the imminent return of the messiah, who would make an end of the sinful world; only those who accepted the Christian faith—and faith was all that was necessary—would be taken up to heaven with him, while the rest would be cast into the eternal fires.

According to Asch and the Gospels, in many of the synagogues the Jews enthusiastically accepted conversion. But in other places the Jews raised an opposition, often creating an uproar in-

149

citing the gentiles to violence against Paul and his followers. They even plotted his murder.

Throughout Asch gives the assurance that Paul buttressed his preachments with proofs from the prophets. However, unlike the Gospels, he never mentions the specific chapters and verses employed by Paul to that end. Nor does he discuss, from the Jewish point of view, the plausibility or implausibility of the interpretations the Apostle placed on the Prophets.

We can readily assume that Paul's sermons did not fail to arouse discussions and disputations in the synagogues. Jews surely did not hurry to accept the new doctrine; they did not just listen to it and immediately change their convictions. To provoke the brawls and assaults which took place, the debates must have been quite heated. There surely must have been Jews in those synagogues with a knowledge of the Torah who rose in violent response to Paul, to defend the Torah, to uphold the traditional interpretations of the prophets, and to refute those of Paul.

We know the substance of Paul's argument and exactly what were his statements, but what must have been the objections and rebuttals? It would be extremely interesting to know, particularly in view of the fact that the Jewish point of view is everywhere bypassed and ignored in the Gospels.

The ancient debates should be the center of Asch's narrative theme for disputed Christianity was an entirely new religion coming to claim the place of two older faiths—Judaism on the one hand, and paganism on the other. "For we have charged both Jew and gentiles, that they are all under sin" (Romans iii, 9). The dispute was primarily a war of ideologies, a struggle of Weltanschauungen. Asch is obligated to present the three-sided conflict of ideas to his readers. He does in fact make that effort in connection with Paul's journeys to Athens and Rome; he does attempt to show Paul in the old Greek capital disputing with the Greek philosophers, and in Rome, with Seneca the Stoic. But the results are unfortunate, and it is agonizing to watch Asch try to prove himself a connoisseur of ancient philosophy.

However, this effort does not greatly concern us. The important matter is Asch's abuse of Jewish prophetism. We know the ideas Paul concocted out of the Prophets, but what of the Jewish response to them?

On this subject Asch is silent. Such expressions as "according to the prophets" are repeated throughout his text, without the

150

disclosure of any source whatever. And there is not a mention of Jewish rejoinder or counterattack. This is the same method employed in *The Nazarene.*

What a magnificent twofold opportunity Asch relinquished in both cases. He might first have corrected one of the most vicious aberrations in man's intellectual history—the Christian method of employing the Jewish Torah against itself to initiate its own destruction, and of forging the entire Hebrew Bible by his misinterpretations into a weapon against Jews and Judaism.

And second, as we have seen, he might have arrayed the actual Jewish arguments and opposed the Jewish case to the Christian. Nowhere in the Christian literature, dating from the New Testament, is the Jewish viewpoint introduced. The Christian approach to Judaism is that of preconceived judgment, and the widespread ignorance of Judaism is appalling. A Christian with an objective mind seldom if ever comes to know the Jewish point of view in the great historic dispute.

But Asch lacked the vision to meet the challenge. And so we must try on our own. Let us take, for instance, the example of Paul's assertion that the precepts of the Torah were of no avail for salvation, and that with the coming of Jesus man is justified by simple belief alone. Paul bases his doctrine on Genesis xv, 6: "And he (Abraham) believed in the Lord; and He counted it to him for righteousness." Belief was all that was necessary. Righteous works did not count in the plan God had in mind for Abraham.

But it is inconceivable that there did not appear a Jew to confront Paul and quote a bit farther on in Genesis (xxvi, 4-5): "Because that Abraham hearkened to My voice, and kept My *charge*, My *commandments*, My *statutes* and My laws." It was not mere faith that made the first Patriarch righteous in the eyes of God.

The above quotations are from the first book of the Torah. In the last (Deuteronomy vi, 25) we read: "And it shall be righteousness unto us, if we observe to do all this commandment before the Lord our God, as He hath commanded us." The same word "Zedakah" is used in both instances. In both "righteousness" is specifically conditioned on commandments and observances.

Did Paul have any answer to these passages? He obviously did not.

A second and equally important pillar in Pauline doctrine

151

is that the Torah was given to be valid only temporarily, and was superseded by the teaching of Jesus. But in Isaiah it is asserted (lix, 21): "And as for Me, this is My covenant with them, saith the Lord; My spirit that is upon thee, and My words which I put in thy mouth, shall not depart out of thy mouth, nor out of the mouth of thy seed, nor out of the mouth of thy seed's seed, saith the Lord, from henceforth and for ever."

Innumerable times the Torah employs expressions such as "It is a sign forever"; "An eternal statute is it unto you"; "Throughout your generations it is a statute of eternity." Forever, throughout the generations, eternal! This is the clear note from cover to cover in both Torah and Prophets. In what manner, by what kind of mental acrobatics, was it possible to describe the Law as a mere temporary expedient?

This appeal to the Prophets is basic with Paul, and therefore with Asch. Let us look therefore at the concluding lines of the last prophet of the Bible (Malachi, iii, 22):

"Remember ye the Laws of Moses My servant!" enjoins the prophet in the final message of prophecy vouchsafed the children of Israel.

Lest anyone imagine that this refers to some new law not the Law of Moses, the prophet proceeds to specify: "Which I commanded unto him in Horeb"—i.e. at Mount Sinai. And lest it be thought the Law for "Jew and Greek" an expression so beloved of Paul, the phrase is added, "for all Israel." And lest it be construed to mean the Torah "in spirit" only, without reference to the precepts and commands, there are the final words, "even statutes and ordinances."

With this utterance biblical prophecy is finally concluded and sealed: a powerful, irrevocable injunction to remember, to observe, and to perform the Law of Moses. Here Paulinism stands eternally refuted.

Is it possible that no Jew demanded of Paul, how he could prove from the prophets something to which prophetism is so obviously opposed?

Here is a transcendent theme for a Jewish writer, a subject for a supreme work on the ablest of the founders of Christianity contrasting the doctrines of this rebellious "son" of Israel, with the authentic defense and counterattack by Judaism. But this opportunity was missed by Sholem Asch who said nothing on behalf

152

of Judaism and little concerning it. He abjectly capitulated to Christianity and wrote as a pious Christian. He even contributed his own falsification of the truths of Judaism.

It has already been alluded to that Asch attained the apogee of his perversion in chapter ten of Part Three, entitled "A Jew Among Jews," which deals with Paul's Epistle to the Hebrews. This Epistle is as complete a statement of Pauline heresy with regard to Judaism as is to be found anywhere in the New Testament. In fact, it is a comprehensive summary of his views, and gives a broader exposition of points raised in other epistles with some crucial ones added.

By "Hebrews" is here meant the Christians in Palestine, most of whom were former Jews. Paul exhorts them to be thoroughly converted to the faith of Christ, which he extols above the faith of the Torah. Here is expounded in detail the doctrine of the New Covenant, and the cancellation of the power and operation of the Old.

Paul quotes from Jeremiah (xxxi, 31-33) : "Behold, the days come, saith the Lord, that I will make a new covenant with the house of Israel, and with the house of Judah; not according to the covenant that I made with their fathers in the day that I took them by the hand to bring them out of the land of Egypt. . . . But this is the covenant that I will make with the house of Israel after those days, saith the Lord, I will put My Law in their inward parts, and in their hearts will I write it."

Paul, after quoting this passage, asks why a new covenant was needed if the old one still remained valid. Here we face the crucial point at the center of Christian teaching. Here is the great dividing line!

On the basis of this flimsy argument and ill-informed interpretation, Paul proceeds to split the world and break humanity in two parts: an Old Covenant and New Covenant; the Old Testament and the New Testament; Jewish Writ and the Gospels; and eventually into Judaism and Christianity with the eternally tragic tension between them.

Jeremiah's real meaning and intent are quite different. He speaks plainly, and uses no "Aesopian" language. He intends no antithesis between the "old" and a "new" covenant; what is eternal cannot become old. The actual antithesis expressed is in the words "by the hand," and "in their heart." In his time, this prophet avers, the Torah had gone no farther than the Jewish hand in which it was laid; but in later days it would enter within them and be inscribed in their hearts.

In the Torah the covenant is termed "everlasting." Jeremiah is able to speak of a new covenant to replace the one that was eternal, and still remain a prophet among his people, because his prophecy accords with the words of Isaiah (LXV, 17) : "For, behold, I create new heavens and a new earth," which in no manner can be considered a contradiction of the words of Ecclesiastes (i, 4) : "And the earth abideth forever." Elsewhere Jeremiah avers: (xi, 3-4) "And say thou unto them: Thus saith the Lord, the God of Israel: Cursed be the man that heareth not the words of this covenant, which I commanded your fathers in the day that I brought them forth out of the land of Egypt."

Thus we see clearly to which covenant Jeremiah refers, for he speaks plainly of the one and only eternal Old Covenant.

Paul, with Asch in his footsteps, bypasses these facts, and so desecrates the holiest of Jewish sanctities.

Note then: In the Epistle to the Hebrews, dispatched to Christian Jews in Palestine, Paul calls upon them to remain steadfast in the religion of Jesus; he speaks of the priesthood of the Nazarene, come to replace the "lower" priesthood of Aaron and the Levites; and he sets the Nazarene above Moses, and the teachings of the Nazarene above the Torah. In truth this Epistle goes counter to everything Judaic. It sets up Christianity as the eternal denial of Judaism, making Judaism and Christianity what they are: Ultimate Opposites.

With utmost clarity Paul expresses his fanatic determination to root out all vestiges of the Jewish Law when he declares, "In that he saith, A *new* covenant, he hath made the first old. Now that which decayeth and waxeth old is ready to vanish away" (Hebrews, viii, 13).

The understanding of Judaism on this matter has been clearly and distinctly formulated, for even the most ignorant men to understand, by Maimonides, in the following passages:

"Therefore, if a man should arise, whether from among Israel or the nations, and he will present omens and marvels, and declare that God has sent him to add or subtract a single divine precept, or he will expound one of the commands in a manner we did not hear from Moses; or if any person say that the precepts commanded upon Israel are not to be everlasting through all gen-

154

erations, but are merely temporary commands:—that man is a false prophet, for he is come to deny the prophetic status of Moses." (Hilchot Yesode Torah, ix, 1).

This is the final law, in its classic formulation. Behind it stand the Torah itself, and the lore and wisdom of all Jewish generations preceding and succeeding Maimonides. In the light of this law Paul's Epistle to the Hebrews becomes the most extreme blasphemy against Judaism.

But Sholem Asch "thinks" otherwise. In brazen ignorance, flouting all Jewish tradition he comments on the Epistle to the Hebrews as follows: "The tone of the Epistle is Jewish. It could have been written by a pious Jew, who had never, in any particular departed from the principles of the traditional faith."

This is the most contemptible piece of spiteful effrontery ever uttered:

Unless it be that he never read the Epistle to the Hebrews.

True to the psychology he learned so well in Yankel Shabowitch's house of ill fame—one of Asch's own creations, in which the impure endeavor to sully the pure—he proceeds to declare that in his Epistle to the Hebrews Paul offers only such teachings as he had inherited as a pupil of Rabban Gamliel. He further asserts, as a final summation, that in all his thoughts and interpretations as contained in the Epistle to the Hebrews Paul had not in the least deviated from the traditional renderings of the Pharisees.

Now what shall we say of these falsifications and deceptions; of this ideological rape and blasphemy of the Torah, its bearers and guardians; of all the new blandishments and traps spread at the feet of innocent Jewish children to seduce them from the way of Judaism?

What need be said, when the prophet long ago said of these that heed not the words of the covenant: "Cursed be the man!"

Before we leave this work, one more offence must be pointed out. In *The Apostle* Asch installs Peter into the very synagogue ascribing to him the authorship of one of the prayers for the Sabbath and the festivals. Reference is to the prayer *Nishmat kol chai* ("The breath of every living being"). A legend was circulated during the middle ages that Peter was the author of this masterly piece of liturgy. So strongly did the tale take hold that it was entertained even by certain Jewish scholars of that period. However, this was only part of the legend, the full story being to the effect that Peter had undergone a change of heart and in this prayer he had completed his renunciation of the new teaching with which he had been associated. The commentator Rashi bitterly opposed the legend, saying: "God forbid that such an idea should gain credence among Jews. Any person who repeats it would in the days of the Temple be liable to the sacrifice of a sin offering." But Sholem Asch, as an additional spite, at this late date revives this defunct legend of the authorship of the prayer, to disseminate it anew among the ignorant and the blasphemous.

It may be doubted, however, if a sacrifice would be accepted from Sholem Asch. According to the law, "when a Jew wilfully turns to idolatry, no sacrifice of any kind is accepted from his hand. Even the burnt offering which is taken from idol worshipers is not acceptable from a (Jewish) wilful sinner." (Maimonides, Maaseh Hakorbanot iii, 4).

Indeed, from a gentile, pagan or Pope an offering would be welcomed in the Temple, but not from Sholem Asch!

CHAPTER III

Mary

In a biography of Jesus the noted Italian author Giovanni Papini complains of the kind of religious books offered for the reading of the faithful flock. This type of literature, he laments, smells of putrefaction, the fumes of a burntout wick, stale incense that taste like putrid oil clinging to the throat. His argument is that readers discard such fare before many pages are gone.

Had Papini lived to read Sholem Asch's *Mary*, he would have exclaimed, "Here at last is something new!" *Mary* is indeed "new" in a thousand ways. It offers new blasphemies against Judaism, new derogations, opprobria, humiliations, and slanders upon Jewish heads, and new agony for Jewish hearts.

Sholem Asch's biography of Mary and incidentally of the early life of Jesus, is in a sense the first book of its kind. No Christian romancer, historian, or theologian has ever struck at Jewish roots and basic Jewish concepts with such bold ferocity as has Asch in this book, for outsiders are not aware of all the tender spots in the Jewish soul, which Asch chooses to stab and wound. He discovers new wonders for Christianity, wrenching vast areas of the kingdom of Jewry, to hurl, with drunken abandon at the feet of the gentiles. He invents new devices for elevating Christianity at the expense of Judaism. He attempts to render Jews and Judaism base by means of new artifices, tricks, and stunts. Gentiles, lacking the knack and the impudence of this cunning heretic, have never ventured so far. Asch opens new perspectives, new approaches for them. He conjures up so many new visions and fancies, so many new miracles and wondrous manifestations, and so many new anti-Jewish refinements, that his book, had it been done at the birth of Christianity might well have found its way into the New Testament as a fifth Gospel. All this Asch does for the greater glory of Christianity, and the greater hurt and imperilment of Judaism. In *Mary* Asch has drifted beyond return.

In addition, he offers new evidence of ignorance, picturesque illiteracies and fantastic perversions of knowledge fit as fare for the entertainment of readers of humorous journals. Here he has attained the stature of the full-fledged renegade, a type well-represented in Jewish tales. There is the story of one who dressed up a dog in prayer shawl and phylacteries and released the animal in the ghetto streets. The tale is also told of a man of the same sort in Shavel, Lithuania, who habitually sidled up to the Rabbi as soon as he had appeared in the street, drew a heavy piece of pork from his pocket, and devoured it in the presence of the holy man. In another town a Jewish girl converted in order to marry the Christian butcher. A famous Rabbi of the town was visited by so many of his followers during the high holidays that he found it necessary to conduct prayer service outside the synagogue. Every Yom Kippur eve, at the height of the services, this female convert drove a herd of pigs past the Rabbi's assemblage and sent dogs after them, the resulting squeals and howling drowning out the divine service.

In *Mary* Asch resorts to these venomous spites so characteristic of Jewish backsliders. Here Asch permits himself what even the Christians avoid. Christianity "took over" the Torah, it appropriated our prophets, it monopolized the Bible, helped itself to our idea of a Messiah, but left us our biblical ancestors.

True, the patriarchs, particularly Abraham, are ultimately made a part of Christian doctrine. They are built into the foundation of the faith. Jesus says: "Abraham waited for this day." But for some reason the doctrine did not take deep root in the soil of Christianity. It could not penetrate the consciousness of the Christian, for Jesus also said: "I was with the Father before Abraham."

It is only in a dim, far off, spiritual sense that the Christian thinks of the Jewish Patriarchs as his spiritual ancestors. To the Christians, Abraham, Isaac, and Jacob have remained pale figures in the distant background. They have never transported Sarah, Rebecca, Rachel, and Leah into their own Christian heaven. They neither etch images of them, nor dedicate candles, nor offer prayers to them.

The doctrine of the spiritual fatherhood originated with Paul. With his characteristic dialectics Paul split up Abraham into

158

two sharply differentiated persons: one before his circumcision, the other after circumcision. For the Christian he appropriated the Abraham prior to circumcision "that he might be the father of all of them that believe, though they be not circumcised" (Romans iv, 11). Thus he made the Christians the heirs of the primal Abraham; they were his descendants "in the spirit," while the Jews were designated the sons of Abraham "in the flesh." Reversing the order instituted by God, Paul set the earlier Abraham above the later. Yet even he admitted for the Jews that "Theirs are the Fathers" (Romans ix, 5). Also: "As touching the election, they (the Jews) are beloved for the Fathers' sake" (ibid xi, 28).

Indeed, there is a singular passage in the Gospels which easily lends itself to an interpretation placing Abraham aloof from, if not in opposition to Jesus' venture on earth. Reference is made to the colloquy held in heaven between Abraham and a rich man who was undergoing treatment in hell, and who pleaded with Abraham to send Lazarus from the dead to warn and enlighten those below:

"And Abraham said to him: They have Moses and the prophets; let them hear them. But he, the tormented, said: No, father Abraham, but if one went to them from the dead, they will do penance. And he said to him: If they hear not Moses and the prophets, neither will they believe, if one rise again from the dead." From this it would seem that Abraham up above was dead set against Jesus' pilgrimage earthward, but his advice was obviously ignored, with disastrous results.

Be that as it may, whatever function Abraham may have exercised ceased with the advent of Christ. "Abraham's bosom" served as the place where the souls of the saints resided, "till Christ opened heaven by his death." Thus the Gospels.

But Sholem Asch here appears on the scene to reevaluate, reappraise, rearrange and reshuffle the positions and the roles of the Fathers in the Christian scheme, and of the mothers, too.

The Gospels tell that on the night of the nativity in Bethlehem, a number of shepherds were tending their flocks near the city. Suddenly an angel appeared before them and related that at that moment the messiah, the lord of the universe, was being born in Bethlehem; and as a sign of his truthtelling he informed them that they would discover the babe in a manger in a stable. The shepherds at once set out in search, and came upon the very scene the angel had described.

159

Such is the story as told in the Gospels. The shepherds remain anonymous. But Asch cannot resist improving upon the Gospels, and to this story he appends one of his own invention. Asch's version has three shepherds distinct from those mentioned in the Gospels. The Gospel group arrives after the nativity, and their actual number is not stated. Asch has his trio come before the birth. They are on the spot before the arrival of Mary and Joseph, and receive the pair with bows and vocal greetings.

The three shepherds are depicted as uncommonly impressive, mystical personages. Though they are not named it becomes quite evident that they are Abraham, Isaac, and Jacob. The "second" of them carries an unmistakable identification, a bundle of wood on his shoulder, the token of Isaac's ordeal when he was about to be brought as a sacrifice by his father. Even clearer light is shed upon their identity when Mary, after the three have departed, remarks to her spouse: "It is a good sign. Shepherds have come to bless the child. *The patriarchs were shepherds.*"

And so, according to Asch's doctrine, Abraham, Isaac, and Jacob were the first to greet the Christ-child upon this earth and to bow before him. They brought him gifts of oil and incense—symbolically, oil for royal and priestly anointment, incense for deification. Abraham, Isaac, and Jacob were the world's first Christians. And the first Christian woman, according to Asch, was Mother Rachel. Rachel, the most afflicted of the four matriarchs, who in a special sense has become the beloved and sorrowing mother of the Jewish people— ("Rachel weeping over her children") —is converted by Asch even before the patriarchs. She appears early in the book, rising from her grave and accompanying the mother of Jesus from the beginning of the divine espousal until the denouement. Rachel gives Miriam-Mary the first intimation that she is to become God's wife. She is matchmaker, escort to the marriage ceremony and the nuptial chamber, and virtually the midwife too. The climax comes when she crowns *Mary* "Mother of Israel."

The crowns worn from time immemorial by Sarah, Rebecca, Rachel, and Leah are removed from their heads and placed on the head of Mary, who thus supersedes them all.

How frivolously, how impudently, has Asch dealt with the most sacrosanct traditions of the Jewish people!

When speaking to Jews, it is not necessary to expound the meaning of the patriarchal tradition in the life of the people; it

160

means everything. From the earliest days, in Jewish eyes and the eyes of all the world, Father Abraham has been the archetype of the Jewish people, with their qualities of mercy, kindness, hospitality, humility, charity, and generosity. Our sages say, "He who feels no mercy toward his fellowmen is not of the children of our father Abraham." A legend has it that Abraham's face was illumined with so much love and pity that the sick and the ailing had only to gaze upon his countenance to be healed. In the events of Abraham's life our sages envisioned a parallel to all Jewish history.

So too are the other patriarchs, each enshrined in the heart of the Jewish people according to his special attributes and his special place in the history of Jewish advancement toward God and godliness, and the fulfillment of the Jewish role among nations and peoples.

Our sages taught that the patriarchs established the three daily prayers of Judaism—morning, afternoon, and evening—in due order. Our right and claim to the land of Israel is predicated upon the divine promise to Abraham, Isaac, and Jacob. There is no end to the sacred relationships of these patriarchs to Israel's life and fortunes. In the most sacred hour of the holiest day in Judaism, in the hour of Yom Kippur's closing (Neilah) prayer, all this is distilled into a single final, despairing and exalted plea: "Naught remains to us except this Torah . . . and the merit of the three Fathers."

All Jewish prayers are based on the merits of the patriarchs. Jews never refer in their prayers to the precepts they have observed and the good deeds they have performed, and they ask for nothing in the way of reward. They only acknowledge their transgressions: and whatever they seek they request from the God of Abraham, Isaac and Jacob because of the merit of Abraham, Isaac and Jacob.

But one dismal day, a day of shame and sacrilege, Sholem Asch appears like Mephisto on the literary scene and with demoniac laughter and scorn he impliedly says:

"In vain have you Jews prayed through all the generations in the name and upon the virtues of Abraham, Isaac, and Jacob—to the God of Abraham, Isaac and Jacob! The patriarchs have long since departed from your prayers and sacred readings, which have become empty verbiage; they have fled your daily prayerbooks, your synagogues and houses of study, now but haunted

161

houses. Abraham, Isaac, and Jacob have long ago made the cloisters and the churches their abode, where they followed the real God of Israel. And whatever merit they possessed they have long taken from you and turned over to the children of Esau, as is 'stated in Holy Writ.' "

And he takes the verses meant for Jacob and expounds them in favor of Esau.

In the same sacrilegious manner does Asch pervert Israel's matriarchs to his purpose.

The biblical matriarchs, each in her own manner, have become symbols of the Jewish people. "Wherefore did Sarah laugh, saying: Shall I of a surety bear a child, who am old?" (Genesis xviii, 13). With this Sarah has become a figure of the Jewish people old yet ever young. And Rebecca, "The children struggled together within her" (Genesis xxv, 29)—the whole history of the world is pictured in these few words—in their mother's womb Jew and Gentile were already embattled for the kingdoms of Heaven and Earth.

Rachel has a special place in the hearts of the Jewish people, for with her has been associated most intimately the idea of redemption from exile. A beautiful Midrash referring to the time of the Babylonian exile relates how angels prayed before the Throne of Glory for the end of the Jewish exile, but their supplications were unanswered. Then Jeremiah woke the patriarchs out of their graves in the Cave of Machpelah to offer supplication before the throne of God. Samuel and Moses rose to plead, but to no avail. "In that hour our Mother Rachel sprang up before God, and spoke and said. . . Then quickly rose the mercy of God, and He said: 'For thy merit, O Rachel, shall I bring the people of Israel back to their inheritance.' "

Jews driven thrice into bitter exile, wept as they passed the tomb of Rachel on their way into an unknown destiny. There were the exiles of Egypt and Babylon, and the longest of all, Rome. Through the two thousand years of the Roman exile Jewish lads in their schools wept in a sorrowful lament when they came upon the words, "And as for me, when I came from Paddan, Rachel died unto me in the land of Canaan in the way, when there was still some way to come in to Ephrath: and I buried her there on the way to Ephrath—the same is Bethlehem" (Genesis xlviii, 7).

Throughout all the ages, Rachel wept for her children, and the children wept for their Mother Rachel.

Yet, ironically enough, in the very year of redemption, the third year of the State of Israel, when the redeemed children from all corners of the world were toiling toward Zion, and passing the burial place of the matriarch on their way back home, Sholem Asch appeared and set up a cross upon her tomb!

Since the placement of an idol in the sanctuary, there has been no greater blasphemy in the house of Israel.

2

New Libels

More than once Sholem Asch has emphasized that his aim in writing his Christological works was to forge closer ties and a better understanding between Jews and Christians. His sole purpose, he maintained, was to turn gentile hearts to the Jews, and Jewish hearts to the gentiles. He was determined primarily, he said, to do away with the slander that the Jews had crucified Jesus. It was his intent to prove that the guilty ones were the Romans and a priestly clique. And once this became clear, he assured, all Christian prejudices against the Jew would fall by the wayside, and "deicide" or "Christ-killer" would no longer be heard in the land.

All these declarations and manifestoes were nothing but "holy lies," in the best Jesuit style. In no way did Asch improve the status of the Jews in Christian legend. Nor could he. For a tree which for two thousand years has grown in crooked and twisted shape will not straighten out at the stroke of a pen. In truth, he could not have altered the situation even had he desired to do so —and he did not. He walked piously in the footsteps of the Gospels. If anything he aggravated the situation.

His Christological exploits were evil enough even before *Mary,* but with this book they became painfully worse: in *Mary* Asch has weighted Jewish shoulders with the heavy burden of new libels, never before thought of in Christendom.

The Gospels tell the story of Jewish persecution of Jesus and his disciples; nothing is said about persecution of the mother of Jesus, Miriam-Mary. But in Asch's own gospel there is a terrifying

163

story of how the Jews persecuted Mary, tried her and came near sentencing her to death.

Nor is there any mention in the New Testament of the toddling Jesus being hooted out of Hebrew school by his teacher and classmates, and subjected to the torments of a child's excommunication. But Asch finds place for this horrible but wholly fictional legend on his splotched and distorted canvas.

And there is nothing in the Christian Bible about the attempt of a Jewish village to stone or hang Jesus long before the trial and crucifixion. Asch turns a mild episode of the Gospels into an horrendous tale of a fierce lynching party. The irate Jews are pictured dragging Jesus out of the synagogue and tossing him into a deep, rocky, slimy crevice, among snakes and lizards. The story is told with horrifying details. But Jesus works a miracle: to the vast amazement and chagrin of the lynchers, he stands up and lifts himself out of the depths, whole, calm, superhuman, celestial. The whole story is concocted as an obvious prelude to the crucifixion and "resurrection."

Asch tells us that it was Mary's divine pregnancy that nearly proved her undoing. When a change in Mary's physical appearance was noticed gossip spread and she was soon brought before a court. She was ordered to reveal whether or not it was her betrothed, Joseph, who was responsible for her condition. If she were in truth betrothed to one and pregnant by another, then, according to the Torah, her crime was great and its penalty death. Asch pictures a protracted, agonizing trial, of a character clearly calculated to cast aspersion upon the Torah. But Mary is rescued from the lion's den thanks to the saintliness of Joseph the groom, who, though innocent, gallantly takes the guilt upon himself.

This narrative, from beginning to end, is both fictional and false, and is without any basis in the Gospels. In the New Testament there is not the faintest intimation that the Jews so much as raised a hand or eyebrow at the mother of the "son of God."

An altogether different story is told in the Gospels. The storm was raised by Joseph, not by the populace. Discovering his bride to be with child, and well aware it was not by him, Joseph was ready to pack up and take his leave. Whereupon the Holy Ghost revealed itself to Joseph, disclosed Mary's secret to him, and bade him remain at her side, which he did.

Asch's monstrous tale is supposedly based on the laws in the

164

Torah, (Deut. xxii, 23-27) having to do with a betrothed virgin violated by another man. For betrothal was considered tantamount to full marriage. If the violation occurred in the field, then only the man was punishable, for it was assumed that the maiden's cries for help went unheard. If the crime was committed in the city, where she could have summoned help, then both were guilty, and the crime was punishable by death.

The episode described in *Mary* could be devised by Asch for only one purpose—to dramatize the "brutality" of the Law, and incidentally of the Jews who threatened the life of the holy mother while the divine child was yet in her womb. Thus a new agony is introduced into the Christian story.

Asch avoids, either consciously or carelessly, the issue raised by his own story. Mary was betrothed to Joseph. How then could God have taken this betrothed virgin Mary unto himself? Are we to believe that God violated one of His own most stringent commandments, one, according to His own canon, the infraction of which is punishable by death?

What devilish caprice inspired Asch to introduce into the Christian epic this cruel, libelous indignity at the expense of Jewry? Only by consciously misreading the law in the Torah could he have developed the line of reasoning which we find in *Mary*. This is a painfully familiar technique, an ancient Christological method. Its purpose is to deprecate the Torah, to give substance to the Christian claim that the Torah corrupts and that only Jesus redeems.

Sholem Asch chooses yet another "terrible" biblical provision which he churns up into a witches' brew, to further vilify the Law in the eyes of Christendom. The Torah, in order to guard the moral purity of the nation and especially to protect the family against the inadvertence of incestuous marriage, prescribes as follows:

"A bastard shall not enter into the assembly of the Lord; even to the tenth generation shall none of his enter into the assembly of the Lord" (Deut. xxiii, 3) .

Asch takes this commandment as his text and builds up a fantastic horror story around it, a bizarre fabrication of devilish savagery to lay at the Jews' doorstep, that must give the detractors of the Jews a gloating sort of relish.

Asch tells of a forsaken child about the same age as Jesus who wandered about Nazareth and who was known to all as "the

165

bastard." Even though he was a Jewish child, because he was a bastard no one in the city felt the least bit of pity for him; no one ever offered him a piece of bread or a drink of water. He was hounded like a wild little beast out of the woods. He went about in filth and tatters, living on anything he could steal or pick up in the gutters. The boy dared not approach a Jewish home or a synagogue, for he was driven off with stones. No other child was permitted to associate with him. No word of learning was imparted to him. And he was not even granted the privilege of a name.

One cannot read this chapter (x, second part) without being stirred to peaks of pity and fury: pity for the luckless child, and fury against the callous, soulless inhabitants of Nazareth.

All these horrors are visited upon the unfortunate boy in order to fulfill the command, "A bastard shall not enter into the assembly of the Lord." It is not possible to reproduce here the full measure of wickedness shown this child. This piece of literary gall must be read to be appreciated. Such vileness toward little children has been conceivable only among the Nazis; only the cremation of the living child is lacking to make the horror complete.

Then one day the child Jesus encountered the little bastard and a great pity welled up in his heart and he befriended the unfortunate creature. This was not an easy feat, for the Jews had reduced the child to the state of a beast living in fear of humans. He would flee in terror at Jesus' advances. But Jesus' persistence at last won the confidence of the child and he finally took him home, where the innocent victim for the first time in his life crossed the threshold of a human dwelling. Mary received the child and with great tenderness washed and cleaned the neglected waif.

At the news of this occurrence, there was widespread indignation in Nazareth. The report quickly reached the school in which Jesus was a pupil, and the teacher placed Jesus on trial, charged with the fearful sin of befriending a bastard child.

The rabbi charges young Jesus: The Torah commands us that no bastard may enter the assembly of God; yet you befriended a bastard, took him into your home, and fed him, and taught him the Shema. You have sinned against God.

And Jesus replies in a manner befitting the future divine revolutionary: "I am not against God; I am for God. I do not be-

166

lieve that God would despise even the lowliest of His creatures, or that He would punish a child for the sin of its parents." A long colloquy in this vein is held. Fellow-pupils testified against Jesus.

It will be seen that Sholem Asch here takes the line traditionally followed by all Christians, that the Torah is a harsh law that knows no pity; it is the law of a stern God of Vengeance, but with Jesus a new law, a law of love and tenderness has entered the world.

After due deliberation of teacher and pupils the accused is found guilty as charged and sentence is pronounced by the teacher: Jesus is expelled from school, never again to cross its threshold, and all the children are admonished to shrink from him as from the bastard. Thus the divine child was excommunicated, and thereafter had no more schooling. This incident, too, foreshadowing the fateful trial that awaited Jesus in later life, has no Christian source, and is entirely the product of Asch's imagination. What can have prompted Asch to perpetrate this monstrous botch?

A tree is known by its fruit, a tale by its effect. And the effect here is devastating, and is plainly calculated to vilify and arouse contempt for the Torah, and to destroy the ancient legend of Jewish loving kindness, mercifulness and charity. It is a course of refined anti-Jewishness pursued behind a facade of literary artistry.

But it is neither literary, nor artistic. It is nothing but a chronicle of sadistic horror, the most offensive attack on the sensibilities of decent readers to appear in a long time, brought out through some sort of perverse folly. Not since the days of the Nazis have such loathsome fiends been paraded in writing for Jews. It is nasty and sickening.

However, this is only one side of this dismal story. There is yet another facet to this poison-penned piece, which is as preposterous a freak on the intellectual level as it is on the artistic. Asch has committed a major blunder, resulting from a lack of knowledge of plain, elementary Hebrew. In other words, we are here once again face to face with his distressing ignorance.

The entire incident here pictured is based on a misreading and misconstruction of the plain words of the Torah; Asch is guilty of reading a false meaning into the word of God, giving wide circulation to a falsehood and malignant distortion. If only we could seek out every reader of Asch's book and tell him that the entire narrative with its orgy of abominable cruelty is false, one-sided and impossible, and that the interpretation used by Asch is completely perjured! Asch simply did not know the true meaning of the biblical words. "A bastard shall not enter the assembly of the Lord." To understand the true meaning of this injunction, Asch had only to turn to the commentary of Rashi, and read the explanation—"He may not marry a Jewish woman." For "entering the assembly of God" is an idiomatic Hebrew expression for entering Jewry through holy matrimony. That is all. Otherwise before the law a bastard is treated in no way differently from other people.

Asch in his ignorance took the words in their elementary meaning. He thought they denied the bastard admission where the "Assembly of the Lord," or Jews, foregather, or entering under the shadow of a Jewish roof. He was ignorant of a plain reading every pupil of a Jewish elementary school is familiar with.

In the same portion of the Torah there is exactly the same injunction worded in the same terms about such as is "crushed or maimed in his privy parts" laying down the law prohibiting matrimony for the sexually disabled. Also about members of certain neighboring tribes: "An Ammonite or a Moabite shall not enter into the assembly of the Lord." And this only meant that no son of these races were permitted to marry a daughter of Israel— "because they met you not with bread and water in the way, when ye came forth out of Egypt; and because they hired against thee Balaam . . . to curse thee." These have destroyed their bond of kinship with Israel by their cruel behavior.

From the use of the masculine and not the feminine in the wording concerning the Ammonite or Moabite, the Talmud deduces that it is only the male of the tribes that is excluded. But the females could, after proselytization, marry male Israelites; e.g. Ruth, who was a Moabitess, entered "the assembly of the Lord" and became the ancestress of King David.

Asch fastened on the bare statement of the law in the Torah and maliciously or ignorantly passed over the interpretations, circumscriptions and delimitations placed upon it by the Rabbinical sages. Thus, "a bastard of known fatherhood shall not enter the assembly of the Lord, but a bastard of unknown fatherhood may enter" (Kidushin, 73a). Again, a bastard whose father is known may enter into matrimony with a bastard where fatherhood is unknown (ibid).

The plain meaning of the passage he employed is not the only

168

thing Asch did not know in the matter of "mamzer" or bastard. He did not know, or willfully passed over in silence, the fact that Jewish law contained many special provisions that show solicitude for the fate of the illegitimately born.

Numerous laws were passed by the sages to safeguard the interests of the bastard. Underlying these laws was the general principle, explicitly stated, that in all matters he was to be considered a Jew. He was to be circumcised; even when the time fell on the Sabbath. He inherited the property of his father, if the latter's identity was known; and, if he were a firstborn, he was entitled to a double portion. He was not only allowed to enter a synagogue as an equal of other Jews, but was also called up to the reading of the Law. He might be ordained as a rabbi, appointed to a minor civil court and, although some scholars dispute it, might even occupy the Jewish throne.

Moreover, the sages declared that a bastard who was a man of learning was greater than a high priest who lacked knowledge. This is implemented in the following provision: If two such men happen to be taken captive, and there is only money enough to ransom one of them, the learned bastard is preferred to the ignorant high priest. Or should both require philanthropic aid, for sustenance or apparel, and there is enough for but one, it is the bastard, not the priest, who is favored. Even the privilege of sitting at the head in the synagogue or at a religious feast, says Rabbi Abin, is granted first to the scholar of illegitimate birth.

And should a bastard marry a non-Jew and thereafter convert the child to Judaism, the child may marry one of Jewish faith, or "enter the assembly of the Lord." It is also said that in the life to come all bastards will be made clean of their stain. In the days of the Messiah, the prophet Elijah will disclose the tribal origins of all Jews, but will not expose the bastard.

How different from the picture of horror painted by Asch, of the gruesomeness of the Torah, and the cruelty of the Jews towards the illegitimately born! The spirit of malice trapped him in the net of his ignorance. Of men like Asch our sages wrote: "He who presumptuously lays down decisions is foolish, wicked, and of an arrogant spirit" (Aboth iv, 9).

These words of opprobrium are hardly sufficient for the author of the malicious diatribe about the poor little bastard. The chapter containing this libel is one of the most horrible pieces

169

ever penned against the Jew. This portrait of the Jew seemed especially vicious at a time when the bloody Nazis, in an orgy of abominable cruelty, had destroyed a million Jewish children.

It is revolting. It is ghoulish.

3

Quotations From Jewish Lore

The fifth chapter of the first part of *Mary* ends with a mighty, triumphant outcry: "A virgin has conceived in Israel!"

This is the axis around which Christianity revolves; and it is the central theme of *Mary*. A virgin has become pregnant, not of a man, but of the "holy ghost," and she has given birth to the messiah.

Were Christianity and its adherents, including Sholem Asch, to halt at this point, it would be of little concern to Jews and Judaism. Many religions have been based upon the doctrine of impregnation of virgins by gods and the subsequent birth of heroes. But Christianity adds: "as foretold by the prophets." In *Mary*, as in his other Christological books, Asch never wearies of playing on the motif—"as foretold by the prophets."

It is this contention which has made Judaism and Christianity forever incompatible. For Christians proceed to claim that this product of virgin birth emerged for the purpose of writing finis to Judaism—"as has been foretold by the prophets."

This entire elaborate system centers around the misinterpretation of a single biblical verse. The notion of a messiah coming to redeem the world was adopted by the Christians from the Jews; but the Jews never insisted that the saviour would be born of a virgin and the "holy ghost". The concept of divine birth, alien to Judaism, found its way into a single Bible verse via Graeco-Roman mythology. This innocent verse, upon which violence has been committed for nearly two thousand years and upon which rests the age-old controversy between Judaism and Christianity, must be closely examined here.

Isaiah vii tells of a great misfortune that befell the kingdom of Judah. Syria and Israel declared war on Judah. The siege of Jerusalem brought terror to the hearts of its people. Then came the prophet Isaiah to comfort King Ahaz, and to assure him that

170

the enemy would be defeated and would soon depart in rout, and that an era of prosperity in Judea would follow. But how long would the present troubled period last and how soon would salvation arrive? Here is the crucial episode as it occurs in Isaiah vii, 3:

"And the Lord spoke again unto Ahaz, saying: 'Ask thee a sign of the Lord thy God: ask it either in the depth, or in the height above.' But Ahaz said: 'I will not ask, neither will I try the Lord.' And he said: 'Hear ye now, O house of David: Is it a small thing for you to weary men, that ye will weary my God also? Therefore the Lord Himself shall give you a sign: behold, the young woman shall conceive, and bear a son, and shall call his name Immanuel. Curd and honey shall he eat, when he knoweth to refuse evil, and choose the good. Yea, before the child shall know to refuse the evil, and choose the good, the land whose two kings thou hast a horror of shall be forsaken. The Lord shall bring upon thee, and upon thy people and upon thy father's house, days that have not come, from the day that Ephraim departed from Judah; even the king of Assyria.'"

Does this prophecy pertain to the Messiah? Obviously not. It is an account of a specific situation at a specific time. And we learn later that events occurred just as the prophet had foretold. The young woman who was to conceive, or who was already pregnant—for the Hebrew "Harah" lends itself easily to both translations—was the king's own wife,—the prophet says *this* young woman, with the definite article, as if he were pointing his finger at her—and the child born was the future King Hezekiah. The miracle of the prophecy was the prophet's assurance that the child would be a boy. There is no mention of a virgin's bearing a child. Nevertheless, to this passage and this prophecy the Christians attach the most fundamental of their beliefs.

When the prophet says, "The young woman is conceived," or "shall conceive," he uses the word *almah,* which the Christians, for no sound reason, insist upon translating as "virgin". Such rendering does not necessarily follow. Anyone with a smattering of Hebrew knows this. No Hebrew dictionary, whether compiled by Jews or by Christians, confines the word to that definition. The true meaning of "Almah" is a young woman, whether virgin or matron. It is used in both senses in the Bible. It is obvious that "almah" does not mean virgin in the following passage from Proverbs: "There are three things which are too wonderful for

171

me, yea, four which I know not: the way of an eagle in the air; the way of a serpent upon a rock; the way of a ship in the midst of the sea; and the way of a man with an "almah" (xxx, 18-19) .

Such is the sand foundation on which has been erected the vast, imposing structure of Christianity. An erroneous translation of a single word, a gross misconception of a lone phrase, culled out of Judaism, has sired a faith which attempts to destroy Judaism and supplant all other faiths of all humanity. As mentioned above, the Christians may entertain the notion that their saviour is virgin born, but they must look elsewhere for proof.

In fact Christianity, slowly but surely began yielding on the point and retreating from the position it clung to so tenaciously for hundreds of years. The Revised Standard Version of the Holy Bible, sponsored by the National Council of the Churches of Christ in the United States of America, and published in 1952, has changed the word "virgin" to "young woman" in the much disputed verse in Isaiah. Thus an eminent group of Christian scholars at long last have bowed to the truth and yielded to the Jewish point of view. However, this change caused bitter controversy among the "Bible believing", or strictly fundamentalist, denominations, who contend and rightly so, that this destroys the very foundation of the central doctrine of the Christian faith. In Rocky Mount, N. C., a Baptist minister burned the page bearing the new, and what to him is a blasphemous version. Other public burnings of the book took place at Phoenix, Arizona, Crestview, Florida, and Akron, Ohio—where a blowtorch was used. These outraged believers point out that in Matthew 1:23 of the Revised Standard Version the word "virgin" is retained in referring back to the prophecy, thus making the Scriptures self-contradictory. The scholars responsible for the new translation explain that Isaiah was translated from the Hebrew and that the Hebrew word was "young woman" rather than "virgin", while the original Matthew text is Greek and does use "virgin". This however, does not heal the inconsistency: it aggravates it.

In The *Catholic Mind* (January, 1945) , Dr. A. Riley stated an incontrovertible alternative. He said: "If Judaism were the true religion in any period following the death of Christ . . . Christianity was based on the greatest fraud of history."

The fraudulent translation of "virgin" for "young woman" is a case in point and is typical of the problems presenting themselves to the mind of the thoughtful Christian. Trying to fit Chris-

172

tianity into the Hebrew Bible is like the proverbial trying to fit a square peg into a round hole.

The idea of a human god born of a virgin, which is pagan in origin, found its way into Christianity through the many idolatrous religions popular in the Roman world of the time. The devotees of the "Mary-cult" literally borrowed the figures of the pagan goddesses from the pagan temples; by a simple change of name, Isis became mother Mary. In seeking a broader base for Christianity, the church fathers looked into the Jewish Bible for justification of the Mary-cult, and there they seized upon the harmless word "almah," which they wilfully mistranslated.

Beginning with this error, the fathers delved farther into the Bible, and with similar mistranslations and tortured interpretations were able to offer creeds and views concerning the eternal theological problems of God, world, man, Jew and messiah—with which Judaism at every turn was forced to take issue.

These misinterpretations and erroneous translations from the Bible were the cause of much evil in the world. It gave rise to Christianity's conflict with Judaism, and it brought about interminable internecine conflicts which have splintered Christianity into hundreds of sects. Similar Christian errors of interpretation were responsible for the struggles of the Church with science, a struggle which resulted in defeat for the Church, causing incalculable injury to the entire cause of religion.

Jewish sages and scholars never saw any reason to fight science. On the contrary, their better knowledge and saner interpretation of the Bible led them to encourage inquiry into and the study of the universe.

To the credit of Christianity it must be admitted that it was instrumental in accomplishing the historic task of spreading the Bible to all the far corners of the world. But on the other hand, there can be no doubt that many of the world's ills today are in large measure rooted in Christian misinterpretation of the Hebrew Scriptures.

It is, therefore, particularly tragic to find a Jewish author joining the Christian chorus to chant the fateful phrase: "A virgin has conceived in Israel!" This phrase is a poisoned arrow, which with one thrust stabs through the Jew and his Bible, while Asch is holding up all his vessels to catch the falling drops of blood, which are miraculously converted into ducats! Neither respect for the language, nor for Jewish tradition, nor regard for Jewish

173

aversion to alien worship could stay his hand. He robs his people of patriarchs, prophets, and Bible, and turns everything over to the Christians lock, stock and barrel.

Of later Jewish literature, too, Asch helps himself freely of all that is good and beautiful to embellish the rival of Judaism. When the first "I am" of the Lord resounded from Mount Sinai, all of Creation suddenly stood still; the birds halted in their flight, the sheep in their grazing, the ass and ox in their plowing, the trees in their rustling, and the grass in its increase—the glorious poetic fantasy with which this Midrash envelops the Revelation at Sinai, is transferred by Asch to the moment when the "holy ghost" descends upon Mary to impregnate her. Thus the divine bedchamber is rendered analogous to Mount Sinai and the giving of the Law.

With the same recklessness, Asch robs a Chassidic Rabbi to give to Jesus. The story of the Seer of Lublin's reciting the appropriate benediction when taking of his mother's breast is assigned by Asch to the child Jesus.

The energy with which Asch hacks away at the ramparts of Judaism is equalled only by the care and solicitude with which he attempts to repair the cracks in the walls of Christianity. For example: Jews find the Christian contention that Jesus is both the "son of God" and a descendant of David irreconcilable. The Catholic reply that Mary is descended from King David is without biblical authority.

Asch takes such great pains in tracing Mary's genealogy to David, that many now credit him with having unearthed new evidence confirming this relationship. Asch offers further "proof" of the descent; Mary owned the oil-cruse with which Samuel had anointed David king almost a thousand years before! Asch would have us believe that this sacred antique if it existed at all, was not guarded in the Temple, nor in the royal palace, but was in the possession of an obscure village girl! Even Asch's vivid imagination could not build a book out of the very few New Testament passages in which Mary is mentioned. For "filler" he helped himself liberally from Jewish treasure. All that ever was glorious in Jewry glory is assigned to Mary; while all ugliness, regardless of source, is assigned to the Jews. The product of this juggling of sources is morally wicked and artistically cumbersome, and altogether a monstrous piece of work.

The Idolator

In Christian literature no particular relationship between the mother of Jesus and the Jews is ever mentioned. In the very few passages in the Gospels allotted to Mary, she is presented only in connection with her son. But Sholem Asch is not content with his sources; he "discovers" new important bonds and connections between Mary and her people. He informs us that Mary was appointed by God "the Mother of Israel" (p. 43).

Elsewhere she is given a more mystic designation, as a "sacrifice for Israel." Remarking her sufferings—after all, she was only a "feeble Jewess"—Jesus speaks to her:

"Your suffering, Mother, will purify Israel, like the blood of a sin offering."

Thus Jesus was destined to serve as a vicarious atonement for the world, while his mother performed the same function for Israel. But well do we know, with bitter knowledge, how often our people have been slaughtered as a "sacrifice" to Mary!

How can she be accounted a "national mother" to us, recalling as we must how during Christian processions in her honor, in the "old country," we little Jewish children used to run into hiding, partly because our presence was forbidden by the ecclesiastical authorities, partly because we were afraid of being beaten up by the devout Christian crowds?

Do children run away from a mother? What kind of mother is she whom children flee in deadly fear?

Yet it may be supererogatory for us to quarrel about Mary with Sholem Asch. Let him "sell" Mary to the Protestants before offering her to the Jews.

One of the most important *causae belli* dividing Protestants and Catholics is the Mary-cult. To the Protestant, Mary is only a Jewess who conceived and bore the messiah. Whether as virgin or married woman, of the holy ghost or of mere mortal, each Protestant sect believes according to its own doctrine. In any case, Protestants maintain that Mary's service to mankind was the bearing of the Messiah. No role is assigned to her in heaven.

In the Catholic Church, candles are lighted before Mary, and devotees kneel before her, offering prayers and adoration. Here Mary-worship has dimmed the importance of Jesus himself. Her images are more prized than those of her son; her statues are said to shed tears, bleed, speak, walk, and heal. Wooden, stone, and metal representations reputedly come to life. To these statues in scattered churches travel believers from all parts of the world, to touch, kiss, and be healed. Often these Madonnas are carried all over the world for good Catholics in their own habitations to view and to adore. The charge is often made that many Catholics consider these images not as symbolical presentations only, but as the actual living presence of the divine mother. In this belief, they are encouraged by the clergy.

Protestants point the finger of scorn at this common, primitive form of idolatry. The more tenaciously Catholics cling to Mary, the more do Protestants belittle her.

Amid this clash and clatter of controversy, Sholem Asch begins to preach Mary-cultism to the Jews!

The historic cleavage between Catholicism and Protestantism on the place of Mary in the Christian scheme came most sharply to the fore in 1951, when Pope Pius XII proclaimed as dogma the assumption of Mary, that "when the course of her life on earth was finished, she was taken up body and soul into heaven."

Outcries against the Pope's pronouncement were heard around the world. In Italy the Waldensian and other Protestant churches raised their voices in objection. The Archbishop of Canterbury and York declared that the Church of England "refuses to regard as requisite for a saving faith any doctrine or opinions which are not plainly contained in the Scriptures." The Free Church Council, representing all Protestant Churches other than the Church of England, also protested.

"We as Lutherans," reads a resolution adopted by the American Lutheran Conference, "must protest that there is no basis for the dogma in scripture or in the ecumenical creeds." And in the famous Riverside Church in New York City, Dr. Robert J. McCracken stated: "There is not a shred of biblical evidence to support it. Its acceptance involves defiance of all the canons of historical scholarship." The Protestant Association of South Africa went even farther, and in a cable to the Pope said that the new dogma was "a legend of pagan origin."

But on one point in the story of Mary the Protestants agree with the Catholics: that there was a moment in the Christian story, indeed in the course of history, when the will of God depended on

176

the will of man, or rather woman. Reference is made to the moment of consummation of the union of the Holy Ghost and Mary. Christian theology rightly maintains that the Holy Ghost did not spread his wings over Mary, or "bestrew" her, as the Gospels have it, without her consent. Without her consent, in earthly parlance, would have constituted rape. The principle that "one may not force a Jewish daughter" applies, as we see, also to God.

Hence it is taught by all Christian theology, Protestant, Catholic, and Aschian, that Mary's consent was requisite to the act, and that, fortunately for God, man, and universe, she offered her consent quite readily.

That Mary, or any damsel, would have refused to bear the saviour seems ridiculous, but theoretically, she could have said no. Thus we see that according to Christian theology, there was a moment in the course of the universe, when all of God's plans and the destiny of mankind, lay not in His own power, but with a woman's will.

This offshoot of the Mary-cult is a part of the agony of Christianity, a religion which derived out of Judaism, but which crucified itself when it departed from the pure Judaic Unity.

Sholem Asch treats Mary with the extreme veneration of the Catholics. Nevertheless, as a novelist, he passes up a magnificent opportunity. Imagine the extraordinary dramatic conflict he could have created by making Mary first say no. He might have followed the style of folktales, having her plead, "Give me three days to think it over!" What a drama that would have been! A woman, an ordinary young woman, delaying the divine plan for all of creation! Has there ever been, or could there be, a more dramatic tension between heaven and earth, God and man, the Creator and Eve? Had Mary demanded the righting of the injustice in the first curse heaped upon her sex ("I will greatly multiply thy pain and thy travail; in pain thou shalt bring forth children!"), she could have imposed her will, declaring, "This is my condition—Remove the curse; give assurance of a better destiny for my sex, or else . . ."

But Asch's genius failed him; he did not grasp the vast potentialities of such an impasse.

We have attempted to sketch the utter confusion of Christian dogma, to indicate why various theologians and sects are at perpetual loggerheads with one another, and to reiterate our question to Sholem Asch: How can you attempt to offer this fare to a people which for thousands of years has tirelessly labored to attain, and has indeed attained, such a concept of divine unity as to rival the sun in luminous clarity?

At a time when non-Jews are questioning the validity of Christianity, Sholem Asch's attempts to lure Jews into the Christian fold seem scarcely opportune. We refer not to communist non-belief, and their attempt to destroy both church and religion. We refer to unimpeachable Christian sources, as for instance the noted Russian religious philosopher, Nicolai Berdyaev, who declared:

"In a certain sense it may be said that Christianity, historical Christianity, is coming to an end, and its rebirth can be expected only from a revelation of the Holy Ghost, which will provide a new birth for Christianity." ("The Divine and the Human," p. 1).

There were others of his stature, men like Kierkegaard and Dostoyevsky, who had a decisive encounter with Christianity when it seemed to them to be at the historic crossroads of inevitable decline or transfigured revival. Can it revive with the slaughter of six million Jews in the heart of Christian Europe?

There is a story told of Semiaticz, a little town in old Russia, where a Jewish youth accepted conversion and moved in with the local priest near the church. Every day his mother took her place before the Church, weeping and wailing, begging her son to come out and return to the fold. But he did not emerge.

Then one day, when her despair had grown unendurable, she tore open her blouse, exposing her breasts; and before heaven and the church she spat upon them and cursed them for having ever given sustenance to her treacherous son.

This action might have been emulated by another mother, from another town, called Kutno (Asch's birthplace), had the devotees of Mary not burnt the town together with the mother.

5

Alcmene and Paulina

Since the doctrine of the Virgin birth is the focal theme of *Mary,* some attention must be given here to this belief in the light of history and comparative religion. As has been noted, this religious creed is not peculiar to Christianity, but is common to many re-

178

ligions of past ages. Divine humans sired by the gods abound in myth and legend. Divine origin was often assigned to men of genius. So widespread was the belief that it has been widely adopted as a theme in classical literature.

The Egyptian Pharaohs accounted themselves descendants of the great god Ra. According to Greek and Roman believers, Zeus and Apollo sired many distinguished men, including Plato, Alexander and Caesar Augustus. Romulus and Remus, founders of the city of Rome, were reputed to be the sons of a virginal temple servitor and the god Mars.

In literature we discover the theme of godly association with earthly females in Amphitryon, a comedy by the Roman playwright Plautus. The gist (or jest) of the plot concerns a general who has gone off to war, leaving his beautiful spouse Alcmene at home. Jupiter, chief of the gods, sees her and lusts after her. Assuming the appearance of the absent Amphitryon, he disports himself on earth as Alcmene's husband. Mercury, messenger of the gods, is stationed as a lookout at the door.

The victorious Amphitryon returns home, sending his servant Sophias ahead to announce the victory. Sophias' encounter with Mercury at the door is quite comic, as is his discovery that there are strange guests in the house. In the end Jupiter confesses all, promising Alcmene that the offspring from the escapade will be a most heroic son. This proves to be Hercules.

But a remarkably similar incident seems actually to have occurred in ancient Rome. It is fully detailed in the "Jewish Antiquities" of Josephus, and is worth reproducing. Here is the story verbatim:

"There was at Rome a woman whose name was Paulina; one who, on account of the dignity of her ancestors, and by the regular conduct of a virtuous life, had a great reputation; she was also very rich; and although she was of a beautiful countenance, and in the flower of her age when women are the most gay, yet she did lead a life of great modesty. She was married to Saturninus, one that was every way answerable to her in an excellent character. Decius Mundus fell in love with this woman, who was a man very high in the equestrian order; and as she was of too great dignity to be caught by presents, and had already rejected them, though they had been sent in great abundance, he was still more inflamed with love to her, insomuch that he promised to give her two hundred thousand Attic drachmae for one night's lodging;

and when this would not prevail upon her, and he was not able to bear this misfortune in his amours, he thought it the best way to famish himself to death for want of food, on account of Paulina's sad refusal; and he determined with himself to die after such a manner, and he went on with his purpose accordingly.

"Now Mundus had a freed-woman, who had been made free by his father, whose name was Ide, one skillful in all sorts of mischief. This woman was very much grieved at the young man's resolution to kill himself. . . . and came to him, and encouraged him by her discourse, and made him to hope, by some promises she gave him, that he might obtain a night's lodging with Paulina; and when he joyfully hearkened to her entreaty, she said she wanted no more than fifty thousand drachmae for the entrapping of the woman. So when she had encouraged the young man, and gotten as much money as she required, she did not take the same methods as had been taken before, because she perceived that the woman was by no means to be tempted by money; but as she knew that she was very much given to the worship of the goddess Isis she devised the following stratagem.

"She went to some of Isis's priests, and . . . persuaded them by words, but chiefly by the offer of money . . . and told them the passion of the young man, and persuaded them to use all means possible to beguile the woman. . . .

"Accordingly, the oldest of them went immediately to Paulina . . . and he told her that he was sent by the god Anubis, who was fallen in love with her, and enjoined her to come to him. Upon this she took the message very kindly, and valued herself greatly upon this condescension of Anubis, and told her husband that she had a message sent her, and was to sup and lie with Anubis; so he agreed to her acceptance of the offer, as fully satisfied with the chastity of his wife. Accordingly, she went to the temple, and after she had supped there, and it was the hour to go to sleep, the priest shut the doors of the temple, when, in the holy part of it, the lights were also put out. Then did Mundus leap out (for he was hidden therein), and did not fail of enjoying her, who was at his service all the night long, as supposing he was the god; and when he was gone away, which was before those priests who knew nothing of the stratagem were stirring, Paulina came early to her husband, and told him how the god Anubis had appeared to her. Among her friends, also, she declared how great a value she put upon this favor, who partly disbelieved the thing, when

180

they reflected on its nature, and were partly amazed at it, as having no pretense for not believing it, when they considered the modesty and dignity of the person.

"But now, on the third day after what had been done, Mundus met Paulina, and said, 'Nay, Paulina, thou hast saved me two hundred thousand drachmae, which sum thou mightest have added to thine own family; yet, has thou not failed to be at my service in the manner I invited thee. . . .'

"Now she began to come to the sense of the grossness of what she had done, and rent her garments, and told her husband of the horrid nature of the wicked contrivance, and prayed him not to neglect to assist her in this case. So he discovered the fact to the emperor; whereupon Tiberius inquired into the matter thoroughly by examining the priests about it, and ordered them to be crucified, as well as Ide. . . . He also demolished the temple of Isis, and gave order that her statue should be thrown into the river Tiber; while he only banished Mundus, but did no more to him, because he supposed that what crime he had committed was done out of the passion of love" (Whiston's Josephus; pp. 535-6).

CHAPTER IV

Moses

It was widely known that following publication of Sholem Asch's three Christological novels—*The Nazarene, The Apostle,* and *Mary*—he had begun a book on Moses, teacher and legislator of Israel. The small number of supporters still loyal to Asch were jubilant. Unabashedly they declared that in the new novel Asch would outwit all his critics. He would portray a traditional Moses, thus placating his people; Jews would readily forgive his earlier works, open their doors to him once again, and leave present "detractors" silent and humiliated.

The shocking cynicism inherent in such an assumption is a sad commentary on the spirit of our time, but is not out of keeping with the character and career of Sholem Asch, a vagabond between two religions. There is no sinner lower in the scale than the one who, with premeditation repeatedly undertakes the cycle of sin and repentance. But even if *Moses* were a true act of repentance, it would change nothing; for there is a profound difference between one who sins on his own account and one who brings others to sin: a man can mend his own ways, but it is not within his power to bring back to righteousness those whom he has impelled to transgress. Of such a one is it said: "He who has sinned and caused many others to sin, is not offered the chance of repentance." Asch, by his works, led many astray from the Jewish path.

However, all conjecturing was quickly resolved when *Moses* finally appeared, and it became obvious, at least to the initiate, that Asch had no thought of repenting at all. For in *Moses* he continues to expound his Christological notions, albeit furtively.

If anything, his sin is magnified: in the three earlier books he departed from his own to extol an alien faith and church; in this volume he brings the foreign concepts home, into the very synagogue. Moses is Christianized.

Asch does not advance the transformation honestly, frankly and directly, but in underhanded manner, through circumlocution, subterfuge and concealment. On the surface, to the uninitiate, everything appears most proper; the unaccustomed eye does not readily detect the foreign matter. Asch appears to be reverently retelling the Moses story as it is recounted in the Pentateuch, with amplifications from other sources and embellished with many gems culled from the midrashim. Nevertheless, it is all a sham and a fraud. Under a "kosher" sign non-kosher fare is served and fed to the innocent. Aside of all other considerations, Asch here makes himself guilty of perpetrating intellectual fraud upon his unwary readers.

Before exploring this matter further, we must make a digression to pay a debt to "Art." There is a school which maintains that all sins and transgressions are inconsequential when set in the scales of the divinity called Art; that insofar as Asch fashions a literary masterpiece all things are permitted to him.

Judaism is not a creed, or primarily a creed, but first and foremost a code of behaviour. But there is nothing of the chilliness of the legal code about it: it is the passion of belief translated into the reality of concrete life.

Therefore let it be said at the outset that even were Moses historical fiction at its very finest and not the ponderous, sprawling chronicle that it is; a masterpiece and not a pretentious botch, it would still be a sin against the very Goddess of Art in whose name Asch is pleading immunity and absolution. For having fictionalized the Bible, or the part of it called the Five Books of Moses, one inevitably invites comparison.

Now whether one holds to the belief that the Books of Moses are a divine revelation or a product of the human mind, there is universal agreement that they present an achievement of highest genius, unapproachable by a mere mortal. It was therefore an act of great presumption on the part of Sholem Asch to attempt to rewrite it. Does God stand in need of a rewrite man?

Moses is a recapitulation of the Bible story, from Exodus to Deuteronomy. It covers the career of the prophet-legislator and the birth of the Jewish people from the departure from Egypt to the attainment of Canaan's borders. When an author undertakes to rewrite the Pentateuch, what can be his ultimate purpose or excuse?

There are three possibilities:—to tell the story better, to tell it as well, or to tell it less well.

It would, of course, be ridiculous to charge Asch with the last intent; the second would have been supererogatory. Obviously he must have intended to improve the narrative, which in this case meant no less than to match powers with the Divine.

Apparently Asch did not think the task was too great for him. He cheerfully goes about expounding the speech of Moses, Aaron and all other heroes moving across the pages of this first part of the Holy Scriptures. With disarming abandon he invents new speech for God Himself and even puts some new ideas into His head. Whole carloads of new conversations, dialogues, monologues, orations have been introduced by Asch into his opus that have no parallel, and indeed no basis whatsoever in the Holy Writ.

Now fancy Asch, or any man for the matter of that, injecting himself between God and Moses, eavesdropping on them as they hold council, prompting God what to say to Moses, and Moses what to say to God, ghost-writing for both at the same time—fancy all that and you have the measure of the colossal vanity that went into the making of *Moses*. Indeed, fools rush in where angels fear to tread. What the prophets and the saints were granted only in rare moments of divine inspiration, Asch attempted to attain by virtue of literary talent. He stormed heaven with a typewriter to give us not a novel, but a bigger and better Mount Sinai. The result is a monstrous bore and the ultimate reductio *ad absurdum* in insolence and arrogance.

Some of Asch's supporters tried to find justification that his *Moses* will at least be of service to those who have never made a study of the Pentateuch, and who will make its acquaintance through his novel. To which we may only cry alas for those who must be reduced to learning about the Bible not through its own pages, but by way of Asch's work.

With this introduction we are better prepared to appraise the significance of Asch's adventure into Bible land. His real purpose in rewriting the Pentateuch was not, of course, simple "improvement," but fundamental alteration: alteration into something Christological.

184

With Alien Heart

The Jewish religion rests on the basic tenet that Moses was the greatest prophet who ever lived. As Maimonides expresses it in the seventh principle of faith: "I believe with perfect faith that the prophecy of Moses, our teacher, was true, and that he was the chief of the prophets, both of those that preceded and of those that followed him."

There has never been unanimity among Jews as to the number of principles on which their religion is founded or as to which among them are obligatory, although the thirteen principles of Maimonides have gained popular acceptance. About Moses, however, there is no division, for his place is established by the eternal verdict of the Torah itself: "And there hath not arisen a prophet since in Israel like unto Moses, whom the Eternal knew face to face" (Deut. xxxiv, 10). Thus no matter what prophet shall emerge in later days, he must be confronted with the unalterable dictum of the supremacy of Moses.

Belief in the eternity of the Torah is inextricably bound up with the belief that Moses was and always will remain God's greatest prophet. For whosoever would posit a greater prophet would have to posit as well another and greater Torah, and would then be in conflict with the ninth principle of Maimonides, "that this Torah will not be changed, and that there will never be any other Torah from the Creator."

Both of the religions derived from Judaism—Christianity and Islam, contend for the seat of Moses. They claim to have been granted testaments of a higher order than the Torah, and that therefore their founders are superior to Moses. Thus Mohammed maintained, or it is maintained on his behalf, that God said to him, "I may not be spoken of unless you be mentioned with me. I have made you the first of the prophets to be created, and the last to be given My mission." To the similar claim made for Jesus, there is added the creed that he is God's son, that he was with God from everlasting to everlasting, that he has taken over the sovereignty from the Father in heaven, and came down to replace the dispensation of Moses on earth.

The conflict concerning the personalities of Moses and of Jesus and their place in the divine plan is fundamental in the relationship between Judaism and Christianity. The position of Moses in Judaism has been noted. The irreconcilable divergence emerges when the following from Paul is placed alongside of it:

"For this man Jesus was counted worthy of greater glory than Moses, by so much as he that hath built the house hath greater honor than the house. . . . And Moses verily was faithful in all his house as a servant. . . . But Christ as the Son over his own house" (Hebrews iii, 6). The Gospel goes to great lengths in establishing the superior position of Jesus. Such is the purpose of the story of the transfiguration. The Gospel relates that at one time the Nazarene ascended a lofty hill, together with his brothers James and John, and Peter. Suddenly Jesus was transformed before them:

"And his face did shine as the sun, and his raiment was white as the light. And, behold, there appeared unto them Moses and Elias talking with him. And Peter answering, said to Jesus: Lord, it is good for us to be here: if thou wilt let us make here three tabernacles, one for thee, and one for Moses, and one for Elias. And as he was yet speaking, behold a bright cloud overshadowed them: and lo, a voice out of the cloud, which said, This is my beloved Son, in whom I am well pleased; hear ye him. And when the disciples heard it, they fell on their face. . . . And when they lifted up their eyes, they saw no man, save Jesus only" (Matthew xvii, 1-9).

Here by the alleged intervention of heaven itself Moses was subordinated to Jesus, indicating time, place and circumstance when he was "unseated." In the mind of Peter, Moses and Elijah were still on a par with Jesus. The purpose of the Transfiguration was to disabuse his mind. Both Moses and Elijah together were sent into retirement, for Moses symbolized the Torah, and Elijah prophecy, both functions being supposedly transferred to Jesus.

This is precisely the line followed all along by Asch in his Christological writings. He had taken that position long before the writing of *Moses*. "Jesus Christ, to me," he states with unusual frankness, "is the outstanding personality of all times, all history, both as the Son of God and the Son of Man" (Christian Herald, Jan. 1944).

"Everything He (Jesus) ever said or did," Asch continued, "has value for us today, and that is something you can say of no other man, alive or dead."

These words carry a complete denial of Judaism, invalidating

186

all its teaching concerning Moses. The best that can be said of Asch here is that he has revealed a gross ignorance of the issues involved. The worst that can be said is that he has deliberately ignored them. Neither hypothesis is particularly edifying. He further declared:

"No other teacher—Jewish, Christian, Buddhist, Mohammedan—is *still* a teacher whose teaching is such a guidepost for the world we live in."

Having taken that position, Asch could not ever write *Moses* in a way to meet the position of Judaism concerning Moses, the Man of God. He disqualified himself completely for the sacred theme.

For the height of inconsistency, let us recall that as late as 1940, by Asch's own testimony, the idea of a Son of God was inconceivable, much less acceptable to him. In a response to critics of *The Nazarene* (published April 6, 1940, in the Jewish Daily Forward) he swore by all that was holy: "I declare, that in no place, neither in my book nor in any other of my public writings or speeches, have I by pen or tongue made the statement that there is any god other than the one God of Israel, to say nothing of assuming the existence of a 'son of God.'

"I recall," he continued, "that I expended great effort and spent many sleepless nights, to discover any support for that idea in the New Testament." He did find some minor references to God's son, and was quite perturbed when he read how Peter had promulgated that idea. "I could never bring myself to utter that phrase on my own, nor could I at all understand how so pious a Jew as Peter was could give expression to the phrase."

But apparently he gradually grew accustomed to the strange idea. In His *What I Believe* (1941) he was already presenting Jesus as greater than Moses, using a simple "proof." Moses and the other prophets, he wrote, could speak only in the name of God—"God spake unto Moses"; "And God said unto Moses"; "The word of God to the prophet"; and like locutions—being only messengers, but the Nazarene could speak in his own name—"You have heard that it was said . . . but I say unto you . . . "—which to Sholem Asch, in line with Christian teaching, indicated a special authority for Jesus received "direct from the lips of God."

Later Asch ventured by degrees to speak more boldly and to give expression to the thought he had previously sought to restrain, openly genuflecting to the "son of God" as quoted above: "Jesus

187

Christ, to me, is the outstanding personality of all time, all history, both as the Son of God and the Son of Man."

The hands that could set down such words as these are not hands qualified to write of Moses from the Jewish viewpoint.

In the light of Asch's mouthings, it is interesting to note an appraisal of Moses by a gentile scholar, Dean Milman, British historian:

" (Moses) a man who, considered merely in an historical light, without any reference to his Divine inspiration, has exercised a more extensive and permanent influence over the destinies of his own nation and mankind at large than any other individual recorded in the annals of the world."

3

Moses and Aaron

Sholem Asch, in his *Moses,* does not recede from the Christological position apparent in his trilogy of the holy family, negating the eternal validity of the Torah of Moses and considering it only a temporary dispensation in advance of the Christian culmination. Moses is not presented as the greatest of prophets of all time, but merely as a predecessor and herald of a greater prophet to come. Consequently the Torah does not contain the fullness of God's gifts to man; the highest fulfillment is left to the Christian redeemer. *Moses* is written in utter disregard of Jewish tradition and in complete disrespect toward the Jewish point of view.

Asch's handling of the Moses theme is in complete contrast to the reverent attitude he displays toward the founders of Christianity. Never in his *The Nazarene, The Apostle* and *Mary* does he dare deviate by as much as a hair's breadth from accepted Christian teaching. He is faithful to his New Testament source, altering nothing, omitting nothing. Where he fails to satisfy the Catholic, he pleases the Protestant, and vice versa. The Protestant dollar, too, is equal to a hundred cents.

Not so in his attitude toward Judaism. Here he permits himself all sorts of liberties. He gives himself a free hand in dealing with Jewish sentiment, Law, traditions. He pays no respect to his

188

people, to the Bible, to the Talmud and the wisdom of all the Jewish ages.

The first assault comes early in *Moses,* in his remarks on the tribe of Levi, of which Moses and Aaron were members. According to the Torah and later tradition, this was the sole group maintaining the patriarchal tradition, while the other eleven tribes, enslaved and befuddled, were inclining toward the blandishments of Egyptian aberrancy. There is a midrash which names Levi as the tribe that always worshiped the true Creator, imparting to all the idea of divine Unity taught by the Fathers; the Levites kept before their brethren the bond between God and Israel, the promise that some day the people would grow great and inherit the land of Canaan. Their faith and assurance of redemption from bondage was the firm foundation of the Israel to be.

So says Jewish tradition. But in Sholem Asch's novel, Levi is the worst of the tribes. The Levites are said to have bowed to Pharaoh and assisted him in enslaving the remaining tribes. "Pharaoh's advisers," we read, "were quick to see that it would be easier to maintain dominion over the alien Hebrews—through their own instruments than through foreign instruments. The government of the Hebrews was therefore placed in the hands of the tribe of Levi; and through the tribe of Levi the Egyptians introduced the system of slavery which finally engulfed the tribes" (p. 63).

In return for specific privileges the tribe allows itself to become the instrument by which their people are held in the iron hand of enslavement and tyranny. These men become the overseers of labor, slavedrivers, guardians and keepers, the "capos" of Egypt.

Moses, bringing the first message from God promising that the people will be redeemed, encounters his first opposition in the ranks of Levi; even his brother Aaron opposes him.

Throughout the book Asch heaps contumely upon the Levites, with special attention to the person of Aaron.

In Jewish tradition Aaron is God's faithful servant, loyal helper in achieving release from Egyptian bondage, Moses' mouthpiece, and a symbol of peace. The sages dwell on Aaron's magnanimity in refusing to envy the choice of Moses, his younger brother, to the distinguished position of liberator of Israel. For that reason, they point out, God's first commandment, that concerning the Passover, was transmitted not to Moses alone, but to Moses and Aaron jointly (Exodus xii, 1). Aaron shared the honor with Moses. For the same reason Aaron was elevated to the post of high priest. The sages pronounced Moses as balanced against all of Israel combined, and they accorded the same glory to Aaron.

But in Sholem Asch's novel Aaron becomes the chief villain and intriguer, not unlike the political underworld characters of modern literature. According to Asch, Aaron's appointment to the high priesthood was an act not of God, but of Aaron himself. He does not wait to be called; he does not wait for the Torah to be handed down, or for the exodus from Egypt. Long before any indication of redemption "he chose for himself the high priesthood, having an eye to the important position which the priests occupied in the life of the Egyptians. He devoted himself to a study of the ritual of the Egyptian priests, and learned their prayers, hymns, and conjurations" (46).

Thus Aaron's aspiration to the priesthood is not conditioned by the call from God or prompted by piety but by dreams of greatness, wealth and might for himself and for his offspring for all time.

"Even in Egypt," writes Asch, "Aaron had already been dreaming of a priestly hegemony in Israel after the pattern of the Egyptian priesthood, with an ordered hierarchy, with rich treasure cities about the temples, and great wealth accumulated from field tithes and other taxes. In Aaron's plan the priesthood was to belong not to the entire tribe of the Levy . . . but to the descendants of a single family, that of Amram, while the other Levites were to constitute a sort of temple slave body, the servitors of the priests" (216).

And elsewhere (299): "But if God did not need the sacrifices, the priests and Levites did; and the sacrifices were brought for them, not for Him."

A capitalistic, monopolistic exploiter, founder of a family trust for expropriating the property and sucking the blood of the common people, this is how Asch paints a pillar of Judaism, one of the most glorified and sanctified personalities of Israel's early history.

In Asch's book, the commands of the sacrifices come not from God, or from Moses, but from Aaron. Aaron, with the aid of his sons, Nadab and Abihu, is finally able to impose these laws on

190

Moses. The ceremonial cult of sacrifices is foisted upon Moses by Aaron. Aaron and his sons adopt the worship of the golden calf in order to prove to Moses that the people must have rites and ceremonies, concrete representations of their religion—"a people cannot live with laws and commandments alone" (270).

Asch would have us believe that the sacrificial cult was forced by Aaron and his sons upon God himself. At first, Aaron resists his sons' urging to erect the calf, protesting that God has commanded on the mount that the Israelites have no other god before Him. But his sons finally convince him of the propriety and necessity of the image.

According to Asch, Moses and Aaron had entirely distinct ideas concerning the ultimate Jewish faith. Their conflict concerning the calf leads them to so heated a quarrel that for a moment Moses is strongly minded to slay Aaron and be forever rid of him.

Not even in his Christological works does Asch so insolently attempt to pervert the personalities and text of the Bible. Any child in Hebrew school can recognize the perversity and falsity of Asch's rendering of the Torah. In the Torah the sacrifices emanate from the same authority and with the same force and finality as the Ten Commandments.

Sacrifices are as old as humanity. They already began with Cain and Abel. Through all ages Jewish sages have sought to penetrate the meaning and mystery of the offerings prescribed by the Torah. Maimonides believed they were commanded in order to woo the Israelites away from the overpowering allurement of idol worship. He bases his view on Leviticus (xvii, 7): "And they shall no more offer their sacrifices unto the satyrs, after whom they go astray." From this interpretation Nahmanides differs. Talmudic sages offer profound explanations of the symbols of the sacrifices. At any rate, they were by all accounts integral parts of Jewish faith and activity until finally replaced by prayer worship.

Why should Asch, two thousand years later, so strongly assail this basic part of ancient Judaism, heaping abuse upon the first high priest, to carry it out?

Christianity provides the answer. It is basic in Christian doctrine that the Nazarene arose to become the final sacrifice and that with his crucifixion the institution of sacrifice was abolished forever. At the same time Jesus assumed the role of the true high

191

priest. He thus became the sacrifice, the priest performing the sacrifice, and God receiving the sacrifice all in one.

The New Testament verse thus fulfilled by Asch reads (Hebrews vii, 11-12):

"If therefore perfection were by the Levitical priesthood. . . . what further need was there that another priest should arise after the order of Melchisedec, and not be called after the order of Aaron? For the priesthood being changed, there is made of necessity a change also of the law."

Aaron, according to Christian theology, was only one of the many high priests of the Old Dispensation, a kind of understudy to the Nazarene, who was to be first and only high priest of the New Dispensation. Aaron's priesthood was but temporary; the Nazarene's is to endure forever.

It is this idea that lies at the basis of Asch's offensive against Aaron. Since priest, Levite, sacrifice and the entire order of the Temple were eventually to be nullified by Christian teaching, as they were to be abolished by historic conditions, Asch fairly exhausted his poetic imagination to make them appear sinister and insignificant in the eyes of Jews.

4

The Barbarian

The Michelangelo statue of Moses is world renowned. Were Sholem Asch to approach it with hammer and chisel, to hack and chop and scrape at the figure until it assume an entirely different configuration from that provided by the master, he would be stoned in public. He would be called savage, barbarian, caveman!

The world boasts of another great master, greatest of them all, the Jewish people. This artist also created a figure of Moses, not in stone or fabric but in life and idea. The living Moses is portrayed in the Torah, and Jewry has vested him in beauty and glory which dazzles the eye and confounds the tongue.

This masterpiece of divine countenance has been so daubed and smeared by Asch in his opus that we can well label the renovator "denizen of darkness!"

We have already noted that Asch allows himself no encroachment upon Christian tradition in his treatment of Christian themes. He approaches these matters with awe and reverence. Only in treating his Jewish theme does he behave like a dipsomaniac.

His handling of Moses shows not only a lack of respect for Judaism, but a complete disregard of art. A prime requisite of art is unity, consistency, but in this volume Asch sometimes writes with the extreme piety of a Torah-true Jew or the reverence of a Christian, and at other times with the blasphemous scorn of the Bible critic. He mystically accepts all the miracles, only to become in the next breath completely rationalistic, and offer scientific explanations of supernatural events. He accompanies Moses into the wilderness, and then, forgetting where he happens to be, leaps over the centuries to recount how the laws of Moses are observed today. A limner and poet at time, he often becomes a mere publicist, a writer of journalese.

For example, he describes the dietary laws, the distinctions among clean and unclean animals, birds, and fish, only to wind up with the heretical comment that these regulations were of but a temporary nature (301).

It must be remembered that the story as told is contemporaneous with Moses, presenting the incidents as they occur, transmitting the laws to the readers as they are proclaimed by the lawgiver. Artistically it rudely breaks the unity of the story to stop and speculate on the duration of the laws or to hold disquisitions on their effect in subsequent centuries. The Torah pronounces its laws eternal. They remain as valid today as they were in the period of their promulgation. Thus, Asch's conclusions about the Law satisfy the requirements of neither art nor truth. The only excuse which Asch can offer for making such aberrant comment is his Christian orientation. When Asch wrote of Moses, it was the Nazarene who guided his thoughts. Holding to the Christian dogma that in a later day Jesus was to arise to annul these laws of the dietary, he wove the idea into the Moses recital. Indeed, they get rougher treatment at the hands of Asch than at the hands of the Christians. While Christianity declared these laws operative until the coming of the Nazarene, Asch granted them a lesser duration: "these regulations seemed to bear the stamp of a temporary purpose, relating to the transition time in the wilderness" (302).

For Asch, the only permanent laws are social legislation—

"valid for every civilization touched with the spirit of God." On closer examination one finds that Asch regards those laws later accepted by Christianity permanent and eternal and those later abrogated by the Christians, though still retained by the Jews, as merely temporary. In his effort to detract from the divinity and eternity of the Torah he cunningly employs other artifices and devices. Moses is shown learning and adopting for Israel the laws of neighboring nations, like the Egyptians and Babylonians, thereby implying that when the Jews were profound they were not original. Departing from the orthodox attitude he maintains in the greater part of the book with regards to the revelation at Sinai, he suddenly shifts to a rationalistic stand to hold that most of the laws were only enunciated in the name of the Lord. Particularly is this true with reference to the sacrificial laws. In no instance does Asch admit any divine origin for them. "The ritual" he writes, "was published in such form as to seem to have issued from the one Almighty God, Creator of heaven and earth" (p. 298). But in reality, Sholem Asch maintains, they stemmed from the Egyptians and Babylonians.

One might argue that Sholem Asch is merely concerned with offering a rational exposition of Moses' activity, a worldly approach to the origins of Torah law.

This argument might be justified were *Moses* a worldly novel, but it is not. It is an artistic anomaly, activated in two worlds, the mystical-religious and the sober and realistic. Asch accepts without question that God spoke to Moses and took a direct part in the vast epic which ranged from the Exodus to the death of Moses. He pictures some miracles from the most orthodox viewpoint. But suddenly the religious opus becomes altogether earthly, rational and "scientific."

However, closer examination reveals a method of subtle manipulation. Here, too, the author demonstrates his complete subservience to the Christian idea. Asch, in full accord with pious tradition, ascribes to God only those laws which have later been incorporated into Christianity, such as the Ten Commandments. But those elements not taken over by the Christians are described as emanating from Moses alone, and not from the Almighty.

Apparently Asch is writing like a pious believer: God, on Mount Sinai speaking with Moses and so forth, but in the next breath it is impiously set forth as if the Torah had been composed by Moses and Aaron and submitted by them to God for approval, like two grand viziers bearing state papers for the Master to sign.

Since the Torah was not given by God to Moses and Aaron, but by Moses and Aaron to God, was not the Nazarene justified in casting it aside?

The slippery ease with which he shifts about in time and moves from the supernatural to the real shows that in *Moses* Asch lacked the fundamental affinity with his subject matter which he was able to work up in the case of *The Nazarene, The Apostle* and *Mary*. The heartstrings that once held him tied to his people, its mind and its destiny, were now snapped. The dual nature of the book—half pious, half atheist—also reveals the split personality of the man, a religious floater, who found it rewarding to dabble in Christianity at the expense of the faith of his fathers.

The two trends running in diametrically opposed directions throughout the book, rob it of every semblance of unity, thus dooming it to perdition not only as a work of ideas, but as a work of art as well.

Perhaps the coarsest piece of blasphemy occurs in the depiction of how the Torah was assembled and recorded. The Torah records: "And Moses wrote this law, and delivered it unto the priests the sons of Levi that bore the ark . . . and unto all the elders of Israel" (Deut. xxxi, 9) ; again: "when Moses made an end of writing the words of this law in a book, *until they were finished; that Moses commanded the Levites . . . saying: Take this book of the law, and put it by the side of the ark of the covenant of the Lord" (ibid 24-26). But according to Asch, Moses assembled a number of Israelites and commanded them to write out of their own knowledge or mind or memory. The elders "examined the problem in the light of Babylonian, Egyptian, or desert usages," but many of the writings submitted were motivated by self-interest: the Levites recorded that they were the elite of the nation, Korah set down a version which made Moses squirm, Aaron and his sons assured themselves of titles and heave-offerings and the most luscious sacrifices. Moses' task was to sift the material presented, and make the needed selections and emendations.

Then we are treated to an odd phenomenon: a tannery is set up in the midst of the wilderness, "before the tent of Moses," where the tanners "scraped, with Egyptian swords, the sheepskins, cleaned them and smoothed them and made them fit to receive the sacred script" (215).

Thus, according to the blasphemy of Asch, emerged the Torah of Moses.

5

The Golden Calf

Riding two horses pulling in opposite directions is likely to become a perilously rough affair. This is precisely what happens to Sholem Asch in *Moses,* where on the one hand he has Christian doctrine in mind and on the other he follows the line of Biblical criticism. The results are disastrous. Every semblance of artistic unity of theme or atmosphere is destroyed. Orthodoxy and free-thinking, mysticism and rationalism are freely commingled, turning the book into a crazy quilt of piety, irreverence and downright atheism. All of which is a measure of the intellectual disorientation of the man and his spiritual dislocation. However, he is consistent throughout in one thing: his detraction and disparagement of the Torah. In this endeavor he even manages to offer something completely original, even though it be in the sense of the most original piece of perverted, irrational, monstrous preposterousness.

The burden of his message is that the Torah Moses bequeathed to Israel is in the real sense of the word not the Torah of Moses at all, but rather the Torah of Aaron. It would seem that the two brothers had entirely different notions of what the religion of a people ought to be. The two leaders worked at cross purposes, Moses at every step being thwarted by Aaron, until he finally had to acknowledge defeat. "Far otherwise," we read, "had been the intentions of Moses toward his people; he had dreamed of very different foundations. He had not succeeded. He began to perceive that Aaron was right" (271). And so Moses departed from the world with a sense of frustration and failure, unhappy over his own Torah and the faith it bears. It was Aaron, besotted as he was with the effects of Egyptian idol worship, who carried the day. It was Aaron who prevailed, and not only against Moses, but against the Lord God Himself. Aaron dictated his own ideas of religion to God and made Him sign on the dotted line.

196

This scheme of discrediting and degrading the Torah is indeed novel and may be fully credited to Asch as his original contribution to the Judeo-Christian theology. In his zeal for the Christian side he failed to perceive that such a view must be offensive even to Christians, who may deny the eternity of the Torah but never its divinity and divine origin. Of such it is said, "Whoso honors the Torah will himself be honored by mankind, but whoso dishonors the Torah will himself be dishonored by mankind" (Aboth, iv, 8).

The turning point in the divine plans about the Torah came with the episode of the golden-calf, with the plain implication on the part of Asch that it was Aaron who purposely cooked up the whole affair, precisely in order to prove his point. After the incident of the golden calf—we are told—both Moses and Miriam give thought to slaying Aaron. Since so many Israelites were consigned to death because of the sin of the calf, why should not the same fate be meted out to the chief culprit? Aaron approaches Moses expecting the worst. Moses, with murder in his heart, listens to his brother, who "can explain everything." Aaron presents his ideas of what the religion should ultimately become. They are what his sons had already suggested to him: "Here is thy opportunity to show Moses that dry laws and commandments are not enough to nourish a people. A people must have a tabernacle, a sanctuary, an altar, a hierarchy of priests; it must have festivals and dances, song and freedom—else it will make itself a Calf image" (257-8).

And Asch continues (271): "Moses did not sleep that night. He lay awake upon his couch. . . . And Moses prayed in his heart, and revolved in his mind the words of Aaron. For otherwise had been the intentions of Moses toward his people; he had dreamed of very different foundations; he had not wanted anything but a pure ritual to express their relationship to God; and the bond between them and God was to have been the heart in its purity. He had not succeeded. He began to perceive that Aaron was right."

The idea subtly suggested here and throughout the book is that the faith Moses really wanted to establish for the Jews was close to, if not identical with that which the Nazarene was later to establish. Moses is made to appear to have sought an abstract faith for the Jews, completely devoid of earthly effects and works, a religion entirely comprised of ethical principles and theological concepts. Aaron, on the other hand, wanted a religion of clay, of

197

matter, of concrete representations—something to be seen and felt, and to create the illusion of an immanent God.

The victory goes to Aaron and the Calf:

"He (Moses) began to perceive that Aaron was right. The people was too young, too unschooled, to attain to that high level of pure union with God through the will alone. Perhaps it was best, then, that the people which had failed and fallen in the making of an idol, should rehabilitate itself by the creation of a tabernacle, and that Aaron, who had occasioned their impurity by his service before the Calf god, should purify them by his worship before Jehovah" (271).

So, instead of slaying Aaron, Moses appoints him high priest. And the Law of Moses, essentially the religion of Aaron, is placed only slightly higher than the worship of the calf; the "highest stage" still to be reached is outside the pages of the Torah, subtly suggesting the Nazarene.

After the lecture by Aaron, Moses becomes a different man; and God (may my words not be reckoned blasphemous) becomes a different God. The Jewish religion goes off on a course completely changed from the original divine plan.

Previously, as Nadab explains at the giving of the Law, when Moses first stood on the mountain "Not a word concerning the priesthood did he let Jehovah utter from Mount Sinai! Not one command concerning ritual, or a tabernacle or priests. And in the ten commandments not a word regarding sacrifices" (246).

But as Asch later notes (286): "A great change in regard to the nature of the sacred ritual had set in since the incident of the Calf god, so far as both the will of God and the conceptions of Moses were concerned. . . . it was as if God was more yielding to the desires of Moses than before the idolatry. . . . Before the incident of the Calf god Moses had declared, in the name of God, that God desired neither gold nor silver. . . . After the incident of the Calf god Moses brought down from Sinai the complete plan for a sanctuary, a tabernacle in the form of a golden house." And also (290): "Now this was an extraordinary circumstance: only a little while before, God had issued the commandment to Moses concerning the making of images. . . . 'Not after the manner of the Egyptians, or of other idol worshipers, shalt thou make the house of God!' There was to be no image of man or beast, no likeness of a living thing. And here Moses suddenly ordered (Bezalel) that images of cherubim be made and set within the curtain which covered the entrance of the Holy of Holies" (290).

In a word—God bowed to the calf!

Why should Aaron have insisted on this lower form of religion? First, as has been shown, as a matter of income: because of the fat parts of the sacrificial animals, the tithes, the heave offerings, the first fruits, the paid redemption of all firstborn. Second, because of the influence of Egypt: he modeled his ritual and hierarchy after the usages of the Egyptian priesthood.

Thus the Torah of Moses, which in Asch's version should really be known as the Torah of Aaron, is presented as a complex of alien laws and Egyptian idol worship.

There is madness in the method, true; but also method in his madness. For if the Torah is more Aaron's than Moses', and more Egyptian than divine, and leaning heavily to the side of idolatry, of what great consequence can it be that Jesus has nullified it?

While he finds Jesus the acme of perfection, Asch finds it necessary to apologize for Moses: "Certainly Moses, being human, could not altogether escape the influence of concepts reigning in his time" (238) ; "Moses was a son of his time . . . No one will be found to excuse or to justify the action of Moses against the Midianites" (477).

The highly moral Sholem Asch, living in the very moral twentieth century, finds that Moses was not moral enough.

Asch's method is to belittle the Torah of Moses through Moses himself. He renders Moses a stranger in his own house who suffers defeat at the hands of a self-seeking brother and his co-conspirators. According to Asch, neither the faith Moses sought to establish, nor the nation he envisioned, was ever made actual and secure.

But the nation Moses founded is here! And, "The Law of the Lord is perfect!" (Ps. xix, 8). There cannot be a more profound harmony than that between Moses and the Law. It is madness to say that Moses was disappointed in his own work. His faith in it was strong beyond the conception of ordinary men. On it he based and warranted the existence and happiness of the Jewish people: "for it is your life and the length of your days," "that it may go well with thee, and with thy children after thee, and that thou mayest prolong thy days upon the land, which the Lord thy

199

God giveth thee, for ever" (Deut. iv, 40). The Torah is also his warrant of Israel's high place in man's esteem: "for this is your wisdom and understanding in the sight of the peoples" (ibid iv, 7).

Thus Asch finds himself helplessly suspended in a tangle of semi-Judaism and semi-Christianity, semi-paganism and semi-atheism, reaching in Aaron and the doctrine of sacrifice the peak of vilification and misrepresentation. In his effort to make a clean sweep of Judaism for the sake of Christianity, he forgets, in his servile insincerity that sacrifice, far from being foreign or repulsive to Christianity, is central in Christian theology, Jesus having been the Lamb of God, offered as a sacrifice for the redemption of sinful men. The sacrament of communion is the symbol of that sacrifice to this day.

6

The Forgotten Chapter and Verse

If the Torah of Moses is not marked by divine perfection, and does not assist mankind to full salvation, where then did God reveal his true and complete will to mankind? Asch points in reply to the Nazarene, to the Christian messiah.

As we have seen, the spirit of Christianity rules through the entire novel. While Asch's subservience to Christian doctrine in the early chapters is indirect, in the final chapters it is less devious. His method is still to illuminate in half-tones, but upon close examination his purpose becomes all too clear. Into the final words and actions of *Moses* Asch weaves the main principles of the Christian religion, exactly as the Church has expounded them for centuries. Four examples will illustrate the unmistakable tendency.

When Asch's Moses bids farewell to the faithful Joshua, who is to take over his leadership, Joshua, with proper humility, begs his master to reveal to him the secret power, the mystic key whereby he was able to overcome the superhuman difficulties on his path. Moses replies:

"The secret virtue wherewith I surmounted all obstacles and overcame all dangers was—love: 'Thou shalt love the Lord thy God with all thy heart and with all thy soul and with all thy might'—and 'Thou shalt love thy neighbor as thyself' " (487).

No such query and no such response are recorded in the Torah but it must be admitted that the exchange is a legitimate one. However, the dialogue appears in a different light when one realizes that though the two principles involved are of Mosaic derivation the same answer in the same words was actually proffered by the Nazarene. We read in Matthew (xxii, 35): "And one of them, a doctor of the Law, asked him, tempting him: 'Master, which is the great commandment in the Law?' Jesus said to him: 'Thou shalt love the Lord thy God with thy whole heart, and with thy whole soul, and with thy whole mind' (Deuteronomy vi, 5). This is the greatest and the first commandment. And the second is like to this: 'Thou shalt love thy neighbor as thyself' (Leviticus xix, 18)." Both dicta stem from Moses.

The query as to the most concise epitome of the teaching of the Law has frequently been brought forward and variously answered by the sages of the Talmud. When Hillel the Elder was asked this question, he replied: "That which is hateful to you, do not to your fellow man. This is the whole Torah; all the rest is commentary."

Rabbi Akiba replied: "Thou shalt love thy neighbor as thyself. That is the great principle of the Torah."

The tanna Ben Azzai responded, "The words in the Torah, 'This is the book of the generations of Adam.' They are the basic principle of the Torah." That is, the Torah is the book of all mankind, not white or black, Greek or Jew, but all men.

We need not here inquire into the differences and subtle distinctions among these various answers. The differences are indeed subtle and profound. Of interest to us in this connection is the fact that when Asch chose one of these replies to attribute to Moses he did not use Hillel, Akiba, or Ben Azzai, but chose Jesus.

Moses is brought even closer to Christianity in the final dialogue he holds with God.

Let us pass in silence over the extraordinary vainglory of an author who undertakes to write a dialogue between God and Moses, and refer again to the great gulf separating Judaism and Christianity. Judaism proclaims that belief devoid of good works is utterly inconsequential. Christianity, on the contrary, considers that works are more or less superfluous, and that only faith and belief in the Nazarene will admit one to paradise.

With this in mind, let us note Asch's report of the snatches of conversation between God and Moses he overheard as he was

201

eavesdropping on them: "I have raised up," saith the Lord, "a fiery wall between life and death, and none shall break through it. And to man I have given nothing to take with him into death save faith and trust. Thus too it shall be with you. Go with closed eyes to thy rest, and nought shall accompany thee save faith and trust" (494).

No such utterance could ever have been voiced in Judaism. From beginning to end the Torah resounds one mighty cry and admonition: observe the precepts, the statutes and judgments. The matters least discussed are faith and death. Asch perverts the Torah of Moses in the very face of Moses.

As a third instance let us refer to later Jewish writings which relate that before Moses died God marshalled before him all the generations to come, all the saints and sages of the future, and revealed to him what accretions would be made to the Torah in all posterity, and all that would happen for all time. Asch, taking over this legend, gives it a Christian tinge:

"And Moses opened his eyes and beheld . . . multitudinous faces, faces not of the flesh but of the Spirit. He beheld their inmost being, their spiritual essences, the hierarchy of their souls, in an ascent which reached no final purpose. And he cried out: 'Father of all created things, I see spirits. Very mighty are those whom Thou has elected as the leaders of Thy people; they ascend on the wings of prophecy and they carry the people with them, even to the throne of Thy glory. . . . I see further: they bring closer, ever closer, the day of fulfillment and perfection, but they themselves do not partake of it. They go on forever, and never do they reach the goal. . . . Will they all fail of the end, even as I have failed?" (483).

Here is an entire cluster of Christian motives. Once again Moses is spoken of as "incomplete." All the great spirits of Judaism appearing in the vision, the mighty leaders, prophets, sages, never "reach the goal." They help along the day of fulfillment, but never attain the Ultimate Goal. This is precisely the Christian doctrine of Judaism as a mere stepping-stone to Jesus.

Asch reports God as answering Moses:

"Know, concerning these spirits which I have shown thee, that each of them has his own separate spirit and his own separate knowledge; but such a one as thou desirest to have for thy successor, a man whose spirit shall embrace the spirit of all the Bnai Israel, such a one as will be able to speak for each of them according to his understanding, and for all of them—such a one shall not arise before the end of days. He alone will be possessed of that spirit which will embrace the spirits of all men."

"Who is he?" asked Moses.

"He is the Messiah," answered God.

Who will not perceive that this colloquy is calculated to converge upon the personality of the Nazarene? The colloquy is almost a transcript of the following passages from St. Paul:

The Pauline Epistle to the Hebrews begins: "God, who at *sundry times and in divers manners* spake in time past unto the *fathers* by the *prophets,* Hath in these last days spoken unto us by his Son, whom he *hath appointed heir of all things.*"

We turn to Colossians (i, 19) : "For it pleased the Father that in him should all fullness dwell: And, having made peace through the blood of his cross, by him to reconcile all things unto himself; by him, I say, whether they be things in earth, or things in heaven."

The idea and the words are lifted almost intact from their Christian source.

For the final key to the author's true intent in *Moses,* let us point out a significant line which Asch failed to use. This one brief verse, this key sentence, must have leaped up from the page to catch his attention, begging to be used in his work, but he strangely overlooked it. That single verse, neglected and forgotten, reveals the entire conspiracy by which Asch so strenuously labored to seduce the Jew to a foreign faith and an alien god. That fateful verse reads:

"And there hath not arisen a prophet since in Israel like unto Moses, whom the Lord knew face to face" (Deut. xxxiv, 10).

Sholem Asch concludes his novel with the death of Moses. According to the Midrash, God bade Moses lie down, extend his arms and legs and close his eyes; then with the kiss God took his soul. Asch reproduces this scene, but fails to set down the eternal judgment of the Torah, "There hath not arisen a prophet since in Israel like unto Moses."

Why has this deathless line been omitted? The answer is simple. This passage, this single verse, undercuts the entire story of the Nazarene. Because of these words alone the Christian redeemer could never gain a hold among Jews. This brief line is a hurdle no pretender to the seat of Moses can ever take.

We are told of one who much before Jesus had aspired to the

position of the chief of all prophets. It is written that King Solomon once sought means whereby he might become like Moses. And there came a heavenly voice, saying, "Son of David, do you not know that it is written, There hath not arisen a prophet since in Israel like unto Moses?"

The same applies to Jesus of Nazareth.

In conclusion:

There is the scene in Asch's novel in which Moses is assembled with the elders in the home of Nahshon ben Aminadav to make final preparations for the exodus. Asch remarks parenthetically that since he is a descendant of Nachshon, his soul was present at that gathering. This totally unwarranted claim is probably made in order to create a sense of awe among gentile readers. Asch would overwhelm his gentile readers with the wonder that his genealogical tree is traced as far back as the Pharaohs. I say "gentiles" advisedly, for as Asch must realize this claim will be laughed to scorn by Jews.

It may not be idle to peer into the hidden motive of this extraordinary flight into fancy. Why should Asch choose to claim kinship with Nahshon, of all men? Why does he not go all the way, and claim kinship with Moses himself?

There is a reason. Asch undoubtedly has in mind the tradition that Nahshon was the first Israelite to leap into the Red Sea on the famous crossing. While all the rest stood shuddering, he alone dared to advance. Symbolically Asch is proclaiming himself a modern Nahshon ben Aminadab; he had the "courage" to take the plunge into a sea, which the Jewish people for almost two thousand years have refused to enter and cross.

But while on the subject of origin and lineage, we may here recall a bit of old Jewish wisdom concerning this topic. An old Jewish saying has it that no Jew ever abandons his faith. Although experience would seem to contradict this saying, the explanation is a sound one: such Jews as do change their faith are not, it is claimed, real Jews, but the offshoot of the "mixed multitude" who attached themselves to the Israelites when the people departed from the land of Egypt.

Tradition also has it that much trouble has accrued to the Jewish people throughout the ages from this "riffraff,"

CHAPTER V

East River

In times of great social upheavals extraordinary revolutions of the human soul often take place. The turmoil in the world at large creates a turmoil in man's psyche, and man swings out of his customary routine into a direction contrary to his previous norm. This often leads to strange phenomena.

A striking example is post-war Italy, the land of Catholicism, where after the catastrophes of fascism and the second World War, many Catholics, in great mental confusion, turned to a religious habitude which may be called contra-Catholicism. The official Church was compelled to take a stand against this strange trend, which it termed "serving Satan."

The ceremonials of this movement resemble those of regular Catholic worship but in a perverted way. The cross is used, but is placed upside down. The same prayers are recited, but they are spoken backwards. And wherever the word "God" appears, "Satan" is substituted, and vice versa; where "good" appears it is read "evil," and "evil" is read as "good." It is a topsy-turvy world, in which divine actions are reckoned sins, and sins become godly commandments. To pervert the concept of the Virgin, a prostitute figures in the service.

Some such psychological perversion must have affected Sholem Asch, whose talent is bigger than his mind and who departed from the house of his fathers and set out on foreign paths, first in his directly Christological works, then in his more secular novel, *East River*, which is as different from his *A Town* as the worship of Satan is from the normal Catholic religious service.

A Town is a glorification of Jewish life, but *East River* is a defamation of it. If one is a blessing, the other is a curse and

205

malediction. The former was written by a native son; the latter by one alienated and outward bound.

East River is a novel of intermarriage. It is a story which idealizes mixed marriages of Jews and Christians. Asch presents intermarriage, which all generations of Jews have considered a basic peril to Jewish continuance and the Jewish spirit, as the loftiest ideal of Jewishness. Arrogantly presuming to see more deeply and feel more justly than Jewry throughout the generations, he brushes aside every religious consideration and national problem involved in it: both God and nation must bow to love.

In his previous Christological works Asch preached "One Church" for Jews and Christians; in *East River* he preaches one sleeping chamber. In one he parades as a religious reformer; in the other as a matchmaker.

Asch is much like Balaam, who, seeing that neither his so-called blessings nor his curses had any effect upon the Jews, advised Balak to call into service the seductive charms of the daughters of Moab.

Now, usually the wise matchmaker will play up the good points of both halves of the match. He will put in the best light before the one and other the high pedigree and general virtues of both sides. But in *East River* the Christian side is so lauded to the skies and the Jewish side so belittled and dragged through the mire that one finds it difficult to comprehend why the Christian should consider the match at all.

In other words, *East River* is an anti-Jewish book, and it may be considered from either of two viewpoints: as a work featuring intermarriage; or as a novel about Christians and Jews.

There is little purpose in dealing here with the theme of mixed marriage as such, for Asch is not the first Jew to preach assimilation and submergence. It is far more to the point to consider what the novel tells us about the strange adventure of a Jewish writer once he begins to look upon his fellow Jews with alien eyes. We shall see that the result is like a metamorphosis from God-worship to Satan-worship.

The book opens with a pigeon race. At New York's 48th Street and East River, a poor district inhabited by a mixture of Jews, Italians, Poles, Irish and Germans, is in close proximity to a quarter inhabited by the rich. Among the poor was Harry Greenstock, who loves birds and animals. His pride, and that of all the neighborhood, is a dovecote in which he is raising pigeons.

206

In the rich section lives a millionaire who also boasts of his pigeons and their home. It is the great ambition of Harry and his neighbors to mate one of Harry's pigeons with one of a rare breed belonging to the millionaire. Harry is convinced that the offspring would prove a new and magnificent species. The story opens with the pigeons from both cotes cavorting together in the air, and relates how the desired match is triumphantly consummated.

This opening scene strikes up the *leitmotif* to the novel's central theme—the mingling of the two kinds of humans, Jew and Gentile, like the mingling of the two species of bird, must necessarily produce a "nobler" race.

Some distance away, on the sidewalk, in an invalid chair, sits a paralyzed youth who is a witness of the scene. His name is Nathan Davidovsky. At his side stands his father, Reb Moshe Wolf. Both take major parts in the story to follow. Reb Moshe Wolf is a pious Jew, Chassid of Ger, a learned man who in Europe had studied for the rabbinate. He is also something of a modernist. He runs a grocery store on 48th Street, which is, of course, closed on the Sabbath. His son, though a victim of infantile paralysis, is a student. He sits with a book on his knee. The conversation between the father and son drifts from the pigeons' game to a discussion of the "Jewish question" and immediately the anti-Jewish stench of the book rises to the reader's nostrils.

The father, who is evidently critical of the game with the birds, takes occasion to remark that in the Talmud "pigeon-flyers" are decried to the extent of being disqualified as witnesses in a court of law.

"Why?" wonders the son.

"I don't know why, but that's what the holy writings say," replies Moshe Wolf.

"Those holy writings of yours!" sneers the son, shrugging his shoulders.

A brief little scene, but very revealing. The gentile, or the un-enlightened Jew, who reads it will probably think that the Talmud must be a strange book indeed to condemn such innocent entertainment as this, and that the Jews are an odd people who are intolerant or are mentally allergic to so beautiful, companionable and pleasant a bird as the pigeon. He must feel that a people to whom innocent preoccupation with pigeons is so serious as to render men unfit to bear witness in a court of justice must be odd, queer, incomprehensible people, indeed.

207

Continuing the colloquy, Nathan Davidovsky virtually hurls the Talmud in his father's face with contempt, remarking: "My Talmud says that play is a necessity for people, just as necessary as food and air. Pigeon flying is play for grownups, like any other kind of play."

Now the entire colloquy about the Talmud and pigeons is one piece of misrepresentation, designed to cast aspersion upon the Talmud and sow contempt for Judaism.

The Talmud nowhere declares that playing with pigeons for mere pastime disqualifies a man's testimony; it only forbids gambling with pigeons, or any other bird or animal, betting on their performance for gain. "If your bird overtakes mine, I shall pay you so much, and if the other way round, you pay me"—this, like wagering on the turn of a card, is gambling, which the Talmud condemns. Besides, it is made perfectly clear that only the professional gambler, plying no other trade besides that, is disqualified as a witness. The Talmud is here clearly aiming at the protection of the being and the dignity of dumb animals. It permits man to use them for the purposes assigned by the Creator—for labor, for food, and even for innocent entertainment—but not for the satisfaction of man's sickly passions.

Had Reb Moshe Wolf been permitted to explain all this to his son, there would have been no contemptuous reference to "Your Talmud!" On the contrary, the son would have gained a glimpse of the splendor of a morality altogether strange to the Christian world. Both Talmud and the Jew would have attained higher stature and esteem in his eyes. Both gentiles and un-Jewish Jews would have learned about one of the glories of Judaism from *East River.*

This would certainly have been the case, had Asch still been writing "Jewish" books. But *East River* is essentially a Christian book, and like most Christian books about Jews, it transforms Jewish virtues into failings, but never transforms Jewish failings into virtues.

This incident is not the only occasion on which the dove or pigeon is employed in the book as an anti-Jewish symbol. Asch labors the theme to the point where pigeons may even become a bar to matrimony among Jews! Harry Greenstock, widower, seeking a mother for his children, temporarily takes his non-Jewish sweetheart into his home to care for them. He defends his act before Reb Moshe Wolf saying: "I could not find any Jewish wo-

208

man who would take care of my children." To which Reb Moshe Wolf remarks, "Better say—take care of your pigeons. You know that a Jewish daughter would never consent to devote her time and effort to pigeons. It is for that reason you took in a non-Jewess." And such indeed is shown to be the case. Harry Greenstock does find a Jewish woman ready to marry him, but when she discovers the pigeons in the family she will have none of him. All of which is nothing but nonsense born out of malice.

Irving Davidovsky, Reb Moshe Wolf's second son, who will emerge as the chief hero of the story, also displays a dislike for pigeons, but his motivation is entirely different: they provide "too much work and too little meat." The sweet charm of the bird, its domesticity and attachment to humans, the moral lesson it bears for man in pure living, all this lies outside his ken. His thoughts are only of money. When one has money, he says, one has everything; and when one has no money, one has nothing. Thus, the slanderous, money-loving Jew so often encountered in Christian novels plays a dominant part in *East River*.

2

Jew, Gentile, and Beast

Harry Greenstock, the man with the pigeons, is not indifferent to his faith and his coreligionists, but his friends in the neighborhood are drawn not from among the Jews, but from among the Gentiles. Asch explains that the Jew's keeping pigeons, and breeding rabbits (which are not kosher) and other "gentile" animals, and displaying affection for birds and animals "brought him so close to his Christian neighbors, and kept him separate and estranged from his Jewish neighbors." That is why Greenstock is called "the goy."

From this it would seem that Jews are allergic not only to pigeons, but to birds and beasts in general. And it is but one step from antipathy to animals to cruelty to them. In Harry Greenstock's areaway there is also a horse which belongs to a junkpeddler, the Jew Zelik. Christian neighbors repeatedly complain that Zelik is beating the life out of the horse, and one Christian woman demands that the Society for the Prevention of Cruelty to Animals be informed of the way he treats the animal.

From all this an atmosphere of evilness and cruelty is created about the Jew in *East River,* and the strange mystery with which the gentile always envelops the Jew is here elaborated by one more alleged abnormality in the Jewish character.

One might imagine these matters to be mere trifles, but nothing in the world is trifling when it comes to the Jew. The Jews' "lack" of sympathy for dumb creatures is a "trifle" with which their adversaries have, for instance, agitated for prohibition of Jewish religious slaughter. Now these adversaries can turn to a page of a book by a Jewish author, and say, "Look: Sholem Asch bears witness that the living fowl and beast are psychologically repugnant to his people; and he even buttresses his words with testimony from the words of the Talmud and 'sacred writings!'"

There can be no greater injustice than to ascribe to the Jew and the Jewish religion so inimical an attitude toward God's creatures. Particularly false is the report that the Jew disdains the dove, for to the dove above all other creatures does the Jewish heart feel a deep tenderness. Jews learn many virtues from the dove. "My sweet little dove (or pigeon)," "sweet as a little pigeon," "quiet as a dove," "faithful as a dove," "innocent as a dove," "they live like a pair of doves"—these are daily expressions in the Yiddish language. The dove with the olive leaf in his bill is the symbol of peace, dating from Noah's ark.

The Talmud and other "sacred writings," far from alienating the Jew from the dove, actually discover a most intimate affinity between them—they always symbolize the Jewish people by the dove. "Wherein is Israel likened to a dove?" asks the Jerusalem Talmud. The profound answer is given: "All other birds, when they grow weary in flying, swoop down to rest upon a tree or rock; but the dove closes one wing and flies with one wing." The Midrash Tanhuma says, "Israel is like the dove. All fowl when undergoing slaughter toss themselves about, but the dove does not toss and extends its throat; in the same way there are none who stretch out their throats to die for sanctification of the Name, except Israel." And: "Just as a dove, after being paired, never changes her partner for another, so is Israel; from the time the people accepted God, they have changed to no other deity."

Were we to gather on one string all the gemlike aphorisms concerning Israel and the dove, not all the pearl bedeckings of the

210

wealthiest kings and lords of the earth would equal it in beauty and richness.

It is a fact worth noting that Jews do not hanker after "roast pigeons." They seldom eat the flesh of this fowl. The psychological reason for this forbearance can only be described as a tenderness verging on piety.

The irony of it all, in the year 1946, after the merciless slaughter of six million Jews in the heart of Christian civilization, for a Jewish writer to attempt to prove the Jew inferior to the Christian in humanity to living creatures!

The historical truth is that Jews were the first to open the heart of man toward beasts.

"The grief of a living creature" is a phrase common in the Talmud, the very Talmud which Asch's hero Nathan hurls into the teeth of his pious father with the contemptuous retort, "You and your Talmud!"

Sholem Asch places these slanderous words in the mouth of a major character, so that they may be repeated by thousands of other Jews, as ignorant as Nathan of Judaism.

Yet the Talmud explicitly states, "Merciful conduct toward living creatures is a command direct from the Torah" (B. Mets. 32).

The "grief of an animal" and poor "dumb tongue," two phrases common in Yiddish speech, are laden with pathetic feeling for the animal, the beast of burden, for all fowl.

From the earliest times Jews have been raised on the penetrating idea that a man's treatment of dumb animals is an indication of his character. When Eliezer, Abraham's steward, went forth to seek a suitable wife for Isaac, he decided to act on the following principle. He would request a drink of the maidens drawing water at the well, and the maid who offered drink to both him and his beasts of burden would be the proper spouse for Isaac. Moses, according to a Midrash, was tested by the same criterion. When Moses raised a weary lamb and carried it on his shoulders, God said: Because you treat with so much mercy the sheep belonging to a human being, you will be the right shepherd for my own lamb Israel.

In Psalms we read, "Man and beast Thou savest, O Lord"— for both are equally essential in the scheme of the world. Elsewhere we read: "The just man knows the mind of his beast."

Some Jews even believe that all living things may attain a

211

reward in the world to come. In a work on ritual slaughter, the author, Rabbi Israel Hamaaravi, ventures the opinion that, "The animal in the hereafter receives reward for the pain it suffers."

The Chassidim tell of Rabbi Joshua Heschel of Apt, who, journeying along a road that traversed a mountain, halted his horse and scaled the mountain on foot. This seemed curious to his sexton, who knew the rabbi to be old and weak.

The rabbi explained. "I descended from the cart," said he, "because I feared lest the horse summon me to judgment in the afterworld, complaining that I had shown him no mercy, and he had been compelled to drag me up the mountainside."

"But," expostulated the sexton, "you could win the trial on the ground that the horse was created for that purpose."

"That may be true," was the response, "but it is hardly proper to win a victory over a speechless tongue."

An old record relates that whenever Rabbi Phineas Koritzer saw a gentile whose oxen were drawing a wagonload of wood through the mire, he would purchase the wood to the extent of his resources, then throw the wood into the mud as relief for the oxen—since, the writer remarks, "a goy customarily thrashes his beasts in the time of miring" (A. J. Heschel: "Phineas Koritzer").

The consideration given to dumb creatures in Judaism is perhaps most excellently illustrated by the laws applying to animals guilty of acts for which death is the prescribed punishment. In cases of capital crimes committed by humans, a Small Sanhedrin of twenty-three judges is ordered; the same number sit in cases of capital crimes committed by animals. The penalty for an ox's slaying a man is its execution by stoning, but judgment must be passed upon it by the twenty-three. A wolf, lion, bear, tiger, panther, or serpent responsible for a human death must also receive its sentence from the full complement of judges (Sanhedrin I, 4). Full respect and equality before the law are accorded to man and beast alike.

There could be no greater tribute paid to God's creatures than the following from the Talmud:

"If the Torah had not been given, we might have learned decency from the cat, regard of property from the ant, chastity from the dove, and good manners from the cock" (Erubin 100b).

Torah, Prophets, Hagiographa, the Talmud, rabbinical literature, and Jewish folklore, are all replete with humane regulations and noble teachings governing the treatment of dumb animals. But Asch does not display toward his people the respect that they show to the cat, as he intimates that a Jew with attachment toward animals is an alien among his brethren, and can be properly understood only by his non-Jewish associates.

The ultimate result of the Jewish attitude toward living creatures has been that Jews never go hunting for sport, adventure, fun, or amusement. No Jew would think of saying, "It's a nice day today; let's go out and kill something," although the expression is common among many gentiles.

As it happens it is Asch's adopted Christian teaching that has no canons of mercy for animals. It makes the strange assertion that man has no duty to beasts, since God Himself is not concerned about them. There is a reference to that effect in Corinthians (I, ix, 9) in the form of a question: "Doth God take care for oxen?"

But the Jewish God *does* take care for oxen. The Torah forbids muzzling the ox while he is threshing; nor may one plow with an ox and donkey teamed. An animal and its offspring may not be slaughtered in the same day. On the Sabbath one's ox and donkey and cattle are to rest even as does the master. And even if it be your enemy's ox or ass that you discover fallen beneath its burden, you must give the brute all aid possible.

Paul assumes that the law against muzzling the ox during the threshing is not intended to extract benefit for the ox, but to furnish a parable to men: he who threshes may hope for a share in his labor. "Doth God take care for oxen? Or saith He it altogether for our sakes? For our sakes, no doubt, this is written" (ibidem).

Because of this passage Catholicism does not teach the Jewish tenet that it is sinful to wreak pain or injustice upon any living creature. On the contrary, it expressly teaches that it is *not* a sin. It is an historical fact that Pope Pius XI turned down a request to form a Humane Society in Rome and that the reason for his refusal was that it was a theological error to assume that man owes any duty to the beast. It is Catholic doctrine that the beast merits no rights because it has no understanding. Westermarck describes the Catholic attitude thus: "There is not even the shadow of sin in giving pain to a bull in sport .. we are not bound to trouble ourselves that the pain be as slight as possible" (Christianity and Morals, E. A. Westermarck).

The Jew cannot conceive such words being uttered in the

name of religion. Such tenets furnish the basis for the legal and moral justification of bullfights and cock-fights, which are permitted to Christians and are carried on in the most religious Christian nations.

A clergyman once justified the chase by discerning a direct "sign from heaven" in the fact that the skin of rabbits beneath the tail is lighter than the rest of the fur, which, said he, was preordained by God so that the hunter would take better aim.

The implication is that hunting is a God-given boon and Christians have even designated Saint Hubert as patron saint of the hunt. When they are already in the saddle, with the hounds straining at their leashes, the gentleman fox hunters are given the priest's blessing in the name of Saint Hubert, with a prayer for a full bag. What chance does the lowly fox stand against such an array of hunters, dogs, saints, and priests?

On the day of his farewell appearance in Seville's bull ring, Pacote, the best bullfighter in Spain, turns to the candlelit image on his dresser, crosses himself, presses his palms together and prays: "Most saintly of Virgins, I don't ask to be good today. This is not like the other days. I only ask that they come out easy, that they don't snag me, that I may live and be able to worship you. Just let me live. Amen." (Barnaby Conrad, in "Matador").

Hunting is a pleasure foreign, in fact repulsive, to the Jewish mentality. It was Heinrich Heine, I believe, who said that the distinction between Jew and gentile is discoverable in this attitude toward the hunt. Westermarck adds: "There is not a sect in Christendom which teaches humanity to animals as a religious dogma."

Judaism, however, contains that dogma, which carries the authority of a basic law from the Torah. Jewish sacred literatures offer many rules and ordinances about the Jew's duty to the beast, one of which prescribes that when a man sits down to his meal he must feed his animals first.

In Christian lands humane societies and laws against cruelty to animals were introduced by the civil or secular power, and are very recent phenomena in which the Church had no part.

Household beasts and pets have always been well treated by Jews; they are protected by Jewish law, in the spirit of mercy over all God's works. The Jew with his history and his laws had no need to feel shame before Asch's German and Pole, whether in Poland, Germany, or on 48th Street and East River in New York.

In Jewish practice concerning animals only dogs were an ex-

214

ception. Jews as a rule did not keep dogs. For they did not wish to frighten the poor away from their doors.

It was important that we dwell at length on this element in Asch's book, because this method of anti-Semitic attack is well known to us in Christian literature, even when it emanates from "respectable quarters." No less a man than Arthur Schopenhauer writes: "The assumption that animals have no rights, the notion that our conduct toward them has no moral significance, or in general that there exists no moral duty to animals, is a repulsive barbarism, *the origin of which lies in Judaism.*" This indictment appears in a discourse in which Schopenhauer demands a moral attitude toward animals, yet he feels no moral duty toward the Jews or, for that matter, to historical truth.

The Torah in ancient times for once granted speech to an animal, permitting it to utter its great grievance against man, and a great cry for right and justice. Balaam's ass spoke and gave expression to the grief of the entire animal world when it asked: "What have I done to thee, that thou hast smitten me? . . . Am I not thine ass, upon which thou hast ridden all thy life long?" (Numbers xxii, 28-30).

But three and a half millennia later, another European philosopher, greater than Schopenhauer, failed to respond to the heart rending plaint. Catholic René Descartes (1596-1650), "the father of modern thought," taught that animals are automata, completely ruled by physical laws and without emotion or actual consciousness; that when they are beaten they feel no pain, and that when they eat they sense no savor; that they only go through the motions, for they have no souls. But the *shame* of responsibility for these theories is laid at the door of Judaism!

The attitude toward the beast is not a trifle but a tremendous factor in the Christian world's assault on Judaism, and it is important that the facts be made clear. Thus, it is particularly painful to find Sholem Asch, too, planting that odious thing at the doorstep of his people.

3

A Jew of Shame

East River must be counted among Asch's Christological works. It takes its place with a certain historical logic as a sequel to *The Nazarene* and *The Apostle.* In the latter Asch was concerned with

Judaism and Christianity; in *East River* he has devoted himself to Jews and Christians.

This is the usual pattern in Jewish history. For some inexplicable reason the world has never left the Jew alone with his faith. From time to time there have arisen religious visionaries determined to "save" the Jewish soul. When Jews refuse to surrender their souls they are deprived of their bodies, and it makes no difference whether the soul-savers arise from among Jewish ranks or from outside them. The pattern is the same. They begin with anti-Judaism and end with anti-Jew. Such is the pattern in *East River*.

One English reviewer remarked astutely that *East River* is "definitely not a Jewish book." But this puts it very mildly, for the bitter truth is that it is a brutally anti-Jewish work and worthily ranks with the worst in "respectable" anti-Semitic literature. One would be hard put to name another book populated with so many despicable and distorted characterizations of Jews as *East River,* or one which places so prominent a part of Jewry as New York's Jewish immigrant population in such an unfavorable light. It is difficult to believe that the same man who wrote *A Town* and *Reb Shelomo Nagid* also composed *East River*. For it was really not the same. The early Asch dissipated and perished and is no more. The *A Town* disappeared in blood and fire; Sholem Asch disappeared in *The Nazarene* and *The Apostle*. Written in temper or pique, *East River* is Asch's most diabolical achievement in slander and malice.

A Town and *East River* cannot both be true, and it is clear which is the lie. It is sure beyond doubt that the Jews of *A Town* could never have degenerated into the Jews of *East River*. They are like two different species. But Satan overwhelmed Sholem Asch, perverted his heart, and confused his vision, turned truth into falsehood, and twisted the natural into the unnatural.

The Jewish woman, above all others, finds her most natural expression in motherhood. The protective affection of the "yiddishe mameh" is world renowned. And this is not a chauvinistic claim, for the peculiarly motherly traits of the Jewish mother may be seen to arise out of simple circumstances: the Jewish child has always had a more difficult lot than the non-Jewish one, and the anxiety of the Jewish mother has been enhanced in consequence; she has had to offer greater sacrifices to rear her children, and she has willingly done so.

216

It is the nature of every mother, Jewish or non-Jewish, to become especially attached to a sickly or crippled child. It is common experience that disabled offspring often elicit the most noble displays of motherliness. Sholem Asch himself depicted many wonderful Jewish mothers, many magnificent, unforgettable types. But that was in *A Town, B. C.*, and not in *East River*, A. D.

The crippled young Jew, Nathan, is a leading character in *East River*. He was already a sizable lad, a student when he was stricken by infantile paralysis. When we meet him we learn that his mother, Deborah, wishes him dead; that she wishes to be rid of her burden.

An Irish "shikse" ("shikse," in the novel), Mary McCarthy, attaches herself to the household. She becomes Nathan's true mother, sacrificing her time and life for him. Thus in Asch's work shikse and mother are placed in juxtaposition and the valid conception of the "Yiddishe mameh" is destroyed.

This distortion is necessitated by the thesis Asch undertakes to prove in the novel: the thesis of the supremacy of Christian love. And he proves, to his own satisfaction at least, that Christian love is a more vital and dynamic force than the celebrated love of the Jewish mother.

For Mary is not just a shikse, nor even just a Catholic. And it is not by accident that she comes into the Davidovsky home. Jesus sent her there, she avows, presumably as a sort of "apostle to the Hebrews" to show Jews what Christian love is, and to teach Yiddishe mamehs how to be real mothers.

There is another gentile woman meandering through the pages of *East River*, Mrs. Krantz, who is not pious, and who, unlike Mary, does not go to church regularly. She is gentile, however, and for Asch that is sufficient justification to portray her as an angel. Just as Mary devotes her life to Davidovsky, Mrs. Krantz devotes hers to the Greenstocks. While Mrs. Greenstock, a chronic invalid, is still alive, Mrs. Krantz regularly goes to her house to clean, cook, wash the children, and give special attention to Rachelle, who, being of marriageable age, requires careful supervision. And when Mrs. Greenstock dies Mrs. Krantz takes over conduct of the entire household. It is clear that without her the Greenstock family would simply perish, for there is no sign of Jewish neighbors coming to offer help or succor.

Later Rachelle goes to visit the Silberbergs, her uncle and aunt. They are stuffed with money, nouveau-riche, but are as

217

swinish as they are wealthy. The rich aunt drives out the poor relative. The girl flees from the house as from a conflagration, to return to the gentile Mrs. Krantz, for succor and protection.

As a matter of historic fact, the situation was just the opposite in the years in which *East River* is set. It is a matter of record that at that time Jews could not pass safely through an Irish district without being pelted with stones. The Jews themselves were in the period of the great immigration to the United States when Jewish family devotion showed in all its splendor and relatives actually stripped the flesh from their bones to bring their kin from Europe. They sent tickets and funds to the "old country;" Jews saved other Jews providentially relocating the seed of the Jewish people and saving it from later Hitlerian annihilation. Where would Jewry be today had it depended upon the Mary McCarthys and the Mrs. Krantzes to transplant it to America?

Sholem Asch would have looked quite differently upon that historic period of tumultuous migration from the "little town" to the city, that immense transplantation of millions of Jews into a new world, had he still gazed through Jewish eyes. He would have seen it as he saw it in his "America," for example; but that was before his "Christian era."

When the Jewish masses started streaming to America, particularly to New York, that city was just a village. It was Jewish energy, and labor, Jewish impetus and vision, Jewish creativeness and enterprise which more than any other factors helped elevate New York to the status of the world's greatest, most marvelous, most spirited, and most progressive metropolis. What an epic Asch could have written about the Jews and New York!

But the actual result is quite different. From *East River* it appears that the Jews came like a storm of locusts that found New York and settled down to consume its inhabitants, drink their sweat, and suck their blood. In *East River* New York groans under the Jewish yoke. Jews are exploiters, oppressors of the working-man, union smashers, sponsors of the sweatshop. No non-Jewish capitalist appears in the book. Had Asch pictured the exploitation then general in America, in the economic satrapies of the Rockefellers and Carnegies, the Jewish share in the situation would have appeared in proper perspective. Passing the others in silence, the book gives the impression that only the Jews were bloody exploiters, the Grand Inquisitors of that dreary chapter of

218

American history. It makes black and depressing reading to Jewish readers, let alone to gentiles.

The inordinate pursuit of wealth is pictured as the all-consuming Jewish passion, and the materialistic Jew at his worst is offered to view. Money is everything, and all means for acquiring it are justified. Even the compensatory virtues are absent as, for example, charity is here given only for business or political reasons. Whatever remnant of religious faith is left to him, the Jew treats as some form of merchandise. Irving is the embodiment of soulless lust after riches. The Silberbergs, Shmulewitzes, and a host of lesser characters about them, are unexcelled in Jewish literature as depictions of cheap meanness. They are portrayed with the vast hatred and detestation of which Sholem Asch is capable; the portraits are vulgar, boorish, unmannerly, rude, brutish, and withal clownish. Just as once Asch idealized Jews and their mode of life so here he bedevils them. Once, before his "Christian era," Asch did not know such Jews. He may have discovered these many distorted, low, mean, repulsive Hebrews in Christian literature. For a Jew like Shmulewitz would be a suitable companion for Yankel (in Gogol's *Taras Bulba*) who is a black "Jewish" blotch in Russian literature. Shmulewitz is a similar somber disfigurement in Jewish literature (or perhaps in English literature, for it is not quite clear to which this book belongs). The entire gallery of these types, in *East River* belongs to a certain "Jewish" genre in world literature—Gogol's *Taras Bulba,* Turgeniev's *Zhid,* Dostoyevsky's Bumstein—types that are the detestation of the gentiles, the terror of the Jews, and the shame of the writers. Sholem Asch joined the company of the literary detractors of the Jew: that way lies success.

4

Two Sculptured Women

Just as the architecture of a church narrows upward to the tip of the cross, so does *East River* with every line stretch and strain churchward. Asch harnesses his best talents to the task of proving the ancient Christian dogma that by decree of heaven, the Church came to supplant the Synagogue; that the God of Israel long ago forsook the Jewish house of worship, and went to dwell in the

Christian house of prayer; that the Synagogue long ago lost its soul and its reason for being, and persists only because the Jews are a stiff-necked people who obdurately oppose the revealed will of God.

This basic dogma has been exploited in all theological and artistic media: in literature, philosophy, painting and sculpture.

One of the best known representations of it is to be found in the Cathedral at Strassbourg. Two gigantic feminine figures in stone appear on the facade. One represents the "Church," the other the "Synagogue." "Church" looks proudly, severely, and reprovingly toward "Synagogue." She wears a crown removed from the head of "Synagogue." In her left hand she holds a cup, also taken from the other figure. In her right hand she grasps a banner of the cross, planted securely on the ground.

The other statue stands with head bowed. Her eyes are bound, for she cannot see the "truth." Her left hand holds a piece of stone, a shard from the broken tablets of the Law, to which she continues to cling. In her right hand there is a long spear—symbol of her onetime hegemony—but the staff is broken and can no longer be leaned upon.

This is the view of Christian theology of the fallen state of the Synagogue. And this is the foundation upon which Sholem Asch constructs *East River*.

To Asch, the Catholic Church is great, mighty, imposing, imbued with healing power; and the Synagogue is small, weak, pitiable, broken, emptied of all moral strength.

In all of New York Asch is unable to discover one worthwhile synagogue or one proper congregation. He does not even find a synagogue with a presentable edifice, to show his readers, but portrays only the "fallen succah." His worshipers meet in a "hall," or in a bedraggled building rebuilt into a synagogue by Shmulewitz, which is later converted into a movie theatre. But his churches are all beautiful!

His priests are all high-minded ethical personalities, one with God and with man. The Triangle Fire, in which a hundred and fifty girls are burnt to death, is brought on by the Jews and their sweatshop system, but the lesson taught by the catastrophe—the need to improve the shops—Asch puts in the mouth of a priest. And as a counterweight to these lofty personalities of the churches, Asch offers on the Jewish side the religious hypocrite, swindler, and blackguard, Shmulewitz.

Although Asch's medium is "literary," it is no less a swindle and a humbug. One can not only be a swindler in religion, but, through misuse of one's artistic gifts, in art as well. When an artist treats one face with soot and another with delicate powder, it is easy for him to prove that the second visage is the more beautiful. In dealing with a problem as cataclysmic as the Judeo-Christian controversy, such a technique is reprehensible and below criticism. By his own literary procedure Asch shows himself closer in character to his Shmulewitz than to the priest. But Christianity long ago provided Asch's excuse: the end justifies the means because it is allegedly only for the glory of God that Asch carries the message to the Church from the ghetto of *East River* that Judaism is nearing its end, and that the full victory of the Church is imminent.

Let us consider the treatment of Mary McCarthy and Harry Greenstock. When Asch tells of Mary visiting the church, he writes reverently and respectfully. With awe he describes the church, its service, and its worshipers. Mary knows why she is attending her house of prayer. When she is in trouble, or in need of anything, she goes straight to the church and prays to Jesus on the crucifix; and always, Asch assures us, her wish is granted. She enters ill, and goes out healed. She comes in impoverished, and departs enriched.

Harry goes to synagogue only in a moment of crisis—the reference being to Yom Kippur—"when it becomes necessary to submit a report to the office of the district attorney of the Jewish God." Asch would never permit himself to write with such cheap cynicism concerning the Christian God. He admits that if Harry were put to the test he would more readily surrender his life than change his religion, but adds that "with this he completed his duty to God." Addressing his God, Harry says, "Everything else pass over. Don't you bother me, and I won't bother you."

Trapped in the Triangle fire, Mary has but to mention the name of Jesus, and instantly she finds the strength to save herself. But her Jewish co-worker, who does not mention Jesus, dies, even though she is directly at Mary's side.

All of which adds up to the inference—sweet music to Christian ears—that the Jewish religion is already moribund, but that miracles can still be accomplished through Christianity. It never occurs to the simple Jewish mother of Nathan, the paralyzed cripple, to turn in hope on his behalf to the Jewish God. She has long since given up her son, and all she asks for him is death. Med-

221

ical science, too, has given up. But Mary goes to Church and prays to Jesus, and (wonder of wonders!) Jesus (with a little sex to help) has Nathan move a limb! After that the way becomes smoother for the effect of medicine, too, until finally he regains movement of his limbs to an appreciable degree.

Nathan lies in the hospital, and next to his bed lies a gentile drunk awaiting death. The drunk speaks to Nathan concerning Jesus, and—another miracle—Nathan, the confirmed atheist, glimpses God! Throughout the years his father, Reb Moshe Wolf, a fine and honorable Jew and a scholar in matters both Jewish and worldly, has argued and philosophized with his sentient son about belief in God, and his seed has been sown on rock. Yet a stranger, an illiterate goy, a gutter drunk, is able to open the boy's eyes! How does it happen? What profound thoughts so affect the freethinker Nathan Davidovsky?

None but the usual Christian palaver. The difference is, however, that his father talks to Nathan about the Jewish God, and the drunk talks to him about Jesus.

Sholem Asch is a true soldier of the Salvation Army, which, in roaming the streets in search of recruits, frequently introduces a "bum" who has "gotten religion," to make an impression.

Asch continues steadily and methodically upon this course all through *East River,* piling lies upon lies and rubbish upon rubbish, until he is able to bring Reb Moshe Wolf himself into the kingdom of Jesus.

The Catholic Mary and Reb Moshe Wolf's second son Irving, whose religion is money, are wed. They make a compact not to interfere with each other's faith, and agree that any child will be reared neither as Jew nor Catholic, until he reaches maturity and is able to choose his own faith—though it is hard to see how he can decide if he has learned nothing about either. The son that is born to them is neither circumcised nor baptized. But Jesus is powerful, and gives Mary no rest because of her failure to baptize the child. At last she goes off furtively and has the baptism done. When Irving learns of this he is outraged and leaves her in anger, and the Catholic daughter-in-law, with her uncircumcised and now baptized child, comes to grandfather, the Chassid of Ger, Reb Moshe Wolf, for succor.

It happens to be the eve of Passover, and in the absence of Grandma Deborah, Mary prepares the seder. (Deborah has quarreled with Reb Moshe Wolf and left him without a seder table

222

at home). Mary, having quarreled with Irving, finds no other place in New York to flee but to her father-in-law's. And thus it happens that Mary and her little Christian spend Passover eve at Moshe Wolf's, with Mary actually preparing the festive meal. She does everything according to the law, more piously than Deborah herself would have done. Then comes the climax toward which the novel has aimed from the beginning: the little Christian sits at the table with his crucifix around his neck. While the Chassidic old Jew, with his Passover reader before him, offers the appropriate benedictions, the lad recites his own benediction, and the pious grandfather suddenly discovers that these are virtually the same prayer to the same God—and he makes peace with the situation.

Thus with a minimum of effort and toil Jesus is enabled to gain the mastery over the most pious type of Jew, the Chassid of "Gerer stock." Only in a fantasy bathed in baptismal water could so clumsy a caricature of the Chassidic Jew be created; only in the churchly hodgepodge to which Asch surrenders his birthright as a Jew, and his right as a Jewish writer, could such nonsense be conceived!

The Jew is deceived and the Christian is duped, and the very concept of imaginative literature is prostituted in a Satanic orgy of mockery and buffoonery. It is because of such fraudulent inventions and vain aberrations, that Plato in his "Republic" proscribes poets and tellers of tales as dangerous to the social organism. In the land wherein belles-lettres began, in that early age, men became apprehensive of the peril that may lurk in unbridled imagination.

Plato's warning against the boundlessness of poetic fantasy, with its power to deceive, seduce, and corrupt, was not the only admonition of that nature. Centuries later Jean Jacques Rousseau developed the theory that when literary art advances to high place in a culture, the nation is on the road to ruin and downfall. Pascal wrote, "The imagination is a master of error and falsity, an arrogant power which is inimical to the intelligence."

Our own Maimonides declared: "Imagination is the same as the evil inclination, insomuch as all our failings in speech or character are the direct or indirect product of imagination" ("Guide to the Perplexed," II, ch. 12).

Schlegel, the romantic who elevated imagination above reason, indicated most profoundly the thought behind his preference, which was the very reason why others condemn it. Schlegel asserted that he would abolish all the laws of logical understanding, and would hurl humanity once more into "the hypnotic confusion of fantasy, the aboriginal chaos of human nature."

"Chaos" is the proper term for Sholem Asch's imagination as it is revealed in *East River*.

Nevertheless Asch failed to take full advantage of the irrational and impossible sitation of this seder. At such an unusual festival meal, he could have accomplished something never before achieved; he could have devised two distinct haggadot (Passover readers), the one extant for the elder, and a new Catholic one for the boy. This would have added a third version to the Seder ritual—the Ashkenazi, the Sefardi, and now the Roman or Popish. This feat could have been achieved with but a slight change. The grandfather would have read the age-old story annually recited by all Jews: "Bondsmen were we unto Pharaoh in Egypt, and *God* brought us forth with a mighty arm." The child, using the Catholic haggadah, would have said instead: "And *Jesus* brought us forth."

For the Catholics have their own interpretation of the exodus. According to their Bible it was none other than Jesus that conducted the Jews out of Egypt. Asch had only to refer to verse five in the Epistle of St. Jude, which reads: "I will therefore put you in remembrance, though ye once knew this, how that Jesus, having saved the people out of the land of Egypt, afterward destroyed them that believed not."

However, Reb Moshe Wolf "accepts" Asch's "thesis." He is content to have a crucifix-bedecked grandson in his house. Prayer-shawl and phylacteries for grandpa's daily use; a crucifix for the grandchild. He is comforted by the thought that another child will be born, who will be Jewish. It will be fifty-fifty: one for the Jewish God, the other for the Christian; in one home one boy with a crucifix, and another with tzizith. But what if there be three children?

At all events the ultra-pious Moshe Wolf is prepared to give up his Jewish people to a foreign God. Such is the confusion to which this Christian-Jewish novel is finally reduced.

It is for reasons of symbolism that Asch chooses the seder night for his family reunion. It was allegedly on a seder night almost two millennia ago that history brought about the division between Jew and Christian, and on a seder night Sholem Asch

224

seeks to reunite them. Thus the climactic point of the story merges with the very pinnacle of the Church. Asch celebrates the final victory on behalf of a Church dogma: at 48th Street and the East River there remained one last full blooded Jew, one remnant of the solid historical Jewish tradition, and Sholem Asch contrives to bring him in the seder night, bent and broken, defeated and surrendered, to the doorstep of the Church triumphant!

But having accompanied Asch thus far we are suddenly no longer able to control our risibilities: who can imagine a "Chassid of Ger" forming a partnership with the Church! A mezuzah and a crucifix together at the seder! A pious Jew consenting to intermarriage, on condition that the children be divided half and half with the Church! This nonsense is simply beyond all endurance.

That excellent representative of the finest in orthodox Judaism, Moshe Wolf, consents to everything, and only the wicked Jew Shmulewitz, and his unscrupulous associates, are in opposition. Shmulewitz is the antagonist of Moshe Wolf and is so loathsome a character that one's skin almost crawls reading about him. The moral of the story is that only a degenerate Jewry still remains obdurate and continues to close the door to Jesus; the upright and virtuous of Israel are prepared to accept him.

It is thus, it appears, on the Christian side, too. The only one who consistently opposes any traffic with the Jews and upholds Catholic tradition against intermarriage is the lazy, wife-beating drunk and outcast, Mary's father.

The entire narrative is a vast burlesque compounded by Satan and his imps, playing tricks with Asch's soul. The Jews are not Jews, the Catholics are not Catholics, the Chassid is no Chassid. Ordinarily a sound fictional craftsman, Asch has here concocted nothing but a stilted story with cardboard figures.

Although Reb Moshe Wolf may have been a good Jew, he has no backbone, and one can prove nothing from the conduct of a spineless fool. The problem of intermarriage could have been presented in all its stress, agony and complexity if Asch had dared to present real people, strong both in character and in faith. The uprooted characters who wander through Asch's narrative express neither Judaism nor Catholicism. They are mere grotesques miming an impossible solution to a problem which is beyond their grasp.

As to the idyl of cross and mezuzah, let it here be noted:

At the end of the second World War, an American Jewish

225

communal worker and writer, Samuel Wohl, went on a tour of Poland, the vast graveyard of his people. He went to a number of cities where it was least perilous for a Jewish visitor to travel. Above all he visited Warsaw. He saw its ruins. Here is an excerpt from his book, "My Journey to Warsaw," recounting his experiences:

"I looked into former Jewish shops. In every one there hung opposite the door a picture of the 'Holy Mother' with a burning lamp, and on many doors there were still attached the little mezuzoth left by the former owners."

Such was the actual peace between cross and mezuzah in the year 1946, the year of *East River*.

CHAPTER VI

One Destiny

An Epistle to the Christians

Dear Mr. Asch:

Your master and teacher, Saint Paul, propagated his preachings in the form of epistles, epistles to the gentiles and to the Hebrews. Following the master's technic, you have subtitled your little book, *One Destiny*, "An Epistle to the Christians." Since your letter bears no mark of "Personal" or "For Christians Only," I felt that I too was permitted to read it. And now I am writing to you about it.

To tell you the truth I do so with no little apprehension. For I recall the way you expressed yourself when you assaulted me for my review of your first Christological book, *The Nazarene*. You said: "Do you know what would happen if I told the Christian world that I was being persecuted by the Jews on account of that book? Why, they would canonize me!"

Later you threatened the "Forward," in which my articles appeared, with a lawsuit.

This, too, is quite in the spirit of your revered mentor. Paul was the first to establish the tradition followed by all Jewish sectaries since his time, threatening on the slightest provocation "to tell the gentiles." When the Jews proposed to try Paul, he said: Oh no! Not me! Since he claimed to be a Roman citizen, any trial would have to be in Rome, not in Jerusalem, he said.

It is always so with Jewish renegades. Once they have gone over the fence, they feel strong and secure with the mighty, and assume a threatening attitude towards their former brethren.

There is more about Paul's methods, which is apropos. Paul, you know, was somewhat unsettled in mind. Now don't raise your hand at me! It is not I that say this, heaven forbid! It says so in your Bible, in the New Testament itself: When brought before

227

the Roman procurator Festus, Paul began to explain and expound, only to be rebuked by Festus, "Paul, thou art beside thyself; much learning doth make thee mad" (Acts xxvi, 24).

Confusion if not affliction of the mind is evident in all of Paul's epistles. They are so enigmatical and obscure, and full of contradictions, that not even the keenest of Christian minds can make full sense out of them (Paul, like you, needed an editor). So much so, that many Christians have long held that Paul only brought disaster upon the Christian religion, and that the disruption of Christianity into something like three hundred mutually destructive sects is entirely due to his baneful influence.

Now, except for the learning, the influence of Paul's mentality is distinctly evident in your own epistle, Mr. Asch. Your epistle, too, is filled with contradictions, confusions, aberrations, falsehoods and ignorance. It also contains statements which in many respects are dangerous to the Jews. I have in mind your reference to the Mohammedans, false reference by the way. I shall not undertake here the space-consuming task of unraveling your confusions and contradictions. Sensible readers will easily enough discover them for themselves. I shall limit myself to some of the more lucid portions of your address to Christendom.

Clear and lucid enough is your explanation to the Christians for assuming the right to address them. "It is the reverence I bear your faith," you say, "it is the love, the pious devotion and faithfulness I feel for the founder of your religion, that gives me the courage and the right to stand before you as a brother speaking to his brethren." What then is left for the "founder" of your own religion, Mr. Asch? Can one attend synagogue and church at the same time?

Lucid, too, is your role of character-witness on behalf of contemporary Christianity. You take it under your wing and attest that "Never since the days of Constantine," you say, "has Christianity attained such elevation and approached so close to fulfillment of the commands of Jesus, in word and deed, as in our days."

This indeed is the idiom of a faithful lover. For love is blind —and it seems, deaf and dumb, too.

Clear too is your presumption to speak "in the name of millions of Jews." By what right? You speak in the name of the Jews who have been slain in our fearsome time, and those who have remained alive. Nevertheless, I find it hard to understand how a

228

man whose face and heart are turned churchward can presume to speak for the Jews of the synagogue.

Indeed, you bear the "good news" to Christendom, false tidings to be sure, that the living remnant of Jewry has almost come near the embracing of Christianity. "I know," you say, "of no time in the history of both faiths when Jewish-Christian understanding and rapprochement became the conscious desire of the leading spiritual powers and the broad masses of both factions more than it has at present. In the minds of the greatest number of Jews, especially among ourselves in America, a revolutionary change of opinion has taken place about the personage who is the symbol of the Christian faiths, as it has, too, about the Christian faiths themselves."

You report that the Jews who perished for the glorification of the Name at Hitler's hands were led to the slaughter with the Prophet Elijah, King David, the patriarchs, the prophets and Jesus at the head of the procession. "Waz you there, Charlie?" You say further that when their souls departed in the flames, "the Messiah" stretched forth his hands to receive them, and they looked up to him. You further claim that the Christian and the Jewish messiahs are the same, Jesus of Nazareth, of course.

Fortunately for you, our holy dead cannot, alas, answer you. But the "greatest number of Jews" alive happily are here and they can speak up.

I am one of these, and if I were worthy to speak for all Jews, or if I were asked for an opinion, do you know, Mr. Asch, what I would do? The first thing I would do would be to call upon gentiles, good "goyim", to reply to you and to bear witness against you. Even in matters of our Jewish faith, a good goy is better than a bad Jew.

I present my first witness. You claim, Mr. Asch, that Christianity today is as virtuous and innocent, as pure and chaste, as it was in its day of innocence. Let us hear from the distinguished writer, Emery Reves, whose *The Anatomy of Peace* was published in 1945, shortly before your *Our Destiny* appeared, and who depicts the selfsame period which you venture to describe, saying:

"The wholesale murder, torture, persecution and oppression we are witnessing in the middle of the twentieth century proves the complete bankruptcy of Christianity as a civilizing force, its failure as an instrument to tame instinctive human passions and to transform man from an animal into a rational social being.

229

"The revival of barbarism and the wholesale practice of mass murder all over the world cannot be regarded as the work of a few godless, sadistic Gestapo men and some fanatic believers in Shintoism. It is being practiced by many churchgoing men of many nationalities.

"Millions of innocent people have been murdered in cold blood, tens of millions have been robbed, deported and enslaved by Christians, descendants of families belonging for centuries to the Roman Catholic, Greek Catholic and Protestant churches. Cruelties, horrible and inhuman beyond imagination, have been committed by countless men, not only German and Japanese, but Spanish, Italian, Polish, Rumanian, Hungarian, French, Serbian, Croatian and Russian. And these deeds, surpassing in ferocity and bloodthirstiness anything hitherto recorded in Western history, have been tolerated, and therefore tacitly admitted, by each and every organized Christian religion."

Do you hear, Mr. Asch? "A Daniel has come to judgment!"

Mr. Reves' book has been widely acclaimed; I am not aware of anyone's having taken exception to the author's views on the Christian church.

Now imagine what would happen if your "Epistle" should fall into his hands—the letter was intended for Mr. Reves too, wasn't it? Imagine his reading that "in our days" Christianity has become the Simon pure faith taught by Jesus. What could he say? Would he not have to reply as did the procurator Festus to your master, something or other "doth make thee mad"? For Mr. Reves would not ascribe your madness to "much learning."

2

The Church and the Jew

What do you do to the Jewish martyrdom of our awful time, Mr. Asch? What use do you make of our unparalleled national tragedy? In your subservience to the Church, you pervert this for use in your Christian propaganda. You parade six million slaughtered Jews about the world, crying, Hurrah for the Nazarene! Long live the Apostle! You are trying to cast a devout Christian aura over the most terrible field of slaughter in all history, where a

230

third of our nation has been tortured to death by Christian peoples, in the heart of the continent that is the home and centre and glory of Christianity. Elsewhere you have devised a scene in which you bring up from the dead in a vast procession the martyred Rabbis and scholars, the slaughtered children, renowned leaders, some of whom you summon up by name, like the martyr Hillel Zeitlin, and all under the pealing of church bells! There is no meaner, nor more callous piece of writing than this in all literature.

I have confronted you with one witness, Mr. Emery Reves, who, decrying the same tragedy, proclaims the "complete bankruptcy of Christianity." You differ with him in only one particular, a rather important one: you envision the handful of Jews that were rescued by good Christians, God bless them, while he sees the vast spectacle of the six million who were murdered. He stabs into the very heart of the tragedy. He rightly probes the relationship not between the rescued and the Church, but between the murdered and the Church. "These deeds," says he, "have been tolerated by each and every Christian religion." Proof supreme of Christianity's failure.

But you may argue: mayhap this man Reves is an atheist, or an heretic, or otherwise an enemy of Christianity. Maybe; since I do not know him personally, I cannot say. Therefore I shall add to his testimony that of a Christian whose loyalty and piety is unquestionable. I present the distinguished Swiss theologian, Emil Brunner, professor of theology at Zurich, and author of a book on Jesus called *The Mediator*. The book appeared as far back as 1927, much before the Hitler catastrophe. As an effort to save Christianity, it became almost a second Bible of that faith. I quote from page 504 of the English version:

"It is quite possible to defend the thesis that, historically speaking, Christianity has been a fiasco. True Christians would be the last to controvert this. . . . Even in the matter of conversion of Christians, Christ has not succeeded."

Understand, Mr. Asch?

But perhaps the testimony of one theologian is not sufficient. Then I can furnish another, and yet another; how many will be needed to convince you, Mr. Asch?

Professor Walter Marshall Horton, noted American scholar, published his *Theology in Transition* in 1943. The very title of the book indicates that all is not well in the faith.

231

"Our *Jewish friends,*" says he, "*are right* when they maintain that if by the Messiah we mean the one who ushers in the Golden Age, then it is rather strange for us to call Jesus the Messiah! . ." (P. 134).

This good Christian sorrowfully admits that the Jews are right, and that Jesus may not be the true messiah, after all. But you, Mr. Sholem Asch, happily proclaim that Jesus is the true messiah and that the Jews are wrong! What will an honest Christian think of you? You may well contemplate it, Mr. Asch. There is no doubt of your standing among Jews.

You say that this Messiah marched at the head of our holy ones in Poland as they were being led to their annihilation. Yes, He went first, but not in the way which you suppose. Were it not for the hatred of Israel, promulgated in His name through almost twenty centuries, Hitler would never have been able to inflict such a holocaust upon us in the space of ten years. You distinguish anti-Semitism and Christianity as two separate entities, mutually exclusive. In reality they are profoundly related. Even in your own books, *The Nazarene, The Apostle,* and *Mary,* the animosity toward the Jews cries out from every page. It is something you are unable to restrain; it is inherent in the very stuff of which your fiction is compounded.

Again I quote the testimony of a Christian to confound you. Karl M. Chworowsky, a Unitarian minister, writes:

"Historically and in its basic doctrine Christianity . . . has been and is anti-Semitic. . . . (Christianity) has at every stage of its history shown contempt for and hostility toward its mother-religion and encouraged its devotees to regard Judaism as a dangerous heresy and to look upon Jews as a 'lesser breed,' as a people forsaken and condemned by God."

You took our holy martyrs and hanged the cross around their necks at the very moment they gave up their souls "Al Kidush Hashem." You forcibly converted them at their deaths. Such was the custom of the Inquisition. The Jews of Poland, with roots in the oldest soil of the Jewish faith and tradition, the pious, the devout, the faithful citers of prayers, the scholars, the sages, the rabbis, the teachers, the Chassidim, the Jews with beards and long earlocks, who donned their prayer shawls as they went forth to their doom—these were the Jews around whose necks you placed the cross! The Nazis desecrated their bodies; you desecrate their souls!

232

And finally, the holy dead themselves testify against you, Sholem Asch. Their voices still cry from the crematoria. Not out of their graves, for they were granted no graves. But from the ghettos, the gas chambers and from the cremating flames. With joyous song they walked into the mouths of the furnaces. And do you know what they sang, Mr. Asch?

They sang no hymns to Jesus, no paeans to the Messiah who had already come. They sang the "Ani Maamin":

"I believe, I believe,
In the coming of the Messiah,
I believe.
And even if his coming be delayed,
Nevertheless I believe!"

This was one of the songs chanted in the Hitler ghettos. It ran in Hebrew, and I trust you still have enough Hebrew to understand, Sholem Asch, that the Jews were awaiting the Messiah whose *coming* is *delayed,* and not the one who has already come.

In their final moments they voiced the most sacred expression of Jewish faith and devotion: "Hear, O Israel, the Eternal is our God, the Eternal is one!"

Understand, Mr. Asch—ONE—One alone. They abhorred any partner to Him.

But you, cynic that you are, try to force a strange god upon them even in their death.

In the sinful, Sodomic period in which we are living, there has never appeared a more cynical narrative than your "Jesus in the Ghetto." You tell of an episode that supposedly took place in a famous red church on Gzhybov Street, Warsaw; the crucified image on the cross came alive, stepped down, donned a prayer shawl, and joined a crowd of Jews surrounded by a mob of Poles incited by the Nazis. When the mob recognized the face of their Lord, they desisted. Thus Jesus saved the Jews from the pogrom and extinction.

Thus, you attempt to clear the Poles of their share in the crimes against the Jews; the Poles, who experienced a unique pleasure in the odor of burning Jewish flesh; the Poles, who betrayed the fighters of the ghetto and never came to their assistance with the promised weapons; the Poles, who amused themselves with the bon mot, "The Germans will strew Hitler's grave with stones because he devastated Germany, but the Poles will strew his grave with flowers because he freed us from the Jews."

233

Through your tale of the revivified crucifix which "rescued" the Jews, you seek to remove from Christianity all responsibility for the Jewish holocaust. Satan's urging must have prompted you to choose as setting for your story that same red church on Gzhybov Street which stood at the very border of the ghetto.

When Warsaw was finally wrested from Nazi hands, and the curtain of fire behind which the most dire tragedy in Israel's history had taken place was lifted, the world gazed upon this scene of horror:

That which had been the ghetto was now one great mass of rubble. As far as the eye could see, for miles of what once had been streets and public squares, nothing remained but stones, stones, stones. And the stones were not whole, nor fractured, but virtually powdered. It seemed that the entire ghetto had been sent through gigantic millstones to be ground into flour. This was the final, mute testimonial to the ferocity of the Nazis.

And beneath the rubble, just as thinly ground, lay the bones of our unforgettable fighters of the ghetto.

But at the very edge of the ruins, against the open horizon of the battered city, there stood, whole, straight, proud and triumphant, its steeple reaching into the sky, the red church on Gzhybov Street, fairly shrieking: Victory!

Yes, the church stood erect and whole and proud, and at its feet lay Judaism ground into dust. A testimony.

Pictures of that scene were sent to all parts of the world. The picture might well be hung in Jewish homes as a memorial, a kind of second Wailing Wall.

And out of this church, looking down triumphantly upon the terrible Jewish devastation, you, Sholem Asch, called forth the Nazarene, and said: He rescued the Jews. You cynic!

But let us restrain our anger. Let us try to speak calmly. From the evidence cited above, Mr. Asch, it is clear that Christianity is now passing through an unparalleled crisis. Some Christian writers frankly admit bankruptcy and defeat, which implies a victory for Judaism. Judaism has conquered in its very defeat. Yet you, Mr. Asch, choose to confuse innocent Jewish boys and girls into believing that Christianity has won the victory over Judaism!

Lest you think I am day-dreaming or indulging in wishful thinking, I shall bring forward another witness, again a Christian, and a theologian as well. He is Dr. J. Ernest Wright, professor of

234

the Old Testament at the McCormick Theological Seminary in Chicago. In 1944 he published a small volume, *The Challenge of Israel's Faith,* in which he urges Christianity to return to the Old Testament for a true concept of God. The Father-son picture, he contends, has degenerated into mere sentimentality. It is a God before Whom one can feel no fear, no reverence. Through Jesus and the entire Christian teaching, says he, "we have persuaded ourselves that this is a lovely world, with nothing at all to fear. God? He is a wonderful Father, almost too good to deny us anything, and far too polite to punish us for misdeeds" (p. 48).

The Jews, alone, he continues, know what the true God is. They comprehend the concept better than the Christians, who ought to learn from them.

You can see, therefore, Mr. Asch, that Judaism is at the threshold of the greatest spiritual triumph in history. A spiritual conflict which has continued for two thousand years, in blood and fire—we furnished the blood and they the fire—is approaching a conclusion in our favor. Naturally this conclusion is not imminent. No lengthy war ends abruptly. But your Church is decayed; and sorely needs a new Reformation to be saved.

At this juncture of history, you, Mr. Asch, come to inform the gentiles, in your "Epistle," that "the greatest number of Jews" everywhere, including ravaged Jewry of Poland, and above all the Jews of America, are today drawing close to Christianity.

Now you are well aware, Mr. Asch, that this is not so. You have convinced no one but Christians with your hocus-pocus. You have aroused false hopes in the hearts of Christians who imagine your words to be true.

You are undoubtedly aware that in some Christian persuasions the second advent of Christ is closely linked to the conversion of the Jews. Jesus will not return to earth again before the Jews, who denied him, do penance and acknowledge him as the true Messiah.

Since the early times Christians have awaited this sign from the Jews, upon whom redemption depends. There is a great division of opinion in Christian theology as to the circumstances of the Jewish conversion. Some say it will happen on a miraculous day when all the rabbis will adopt a resolution for the whole of Israel —We surrender! Others say that the conversion will be a slow gradual process. Still others hold that it will not be necessary to

235

wait for the conversion of all the Jews; a majority will prove sufficient. Another group asserts that a few, just the elite, will be ample.

Now, Mr. Asch, you bring to the gentiles the cheering message: "Here are the Jews! They are yours for the asking! Come and get them!"

3

Seducer and Perverter

You have brought the Christians the glad tidings, Mr. Asch, that "in the minds of the greatest number of Jews a revolutionary change of opinion has taken place about the personage who is the symbol of Christian faith." In your epistle you designate Him also the redeemer of the Jews, promised by God to the patriarchs, and foretold by the prophets, as consolation and reward for all their sufferings. To pious Christians this is most welcome and long awaited news.

If you are indeed able to deliver to the Christians "the greatest numbers" of Jews, I say that this will prove more world-shaking than even the atom bomb. For it is no little matter for Christ to come down from heaven and inaugurate the beginning of man's ultimate redemption.

Obviously, the first phase of the revolution will transpire among the Jews themselves—that is, those who wish to go along with you. First they will have to unlearn and discard everything Jewish and begin to acquire all that is Christian, everything that the Christians have long known by heart. They will be required to start from the very beginning. Kindergarteners who will open up their primers.

That the Books of the Law and the Prophets foretold all that was to happen with Jesus is a basic creed of all Christians in all their denominations. The mission houses which infest Jewish districts display legends such as the following— "We have found the Messiah of whom Moses and the prophets did write." When asked to name the chapter and verse to which they refer, they point, for instance, to the scene at the bedside of the dying Jacob. When Jacob blessed Joseph's sons, Ephraim and Manasseh, he placed his hands upon their heads crosswise. This, they say, was the foretelling and a prefigure of the cross.

236

Or, as Thomas Aquinas says, the candelabrum in the Temple was a prognostication of Jesus; just as the menorah brought light, so did He bring light. The twelve loaves of shewbread, in another interpretation by this outstanding medieval Christian philosopher, were prophetic of the twelve apostles. And so on.

In general the Christians have turned the Jewish Bible into an instrument to plague the Jews. From the first there have been, they say, the exoteric and the esoteric. The superficial version is for the Jews; the hidden, mystic exposition is for the Christians.

Even in the days of Paul they were discovering two distinct meanings in Torah and Prophets, one intended from the first for the Christians, the other for the Jews. In a most unusual way Paul attempted to use the Torah itself as basis for this idea.

The Torah relates that when Moses descended from the mountain with the second tablets, his face was illuminated; and that when the Israelites beheld this phenomenon they grew afraid to approach him. Thereafter Moses wore a veil over his face.

Now Paul interprets this veil as a symbol of the concealing from the Jews of the actual meaning of the Torah. Only in Jesus the messiah was the veil removed and the true teaching revealed. Says Paul: "But their (the Israelites') minds were blinded: for until this day remaineth the same veil untaken away in the reading of the old testament; which veil is done away in Christ. But even unto this day, when Moses is read, the veil is upon their heart" (II Corinthians iii, 14-15).

Paul's explanation is a complete perversion of the text. For in the same chapter a few verses later, we have Moses speaking to the Israelites to transmit God's word *minus* the veil over his face (Exodus xxxiv, 34). But to torture a sentence or phrase of Scripture meant nothing to Paul.

And so began the legend that the Torah was never fully revealed to the Jews.

Later Christian apologetics provided another crutch to support Paul's lame conjecture. In the same portion of the Torah Moses asks God to show him His glory; and God replies, "Thou shalt see My back; but My face shall not be seen" (Exodus xxxiii, 23). Hence, say the Christian theologians, pointing from the verse to the Jews, and from the Jews to the verse, the Jews were allowed to see only the reverse side of God and the Torah.

But, alas, this Christian triumph, too, lasts only until one points out other verses in the Torah. For in the same chapter it is

237

told (11) : "And the Lord spoke unto Moses *face to face,* as a man speaketh unto his friends." And in Numbers xii, 8, God says, "With him do I speak *mouth to mouth,* even manifestly, and not in dark speeches; and the *similitude* of the *Lord doth he behold."* Also we read in Deuteronomy (xxxiv, 10): "And there hath not arisen a prophet since in Israel like unto Moses, whom the Lord knew face to face."

However, it is not my aim, Mr. Asch, to demonstrate how the Christians get themselves hopelessly entangled in our verses. My intention is to give you a sample of Christian exegesis of Jewish Scripture. Perhaps a few more examples will not be entirely out of place here.

Take, for example, the story of Cain and Abel. The Christians say, "The murdered Abel is a figure of Jesus Christ, while Cain is a figure of the traitor Judas and the Jewish people, who put our Saviour to death" (Bible History, by R. Richard Gilmour, D. D.). Do you see how easily Israel is made the Cain of humanity? Do you approve, Sholem Asch, of this Christological Torah exegesis?

Again, the Christians say, "Noah is a figure of Jesus Christ, a symbol of the Nazarene, as the ark is a figure of the Catholic Church."

Unique, too, is their exposition of the story of Jacob and Esau.

"This transfer of Esau's birthright to Jacob was symbolical of the Jews, who, in the time of Christ, rejected the Gospel, and their rights were transferred to the Gentiles, who were chosen in their stead."

You see how they confound the facts: They make an Esau out of Jacob, and a Jacob out of Esau.

The aim of the Christians is quite obvious—to pre-empt the Bible for themselves. And they make no secret of it. Our Bible, they say, has become theirs. Everything, they claim, belongs to them: the firstborn status, the election, the covenant, the Holy Writ, even the name of Israel. They claim to be the true Israelites. They may detest the Jew, but they like to glorify themselves with his name. Without obeying the Jewish Bible, they lay claim to it. It is theirs, not ours; and every time, Mr. Asch, that you say that the Nazarene came just as the Prophets had foretold, you plead their cause and wrest our sacred Book from our hands, saying in effect, "You no longer possess it; it belongs to the gentiles."

238

Shall we take another example, Mr. Asch?

To Christians the life of Joseph is a picture of the life of Jesus. Joseph was hated by his brothers because of his dreams; Jesus was hated by the Jews because of his teachings and the prophecies related concerning him. Joseph was betrayed, sold and tortured; so, too, was Jesus. Joseph was ultimately triumphant; so was Jesus. Joseph became ruler over Egypt, Jesus became king of heaven and earth. Finally, Joseph saved his brethren, Jesus became the saviour of all humanity.

These turns and twists, crooked as they seem, are simple to construct. Proceeding in this manner, the entire Bible has been subjected to the same treatment; the Christians have deprived us altogether of our Scripture, outrageously denying us any share in it whatsoever.

Thus we find Professor Adolf von Harnack, famed theologian, writing:

"The Bible, from cover to cover, has absolutely nothing to do with the Jews. Unjustly and insolently did the Jews claim it, confiscate it, and present the claim that it was their possession. They falsified the facts through their misinterpretations, and even made changes and omissions. It would be a sin for any Christian to declare—the Book belongs to us and the Jews. No, the Holy Writ belongs, now and forever, to none but the Christians!"

Von Harnack's reasoning runs as follows: Since it was destined from the very days of Creation that the Jews would deny the Nazarene, and that they would lose their birthright and election to the Christians, it is clear that everything, including the Bible, was eternally intended for the Christian; what business can the Jews now have with the Bible?

But this is nothing compared to Martin Luther's diatribe on the same subject. Von Harnack oozes high minded Kultur, while Luther takes us directly to the pigsty. The father of Protestantism, after translating the Bible into German with the copious help of Jewish scholars, declared the Bible to be strictly a German book, in which the Jews have no share at all!

"The only Bible to which you have any right, he informed the Jews, is that to be found under a pig's tail; the letters dropping therefrom you are entirely free to eat and drink" (Griesser, "Luther," Book 4, p. 285).

Now you see, Mr. Asch, what fine company you have joined. And now, pray tell me, if you will, why do Christians find

239

it so desirable to preen themselves with our plumage? They tear the holy garments from our bodies, and proceed to adorn themselves before the entire world with our raiment. In broad daylight they would expel us from our holy of holies and sprawl out in those sacred precincts as though disporting in their paternal vineyard. Why? Why would they not leave us alone?

Let us take the Passover seder, as another example.

Are you aware of what they do with our Passover seder?

It, like our Bible, is theirs. I have seen all the rites of the seder interpreted as Christian symbols. I am convinced that this is the doing of some Jewish renegade. First, it is asked why three matzos are laid out as part of the ceremonial. The Sabbath and festival loaves are ordinarily two, yet of matzos there are three. And why is the middle matzo the first to be broken? And why is a portion of it—the afikoman—wrapped in a white cloth and hidden until the end of the meal? Later, the "afikoman" is recovered from its place of concealment, and all partake of it: Why? And why the custom of "stealing" the afikoman?

These are the four questions of the meshumed, the convert. There are of course many learned and wise explications of these customs. But they do not satisfy the meshumed, who proceeds to provide his own as follows:

The three matzos represent the trinity—Father, Son, and Holy Ghost.

The breaking of the middle matzo symbolizes what happened to the second person, the crucifixion.

The wrapping of the afikoman and its concealment shows the Son being taken down from the cross, wrapped in white garments, and interred in a grave.

And the stealing and subsequent eating of the afikoman reproduces the resurrection of the crucified and buried Son on the third day, His ascension into heaven, and His return to serve as the bread of life to be consumed by all the nations.

"And thus," concludes the meshumed, "is the mystery of the seder solved!"

But to what end do the Christians and the converts seek these interpretations? Why do they feel so insecure in their "true" faith that they must forever find new justifications in Judaism?

And how odd it is to discover that you too, Mr. Asch, are in the same company as these, and that you sing the same song in the selfsame chorus!

The aforesaid meshumad played tricks with Passover; you do the same with Chanukah.

By the way, speaking of the seder I am reminded of a point I always meant to ask you about. In *The Nazarene* you describe the last seder celebrated by Jesus and his disciples, the seder that was later to be known as the Lord's Last Supper. It is not a bad description you have there, though as usual you have overcharged it with messy emotion and made it wearily decorative. But while at it you must have known that you were describing what, according to Christian teaching, was the last valid passover and that there and then Jesus instituted a memorial celebration (that of his flesh and blood) that from then on was to replace the passover. You must have further known that according to the same Christian philosophy all the passovers the Jewish people have been celebrating since then, since, that is, the year 33, have, by the same token, been invalid, futile and even blasphemous? Did you ever enlighten your Jewish readers on this point? But to go back to Chanukah.

The sages ask, "What is Chanukah?" and they give the well known exposition of the festival. You ask the same question, Sholem Asch—may the sages forgive the juxtaposition of names—and provide your own answer:

In brief, your thesis is this: had there been no victory of the Maccabees, and had the Jews been assimilated by the Hellenic civilization, the plan of Providence would have been broken, and the *Nazarene would never have been born!* ("One Destiny" 55f).

Thus you avow that not for the sake of Judaism did Providence grant victory to the handful of Jewish heroes who set themselves in opposition to Antiochus Epiphanes, but for the sake of Christianity. For otherwise, you ask, "what would have become of the promise, made by the prophets in God's name, to bring forth the Messiah (Jesus)?"

So that is your idea of Chanukah, Mr. Asch! It was merely preparatory to Jesus. You take it from the Jews and hand it over to the Christians. And when you gaze at the Chanukah lights, you see no candles there, but little crosses dancing before your eyes!

Tell me then—how do you differ from the meshumad mentioned above?

Our Chanukah you give to them; their Christmas you give to us. Who would have imagined you to be so generous?

But permit me to say that this is by no means an original

241

idea. It is old, traditional Catholic doctrine. That is why the Church has included the Books of the Maccabees in its Bible. Many Christian historians have long reckoned the era of Christianity to have begun with the Maccabees.

Basic to this is the concept of the so-called "sacred history" of religious-Christian historians, of whom Bossuet was the first. The entire course of the universe was directed toward the climactic emergence of the Nazarene. The midwife of that emergence, so to speak, was the Jewish people. One might call Jewry the axle on which the Christian wheel was to ride Christianity into the world.

Well, it appears that you think the same, Mr. Asch. You too consider the Jewish people as appearing not for its own sake and for its own message, but solely to serve as forerunner and servitor to the Christians. But the Christians add the declaration, "The Moore has done his duty; the Moore may go."

You have been maintaining all along that with your Christological writings you are endeavoring to mitigate Christian rancor which is likely to strike at any time and at any place. In seeking to better the status of Jews in Christian eyes, you have come forth with a novel compromise theory that Judaism and Christianity are really one and the same, the two halves of an integer, the two sides of a single coin. You have given a new twist to what is often called the "Judeo-Christian concept."

But did it never occur to you, Mr. Asch, that the two sides of a coin are ever turned with their back to each other and never look in the same direction?

You warn the Christians that without Jews their own faith would be imperiled. But at the same time you proffer a warning to the Jews as well. "The preservation of Israel and the preservation of the Nazarene are one phenomenon. They depend on each other. . . . Christianity would become petrified if the Jews, God forbid, should cease to exist . . . so would Jewry itself become petrified, barren, and dry if there were no Christendom to fructify it. Without Christendom, Jews would become a second tribe of Samaritans" ("One Destiny," 9).

The difficulty with this amiable theory is that it is only half true. It is true that without Judaism there would probably be no Christianity, at least in the form in which we know it; but it must not be forgotten that Judaism existed for fifteen hundred years before Christianity ever appeared on the scene. Remarkable in-

242

deed is your conclusion that "no deliverance, no peace, and no salvation can come until the two halves (Judaism and Christianity) are joined together and become one part of God."

On another occasion you said that Christian and Jew ought to have one church. Exactly what do you mean by all that, Mr. Asch? Do you suggest that the Christians be converted to Judaism, or that the Jews go over to Christianity? Which?

Listen to what an honest Christian has to say on the subject. The famous Catholic philosopher, Jacques Maritain, writes: "The final goal of all God's ways with man . . . and the ultimate redemption of the world . . . are dependent upon Israel, Israel in the flesh, turning to Jesus the Nazarene" ("A Christian Looks at the Jewish Problem").

Maritain knows better than you do, Mr. Asch. He does not maintain that Judaism and Christianity are the selfsame entity. He is perfectly aware that they are mutually exclusive. Therefore he does not suggest any merger. His are the words to be expected of a Christian—that Jews must surrender their own heritage and become totally immersed. He speaks as a Christian should; but you by no means speak as should a Jew.

The truth of the matter is that Judaism and Christianity are identical in your eyes because you have no real concern for either. You neither don phylacteries, nor do you wear the cross. You have neither faith nor works. The whole thing to you is just an interesting and remunerative divertissement. But to people of my ilk, your activity is a black mark in a black day.

The two faiths, Mr. Asch, are worlds apart in everything that is basic to religion. They differ in their concept of Deity. They differ in their outlook on the world. They look with different eyes upon the nature of man. They are far apart in their ethics.

Yet to you they are only two halves of the same entity. Childish prattle!

You say that your only criterion of a religion is belief in a messiah. A most odd criterion, indeed. You go on to say that since Judaism believes in a messiah, and Christianity believes in a messiah, the two religions are but one religion.

But the messiahs themselves are quite different, Mr. Asch.

On the basis of your messiah-concept you strongly assail Mohammedanism. You call it a religion without a messiah, and angrily ask, "But what have I to do with Mohammedanism? . . . Is Mohammed a product of the Jewish spirit? . . . Are the Mohammedans my brothers, sharing equally with me in the heritage of the patriarchs? What have I to do with the desert tribe? The Christians are my brothers" ("One Destiny," 51-52) .

Your anger at Mohammedanism, Mr. Asch, is Christian, not Jewish. And your ignorance of this faith is hardly becoming to either Christian or Jew. Your horrible incitation against the Mohammedans is most unjustified. Would you instigate a religious war between Judaism and Mohammedanism at the very time that Jews have reestablished their nation in the heart of the Mohammedan world?

In brief, my purpose in writing to you, Sholem Asch, is to assure you that your labor is in vain; you will never be able to deliver the Jewish people to the Christians!

I cannot imagine my old Hebrew teacher, Notteh the melamed, teaching your doctrine to the little Moseses and Solomons. He would react to your proposals as did another Jew to another missionary. In a mission paper I once came across a piece complaining that Jews are as obstinate today as ever: even when you have one practically convinced, it said, he suddenly scratches at his beard and remarks, "Somehow I just can't believe it!"

I am sure your own father and mother would react in the same manner.

For example, take the holy "bread and wine" which every Christian is required to eat and drink. The priest takes a wafer and wine, recites a verse over them, and they are at once transformed into the "flesh and blood of Christ." Into actual flesh and blood—so must the pious believe. I am referring to the doctrine of transubstantiation.

Mr. Asch, I cannot imagine your dear, pious mother, who used to soak meat for half an hour and keep it in salt for a full hour to remove all traces of blood, partaking of improperly prepared meat—not to mention human flesh, or God's flesh.

Your mother, were she alive today, would never follow you in your Christian endeavors, Mr. Asch—nor would your father. They belong to us. They stay with us.

Now, Mr. Asch, you will understand that I have chosen concrete illustration both exegetical and ceremonial, so that we may understand that being a Christian involves more than just bandying about vague phrases concerning the messiah, redemption, and the prophets.

244

Do you now perceive where your Christological ravings lead you?

I am afraid my remarks on your "Epistle" have grown to the size of your "Epistle." Yet I beg you to indulge me by attending to the discussion of one more point.

4

The Impostor

The word "impostor," Mr. Asch, can mean many unpleasant things—liar, intriguer, embezzler, seducer. No doubt Thomas Jefferson, who applied the word against St. Paul, is now roasting in hell for his mortal sin.

But you, who are so righteous a man, will surely not reject your great mentor, Thomas Jefferson notwithstanding. On the contrary, you will probably accept for him, and even for yourself, this crown of thorns. You will assert: if Paul is in truth an impostor, I too will be called by that name; one must be prepared to make every sacrifice for one's faith!—for you are notorious for your talent for martyrdom.

I bring this up because I feel the urge to call you by some strong yet fitting name. But I am reminded of a small-town wagoner who was driving a passenger arrived from Paris. On the way the driver discovered that he had lost the Parisian's valise. Wishing to soften the blow for the passenger, he said:

"Mister, you come from Paris. How do they say 'lost' in French?"

"In French," was the reply, "the word is 'perdu'."

"Then," said the wagoner, "allow me to report that your valise is perdu!"

I wish to be equally easy with you, Mr. Asch. I shall not call you any harsher name than that made available by Jefferson for the subject under consideration: Impostor.

And it happens, Mr. Asch, that you are an impostor both to the Jew and to the Christian.

You deceive the Christians, because you try to make them believe that the majority of Jews have revised their understanding of their redeemer and their faith. This is liable to arouse false

245

hopes among them and whet their appetites. And when they discover how completely they have been duped, they may nurse even greater rancor towards our people.

But you are a far more vicious impostor in regard to Jewry. Your books bring to Jewish young people in America, ignorant of the facts, a totally false conception of Christianity. In *The Nazarene, The Apostle* and *Mary,* you present the narratives of Christianity as constituting so clean and pure and uplifting a religion—as contrasted to their own—that they may feel encouraged to abandon their own faith for the faith of the Church. You portray the Christian faith in all its earliest pristine beauty and virginal purity.

But, Mr. Asch, something has happened to Christianity since that time. Since that early day, Christianity has been subjected to such profound criticism from within and from without that there is not a trace remaining of innocent virginity. Yet you choose to ignore the experience of almost twenty centuries, and to confuse the minds of the ignorant and the innocent.

There is a vast Christian literature to testify that the kind of Christianity you portray has never existed on earth. You need only read the last chapter of *Christianity Past and Present,* by Charles Guignebert, professor of the history of Christianity at the Sorbonne. "The European nations," says he, "were never, properly speaking, Christian." From the very first, he explains, the religion was permeated by so much paganism that the nations, while calling themselves Christian, have remained pagan to this very day. Rarely, very rarely, did they become imbued with any of the spirit of the Bible. Despite its great power, says Guignebert, the Catholic Church is tottering, and the Protestant wing is also in deadly peril.

But these are conclusions you do not pass on to the Jewish youths who constitute the majority of your readers. Perhaps you will say in defense that these observations belong to later periods and do not come within the scope of your first Christological books which deal only with the narratives of the New Testament. But you even mask problems concerning the Christian Bible. I have before me Ernest P. Scott's work with the self-explanatory title, *Varieties of New Testament Religion,* in which he demonstrates that in the New Testament itself there are several religions; that there is no way of telling which is the true Christian faith; and that

246

the several faiths can never be reconciled or rendered at peace one with another.

You are an impostor when you attempt to convince the Jews that Christianity is completely free of animosity toward the Jew, and when you pretend not to understand whence derive the Christian persecutions of the Jews. This is the main thesis of your "Epistle to the Christians." I dealt with this subject elsewhere and shall not elaborate on it here. Personally, I think that the Christians are far better to the Jew than Christianity. But let me just exhibit here a couple of choice samples that will point up further the grotesqueness of your position.

Exhibit A. Elucidating the Pauline doctrine of the Law or Torah as a curse, Agobard, Archbishop of Lyons, in the 9th century describes the workings of the curse as follows:

"All who are under the Law (i.e. Jews) are under a curse, and are clothed with the curse as with a garment. It has entered, like water, inside them, and like oil into their bones. They are, moreover, cursed in the city, and cursed in the field; cursed in coming in and cursed in going out; cursed in the fruit of their womb, the land and flock; cursed are their cellars, their barns, their medicines, their food, and the crumbs that drop from it, and none of them can escape from this appalling, this ghastly curse of the Law except by Him who was made the curse for us."

Exhibit B. Martin Luther writes: "What are we to do with this damned, reprobate people? If we tolerate them we become parties to their lies and blasphemy. We can't convert them; we must practice a sharp method, if we are to save any of them from the eternal flames. First let their synagogues and their schools be fired; what won't burn must be pulled down and covered with earth. This shall be done to the honour of our Lord, so that God may see that we are Christians and have not assented to their lies. If we protect these houses in which they spit upon and desecrate Christ, it would be as bad as if we did ourselves. Their homes are to be dealt with in the same way, because they carry on the same practises in them. Moses said that if a city practised idolatry, it was to be entirely destroyed; if he were alive today, he would be the first to demand the punishment of the Jews." (Brian Lunn, Martin Luther, p. 324)

Exhibit C. "For nineteen hundred years the blood of Christ has been upon the Jews. Driven from Judea—without a land, without a home—strangers among strangers—hated yet feared—

247

they wander from people to people, bearing with them the visible marks of God's curse. Like Cain, marked with a mysterious sign, they will thus wander to the end of the world." (Right Reverend Richard Gilmour, D. D. Bible History, p. 209, textbook used in Catholic schools in America today.)

And now for a last question.

When you speak of Christianity you do so always in the most general terms. Nowhere do you as much as make mention of the fact that there is not one, single, uniform, coherent Christianity, but that there are many conflicting denominations and persuasions that are mutually destructive and which oppose each other as strenuously and as bitterly as, combined, they oppose Judaism. When you call upon the Jews to turn their faces towards Christianity, exactly what brand of Christianity is it that you invite them to?

I must confront you again with that great man, Thomas Jefferson. In his "Notes on the State of Virginia" he states: "Millions of innocent men, women and children, since the introduction of Christianity, have been burnt, tortured, fined, imprisoned, yet we have not advanced one inch toward uniformity."

And lest one President of the United States not be enough to convince you, permit me to offer the testimony of another. On September 28, 1951, President Harry S. Truman delivered a speech to the Pilgrimage of American Churchmen, in which he said: "For some time I have been trying to bring a number of the great religious leaders of the world together in a common affirmation of faith and a common supplication of the one God that all profess. . . . It has not yet been possible to bring the religious faiths together for this purpose of bearing witness that God is the way of truth and peace. Even the Christian churches have not yet found themselves able to say, with one voice, that Christ is their Master and Redeemer and the source of their strength against the hosts of irreligion and the danger of a world catastrophe. They have not been able to agree on a simple statement like that."

It is a chief feature of American democracy that final decisions rest with the courts. Well, it so happens that an American court had to decide the question: What is a Christian? On the answer depended $75,000. When William B. Small, a prominent Methodist layman of Waterloo, Iowa, died in 1939, his will directed that the income from $75,000 of his estate should be distributed "to persons who believe in the fundamental principles of the Christian religion and in the Bible and who are endeavoring to promulgate same." When his wife died in 1949 ten nephews and nieces sued to break the will. Their argument was: "There is no common agreement as to what constitutes the fundamental principles of Christianity."

After a prolonged trial, with many religious leaders testifying as experts, Iowa Judge Shannon B. Charlton had to nullify the will on the ground that there is no common definition as to what constitutes Christianity or a Christian. "Among Christians," he said in his verdict, "there is widespread lack of accord in their characterizations of the man Jesus and in their interpretations and applications of his teachings." (Time, Dec. 10, 1951).

And here is further corroborating testimony direct from the Church. Many sincere efforts over a long period of time have been made to discover the common denominator of Christianity and bring about Christian unity among its countless divisions and subdivisions, but all to no avail. The Third World Conference on Faith and Order, held in Lund, Sweden, in August of 1952, and sponsored by the World Council of Churches, considered reports drafted by its five subcommittees on how to attain unity among Christian churches on doctrine, worship and communion. The reports revealed such wide divergencies in concept and interpretation that Archbishop Athenagoras of the Orthodox Church of Cyprus asserted: "We may look for church union two centuries hence, but not before." As the meeting closed, its report sadly admitted that "we have not resolved our differences nor brought forth before the world a simple method of achieving unity. . . . We have now reached a point at which our divergencies stubbornly resist easy solution."

The standard slogan of the Christian missionary is, "Come to Jesus and He will give you Peace". There are 256 variants of Christianity now being preached, all factionally embroiled, quarreling, competing, denying each other, often reviling and even persecuting each other. Where is the peace of Jesus?

Now, Mr. Asch, you have kept all this and more concealed from the readers of your Christological writings, among whom there have been hundreds of thousands of innocent Jewish youth. It is for them that I am concerned. On their behalf I label you Impostor.

249

CHAPTER VII

"A Jewish Holiday"

In honor of Christmas of the year of bloodshed, 1945, Sholem Asch contributed this manifesto to the Chicago Daily News:

"I consider the birth of Jesus a Jewish holiday also. In this happy event we Jews have an equal share with all the people in the world, and we have good reason to thank and praise God therefor."

Elsewhere in his statement Asch declares that in these exceptional days, of the Second World War, when humanity is passing through revolutionary events, Christmas has a deeper significance than ever before: "That is the reason I believe that in these days Christmas has greater meaning than previously, for all the people in the world." He includes the Jewish people.

Sholem Asch here appears in an entirely new role. As though he embodied in his own person that great and august body, the "Men of the Great Assembly" of Jewish antiquity, Sholem Asch undertakes to prescribe a new holiday for Jewish observance. Self-absorbed, self-important, shallow, vain, humorless and utterly godless, he dares invade the holy precincts of religion and dictate new precepts and statutes to Jewry.

Every time semi-Christian men like Asch elaborate such counsels to Jewry, it is instructive to learn what true Christians have to say about them. *The Laws of the Ancient Hebrews,* by the Rev. E. C. Wines, is a book one hundred years old at the present writing (pub. 1853). From it we learn that one hundred years ago in the United States Jews were showing a tendency to imitate their Christian neighbors in their celebration of Christmas, by putting up Christmas trees in their homes. The author clearly did not like it. Speaking of the Jews in Christian countries, he said:

"Their peculiarities are invaded by Christian institutions and manners. In our country, for example, the festival of Christmas

250

is extensively observed by them, though it is, strictly speaking, no more a part of their religion or manners than the festival of Baalpeor. I was myself once invited to the celebration of this festival in a Jewish family. On my venturing to call the attention of my host to the incongruity of such an observance by a Jew, he admitted it, and added, that he had said the same thing to the children that very morning, when they had asked him for Christmas presents. Their reply to him was, 'that all children received presents that day, and they wanted them as well.' This conversation let much light into my mind on the dedication to idolatry of the ancient Israelites" (p. 468-9).

Writing almost a century later, another Christian scholar, Professor William Kelley Wright, in his *A Student's Philosophy of Religion* (1922), has the following to say on Judaism in general, and with reference to Christianity and Christmas in particular:

"The great strength of Judaism, as we have seen, is on the side of Agency; its conception of God is at once sublime and yet humanly intimate and accessible. The religion has been preserved through its Law and other sacred scriptures which have been taught in the synagogue and home and which have become ingrained in the affections of Jewish children. The observance of Sabbath and other rituals, especially that connected with the preparation of food, has kept the Jews a distinct and peculiar people. Judaism commands high admiration for the purity and tenderness of its family life; and the worship of the home, especially the Passover, conserves the values of the family more effectively than is done, probably, by any other religion, not excepting Christianity.

"The festivals observed by the synagogue, such as the Day of Atonement, the New Year's Day and the Feast of the Weeks still retain their impressiveness, and deepen and strengthen the faith of the worshipers; while even the most important days of the Christian year, like Easter and Christmas, regrettably have for most Christians lost their spiritual significance and become merely holidays" (pp. 146-7).

Thus, at a time when Christian scholars tell us that Christmas has in the main lost its power over Christians, Sholem Asch calls upon Jews to accept the festival! A thoroughly godless man, he can presume to legislate in religious matters because neither religion actually means much to him, and he can thus skip merrily between two sides, as did the false prophets of Elijah's day.

By proposing Christmas as a holiday for the Jews, Asch makes

251

it incumbent upon us to examine the nature and origin of the festival more closely. He apparently accepts the popular assumption that Jesus was actually born on the day known as Christmas, although no serious Christian scholar today entertains any such notion.

There is no firm and assured explanation of why December 25 was chosen as Jesus' birthday. The New Testament says nothing of it. For its first two and a half centuries the Church had no Christmas and displayed no interest whatever in celebrating the day of Jesus' birth. The first prelate to introduce the festival of Christmas was Hippolytus, bishop of Rome, in the first half of the third century. His choice, however, was January 2. Others hit upon May 20, April 18, April 19, March 25, and March 28. For a short period Christmas was celebrated on January 6, which date is retained by the Greek-Orthodox Church to this day (See *Encyclopedia of Religion,* edited by Vergilius Ferm, "Christmas," p. 164).

But Sholem Asch seems to be satisfied that the "happy event" took place on December 25. How, then, did the currently used date come to be popularly accepted? Certain "wise men" as wise, no doubt, as Sholem Asch employed a variety of fantastic reckonings to prove that the earth was created on March 25; and since Jesus was "the new creation of the world," it was obvious that his mother conceived him on that date, and that he must have been born nine months later, on December 25.

But no serious, objective Christian student of the subject denies that the origin of Christmas was completely pagan, the festival having been taken over by the Church from the contemporary Greek-Roman-Egyptian mystery cults. These cults had nature ceremonials celebrating "the birth of the spring and of the sun." They knew December 25 as the shortest day of the winter, after which, as a promise of the resurrection of the abundant Nature that had died, the days grew steadily longer.

In Rome the day was known as the Saturnalia, and it was observed with the loss of self restraint. The same festival in Greece and other Hellenistic lands was bound up with Aphrodite, mother of life, and her consort Adonis. It was imagined that every year Adonis died and Aphrodite, at once ceased to be fruitful, producing the winter season. The believers mourned the passing of Adonis. But when the days grew longer, it meant that Adonis was to be reborn; hence the joy over the turning point of December 25.

252

When the Christian church arose it simply took over the pagan festival in its entirety, substituting Jesus for Adonis. Such was the origin of Christmas.

This was one of the methods whereby Christianity was able to spread among the heathens. The Church adopted much of paganism, which it then syncretized with the few Jewish elements taken from the mother religion.

It is because of these antecedents of Christmas that today there are Christian sects who ignore the holiday. Among them are "Jehovah's Witnesses," a sect which was initiated in America in the last quarter of the nineteenth century, and which later spread to other lands. The Witnesses find Christmas utterly un-Christian, and they detest the observances clustering about it. They neither give nor accept Christmas presents. They exchange gifts freely on any other day of the year, but on Christmas such giving is counted a sin. To them the Christmas tree represents the legendary tree which shot up in Nimrod's garden when that wicked man passed away. They believe that because of Nimrod's tree, the tree has become a symbol of the enduring power of wickedness over the earth, and that a Christmas tree in the home implies that the owner is prepared to worship evil. The use of lights and candles on the branches, they continue, derives from a pagan custom of a Germanic tribe, the Belths, who, centuries ago, worshiped Satan, and who in their villages on winter nights attached burning lights to green fir trees in the belief they could drive off the evil spirits of the night. The Witnesses argue, therefore, that anyone who today illumines a Christmas tree in his home is unwittingly practicing a pagan ritual against evil spirits.

The Witnesses are equally critical of the concept of Santa Claus. They see no relationship with Christianity in a festival deriving from the Saturnalia, Aphrodite and Adonis, and other pagan beliefs.

This dynamic sect carries on loud and extensive propaganda against Christmas. They assail the festival with argument and mockery, in the hope that ultimately it will disappear from Christian observance.

Sholem Asch apparently seeks to create new adherents to take the place of the deserters, but this is not entirely new in Jewish history. The classical God Adonis was known to the Babylonians as Adumuz, which in Hebrew is Tammuz. As long ago as the days of the Babylonian exile Tammuz was fashionable among Jewish women, who, according to the prophets, mourned his demise. Says the prophet: "And he brought me in by the door of the gate of the Lord's house, which looked to the north; and behold women sat there mourning for Tammuz." (Ezekiel viii, 14). Tammuz, here represented by an idol, is Adonis, the favorite of Venus. He is slain by a wild boar (winter) and is lamented by the female worshipers of the Goddess.

Thus when Sholem Asch invites Jewry to adopt Christmas, he is in reality trying to return them to the ancient paganism of Tammuz, for whom, to the disgust of the prophet, errant Jewesses once wept.

Perhaps Asch, and all Jews who adopt the holiday as their own, should contemplate the observations of the prophet on the sight just reviewed:

"And He said to me: Surely thou hast seen, O son of man: is this a light thing to the house of Judah, that they should commit these abominations which they have committed here: because they have filled the land with iniquity, and have turned to provoke me to anger? And behold they put a branch to their nose" (ibid: 17).

A branch—might it not be the Christmas tree?

"Therefore I also will deal with them in my wrath: my eye shall not spare them, neither will I show mercy: and when they shall cry to my ears with a loud voice I will not hear them" (ibid: 18).

It happens that it was at the climax of the Hitler war, in 1945, when it was established that six million Jews died at the hands of European Christendom, that Asch saw fit to encourage Jewish acceptance of the merry Christmas festival.

Surely Sholem Asch did not lack a Christmas tree in "Anno Domini" 1945. The tree is a German device, instituted in the seventeenth century by the Huns as their contribution to the holiday of the "redeemer"; from Germany it spread into all Christian lands. However, during the Hitler massacres the Germans added a new "decorative" detail: In their concentration camps, side by side with their "Weihnacht-Bäumer," they set up gallows on which to conduct Christmas hangings of Jews.

In the very year when Sholem Asch proclaimed Christmas a "Jewish holiday."

Leaving aside the Aschian trash, we may now take a realistic view of Christmas and the Jew in a Christian society.

254

What a relief it is to pass from falsehood to truth, from sham to deep-rooted conviction! For a statement of a genuine Jewish attitude towards Christmas as opposed to the distorted preaching of Asch, let us turn to a brief essay by Rabbi Usher Kirshblum of the Jewish Center of Kew Gardens Hills, N. Y.

For sheer beauty of form, incisiveness of style and power of expression, it is unsurpassed among the classics of the pulpit. As a guide to mutual understanding between Jew and Christian in a specific and delicate situation it is deeply persuasive. The wealth of ideas within its brief compass makes it a literary gem of a rare order. Entitled "For Christians Only," it is here reprinted in full with the kind permission of the author:

"The holiest night of the year in the life of the Christian is Christmas Eve. It is the festival of the nativity of Jesus around whom all of Christianity pivots.

"The Jew, who detaches Christmas from Christianity by declaring it a general, non-religious holiday is unwittingly hurting the feelings of his Christian neighbor to whom Christmas is the Mass of Christ. The tree, the holly, the wreath, the lights, the mistletoe and the gifts are Christian symbols alluding to the birth, life, and death of the founder of Christianity. Aware of their significance to Christianity, no Jew has a right to deny or minimize them simply because he desires to introduce them into his home.

"Christmas calls for observance and reverence on the part of every faithful Christian. I have no respect for the Christian who remains untouched by the depth and richness for the Christian of this holiday, who refuses to blend his voice with those of his Christian brothers in song and prayer on this most solemn night. But by the same token, I have no respect for the Jew who, unmoved by the Jewish holidays, tries his utmost to outdo his Christian neighbor in the observance of a holiday which is not his.

"The Jewish religion aims to develop within us a deep sense of love and loyalty for our own faith and a profound sense of understanding and respect for the faith of our fellow-man, without cheap and meaningless imitation.

"Thus we can admire the beauty of the Christmas holiday of our neighbor without misappropriating it for ourselves. And when our children, envious of their Christian playmates, request the observance of Christmas, we need not be afraid to tell them that it is not a Jewish holiday. They will never resent our answer

255

if we implement it with the introduction of Chanukah lights, games and parties. They will not feel cheated if we will acquaint them with the Sabbath candles, Purim noisemakers, Seder tables, and Simchat Torah flags.

"Judaism offers beauty and pageantry for us and for our children. Our children will not have to look longingly at, nor want to borrow part of the beauty and charm of their playmates' homes, if we only bid entrance to some of our sacred traditions.

"At the approach of the Christmas holiday, may I extend greetings to all my Christian neighbors and friends. May the spirit of Christmas linger on throughout the year—Peace on Earth, Good Will to All Men!

"To my fellow Jews I extend best wishes for a Happy Chanukah. May we be imbued with the spirit of the Maccabees who fought so valiantly to preserve the faith and traditions of Israel."

This little essay reflects a mind perfectly poised in the face of a most complex problem. In language as human as it is inspiring the author states in frank, lucid and direct terms what must strike both Jew and Gentile as sound wisdom and true religion.

The burden of Rabbi Kirshblum's message lies in its admonition to Jews concerning their invasion of the Christmas holiday, thus running counter to Asch's preachment. In some Jewish quarters the idea got a foothold, that, since Christmas has lost much of its religious significance and has become more and more a national American feast, Jews, too, should observe it. This is a false and even dangerous doctrine, without any justification from either the Jewish or the Christian point of view. Christmas is definitely a Christian holiday, whatever its origin, and for non-Christians to advance the idea that it has become little more than a civic celebration, is to offend the feelings of the hundreds of millions of genuinely religious people for whom Christmas has retained all its religious sanctity and who labor for a revival of its true spirit where it has become lax.

Every year, come Christmas, the protests grow louder and louder against the tendency for overcommercialization and secularization of the Christmas spirit. "It is real sacrilege"—complains one clerical dignitary, inveighing against "this merciless repetition on the radio and television of Silent Night and similar Christian hymns by crooners, hillbillies, dance bands and other musical barbarians", using it to sell toothpaste before Christmas. "Many groups and individuals"—writes the Detroit, Mich. *Free Press*

256

(Dec. 1, 1951) "seem to feel that the religious origin of the holiday has been obscured in the modern binge of secular celebration which attends Christmas".

It took the outspoken Jehovah's Witnesses to point the finger directly at the Jews as a measure of the decline of the religious spirit of Christmas. Holding forth against celebrating Christmas on general principles, "Awake!" (December 22, 1952) poses the question:

"And how much of all this display is sincere? . . . How many partake in the festivities that do not even claim to be Christians one day in the year, such as Jews, agnostics etc., doing so only because 'Everybody is doing it'? Yes, how much sham, how much hypocrisy is there about all this Christmas Celebration?"

The reckless rush of some Jews to embrace Christmas is thus seen to be a potential source of irritation, if not actual danger. The growing resentment of Christians at what to them cannot but appear as a profanation of the most sacred day on the Christian calendar, is a sign of the times that no Jew dare ignore.

The Jews themselves jealously guarded against intrusion upon their religious ways by outsiders. This sentiment is behind their aversion to proselytizing and their reluctance to accept converts. The same spirit is reflected in the saying: "An idol worshiper who observed the Sabbath has made himself guilty of a mortal sin" (Sanhedrin 58). Of the Sabbath it is said in a prayer: ". . . and the heathen shall not participate in its rest, but Thou hast graciously given it to Israel Thy people". This emphasis on the Sabbath was made all the more necessary by the fact that the Christians had abrogated the Sabbath and instituted Sunday as the Lord's Day, thus changing not only the day but its very meaning. For while Sabbath celebrates the completion of creation, Sunday represents the Christian teaching of the resurrection of Jesus. The ancient Jewish plea against invasion by outsiders of one's faith and religious practices, is one of the earliest expressions of the spirit of true democracy and religious freedom.

CHAPTER VIII

Message on Walls

From my youthful years in a small Ukrainian town, I remember children singing a rhyme about a girl convert called Saraleh. I do not recall whether this was a general folk song about all renegades, male and female, or whether a woman named Saraleh who had turned to Christianity had actually lived in the town, and had inspired a song the chanting of which was limited to the locality.

The song was an odd concoction of prose and verse, combining narrative and lyric forms. First one of the boys would relate the story, then they would all burst into the chant. The story ran something like this:

"After Saraleh got herself converted, she climbed to the steeple of the church, and there she sat and combed her hair with a golden comb, taunting the Jews as they passed by. And her sorrowing father and mother rushed out to where she was, and wringing their hands they sang a wailing song."

Here began the song. I still remember the words and the tune:

"And the father came along,
Very sad and weeping strong—
    Saraleh, my dear,
    Come home from here!"
To which the maiden replied:
    "Even were ten bells ringing
    And ten cantors singing,
        I still would not come down."

Then followed a colloquy with the mother. At the end there was a prose epilogue. A second lad would ask, "And why didn't she want to go home?" To which the first would reply, "Because they gave her a golden comb!"

258

The two churches in our town were very tall, and my juvenile understanding could not comprehend how the maiden managed to climb so high. I inquired of my mother, who said: "When a Jew accepts conversion, he becomes an Esau, with all of Esau's strength. Then he is able to scale the highest steeple."

My father supplemented this explanation with the talmudic saying: "Whoever does evil to Israel, rises very high." And he added: "That his fall may be all the greater."

*　　*　　*

It is long since I forsook that little town so distant from New York. But one beautiful morning, through a strange circumstance, the song suddenly came to my thoughts and my heart. In the midst of New York's East Side I caught sight of a Jew who, like Saraleh, had mounted high on a smooth wall, to taunt the Jews. It was the wall of an ordinary dwelling house, and not of a church; but this Jew performed an unusual trick—he ascended bearing the church with him!

It was Sholem Asch—his image, of course, huge, grandiose, and haughty.

"Look up, you little Jews!" it fairly shouted down. "Here I am with my church, and what do I care what you think or say or do!"

The spot picked for the effrontery was Hester Street—poor, old, Jewish Hester Street that many Jews have renamed "Esther Street."

The vantage point from which I gazed upon the spectacle was the building of the "Jewish Daily Forward," which overlooks Seward Park. My glance fell on a tall, smooth, windowless wall across the park. For years it had stood there, a bare, ugly, dilapidated eyesore, at which no one deliberately stared.

But one day the wall suddenly came alive. Laborers appeared and stretched ropes and platforms from which they began painting. No one could see what they were painting, for they were hidden from onlookers by great canvas shields. This lasted a number of weeks. Then came the crucial moment when the coverings dropped, and in astonishment we beheld:

High up in the left upper corner of the wall, seated in sparkling array, and fairly shrieking at us, a portrait of Sholem Asch!

Opposite, in the right corner, in heavy format, two books by Sholem Asch. One might have expected them to be such works as *A Town* or *Kiddush Hashem*, works that helped carve his niche

259

in the temple of Yiddish literature. But they were *The Nazarene*
and *The Apostle*!

Thoroughly amazed, I crossed the park and quietly took a
place before the wall. Across the entire length and width of the
six-story edifice, from the books almost to the ground, there was
inscribed in flaming letters, in English and Yiddish the announcement that Asch, the author of the books portrayed, formerly with
the anti-communist Jewish Daily Forward, was now writing for
the communist "Morgen Freiheit." For when Asch arrived at the
parting of the ways with the former, he set up house at the latter
where for a number of years he made Jesus rub shoulders with
Stalin. It was apparent that the whole scheme, the choice of spot
and books, was a calculated piece of spite such as Jewish renegades
since time immemorial have indulged.

It was when I looked upon the refurbished wall in all its
splendor, with Asch parading Christological works and communist
hosts at the same time, that I remembered the old song about
faithless Saraleh. I stood there for a long while half expecting to
see Asch's father and mother nearby, wailing:

> "Saraleh, my dear
> Come home from here!"

But there was no one there, of course. It was quiet and lonely
at the wall. Yet I imagined that from Asch's lips there issued the
defiant response—

> "Even were ten bells ringing
> And ten cantors singing,
> I still would not come down."

Here was a veritable mirage of Saraleh come back to me,
complete even to the golden comb; for over to the left on a structure adjoining the Asch legend, the advertisement of a bank was
painted, like a mocking trick of Satan!

* * *

As I continued to gaze at Asch on the wall, I felt that there
was something familiar in the arrangement and composition of
the portrait and the volumes alongside of it. At first I could not
recall the memories that were stirring; they were half-remembered
forms without time or place. Finally, in a rush of memory, I realized that I beheld something known to Jews all over the world;

260

something as familiar, beloved, and revered as the Asch concoction was reprehensible. A Pentateuch provided the key—the kind of Pentateuch with a frontispiece bearing the likeness of Moses and Aaron, or sometimes only a representation of Moses bearing in his arms the Tablets of the Law. This is a representation with which the Jew—in fact the whole world—is well acquainted, for it has often been successfully attempted in art—as, for instance, Doré's "Moses." The portrait of Asch displaying his Christian documents had been painted in imitation of classic representations of Moses and the Tablets! Moses with his Law, and Sholem Asch with his rival law!

And once I discovered the intent of the technique, the message of the wall emerged clearly: Sholem Asch coming from the mountain like a modern Moses, bearing new tablets to the people of Israel! A new Mount Sinai on Hester Street! A new descent from heaven—for the large, open sky could be seen in back of the huge painting. On a day with low clouds it would almost seem that Asch was coming down from heaven through the clouds. The effect would be heightened by thunder and lightning in Seward Park, to give Asch the grandiose, monumental effect once reserved only for Moses!

And when the sun set with the last rays gilding the top of the wall, Asch's brow would be illumined with the horned rays of Moses. And when lights were added at night, passers-by, and the pious men blessing the moon from their roofs, would behold Asch's head enveloped in holy radiance, as though the Holy Ghost lent his radiance to his brow.

The entire effect had been carefully planned and executed.

* * *

A wall has two sides. We have been looking at the outside, but let us wonder now what was to be seen on the other side. Let us use a little imagination.

The neighborhood was a thoroughly Jewish district populated by Jews of deep piety. The house of the Asch-wall was inhabited by Jews. It is entirely possible that on the inward side of the wall there were hung pictures of the Gaon of Vilno, that mezuzot were nailed on the door-posts, that the wall was lined with sacred tomes, that some old Jew was seated at a table over a Talmud or a Book of Psalms, and that often in the stillness of the night someone recited the late evening prayers. There was perhaps a miniature sanctuary set up by a pious Jew, with a "minian" holding services behind the Asch advertisements of the Nazarene and St. Paul on a Sabbath or holiday: Just the breadth of a brick separated the two, but that space held two thousand years of bloody history.

If one glanced about the neighborhood, a door away from the Forward building one saw a kosher restaurant. Every day observant Jews came in to dine—rabbis, yeshivah principals, their students, scholars with long beards and patriarchal features. They came not only to eat, but also to discuss Torah, and the trials and tribulations of their people.

Yet directly across from the windows of this eating place Sholem Asch's portrait looked in—his face and his new tablets. And when the rabbinic Jews within washed their hands before eating, and when they recited the final grace, Asch held before their eyes the Nazarene and the Apostle, pointing to the new god to whom they should truly have offered their prayers.

This was at the very time that the communist "Freiheit" began to "warm up" to the rabbis. It was the "line" of the moment. The paper went on a stillhunt for rabbis, and whenever it could grab a rabbi, or obtain a kind word from one, it was in festive spirits. The combination was amazing—rabbis, and Asch's Christological works as chief attractions. (Did the Freiheit hope to convert rabbis into priests?) Sholem Asch lent his aid to the fraud, for by serializing *The Nazarene* and *The Apostle* the paper became the most serious missionary agency ever to appear among Jewry. No matter how insignificant that paper had been, never before—reckoning all the machinations of the regular missionaries —had the doctrines of Jesus been introduced into as many Jewish homes as the Freiheit reached. Did the paper seek a rabbinical "nihil obstat" for its work among the Jews?

A few doors from the restaurant, to right and left, stood yeshivot and Talmud Torahs—Jewish academies and Hebrew schools—including the institution called Yeshivah Tiferet Jerusalem. Hundreds of young boys, wearing earlocks and skullcaps, played all day in the surrounding streets. Little Jewish lads studied the Torah to rebuild the Judaism that was destroyed in Europe.

But over their heads in the distance, there beckoned the figure of Sholem Asch, dangling before their eyes his two tablets of a new law, *The Nazarene* and *The Apostle*.

Parallel to Hester Street runs Canal Street, dotted with Jewish booksellers. Jews from everywhere come to purchase

262

Jewish books. It is a market place for Torah. In the stretch of several blocks is gathered most of the sacred literature of the Jews—everything from the biblical, talmudic, and later sages, to books of wisdom and morals, ranging from Moses to the most recent commentary of an obscure Rabbi. High above these there towered the visage of Asch, with the tablets of a new dispensation.

Near Hester Street is Norfolk Street, where the noted Bet Hamidrash Hagadol stands, and where the market place of Jewish sanctities is located. Shop after shop purveys scrolls of the Law, their mantles, holy arks, their curtains, prayer shawls and phylacteries, wine cups for sanctification of the holy days, and every other requirement for worship and religious observance. Over all were the tablets of Sholem Asch!

In every direction one comes upon synagogues and houses of study and Chassidic "rooms," many filled with refugees from the Hitler massacres. One sees everywhere, along East Broadway and adjacent thoroughfares, the escaped rabbis and pious men and women with the bearing of Jews of worth. And all these were compelled to look upon the strange glories of Sholem Asch.

Sholem Asch appeared on the wall just before the High Holidays, in the period when Jews from all of New York and from adjacent cities came to the East Side to provide themselves with religious necessities from neighborhood shops. And what is it that Asch said to the people from his imposing height?—"You have clung long enough to your old Torah! Cease purchasing your outworn objects of holiness. Instead of Siddur and Machazor, go and buy my *Nazarene* and my *Apostle*! I bring you a new Torah!

"The sainted apostle has annulled all that came before. Your Torah has been made void. So too your Talmud, your legal codes. Your vessels are no longer beautiful in the eyes of God. Your prayers, not properly directed to Jesus, are not acceptable to your Father in heaven."

Such was the implication of the Message on the Wall.

On Rosh Hashanah and Yom Kippur Jews attended the great and small synagogues which dot the entire district, to pray for a happy new year. From every window one harkened to the wailing blasts of the sacred ram's horn. Succoth found the entire neighborhood redolent of myrtle and citron and willow. On the day of the Rejoicing of the Law, Jews happily paraded the streets with the sacred scrolls. But perched high above their heads was Sholem

263

Asch, mocking all their doings and performances, descending to the farthest depths of shame.

* * *

On his first advent Sholem Asch sought only the pious Jews of the New York East Side, but he actually sought all Israel. He wished to spread his wings even over the deviating Jew. He must have thought Coney Island a locale for the more errant members of the race; so there too he scaled a wall from which to gather-in the sinners.

There was, (and still is), an avenue in Coney Island called Surf Avenue. On it, near 22nd Street, a missionary house had long been established. Close by rose a large flat wall on which the missionaries painted their legends calling upon all Jews to accept baptism, to come and bathe in the waters of conversion. The success of their endeavors was negligible, but the holy ghost quickly brought them succor.

Only a block away, at 23rd Street, stood another such wall, flat, empty, available. Asch came and settled down on it with his tablet, and the same picture which had disgraced Hester Street. Then there were two walls facing each other blaring out their message of salvation at passing Jews, and calling upon them to depart from their sinful ways and travel along the proper road to their salvation.

Thus Asch with his great eyes surveyed the broad vista before him. On a sultry day, when hundreds of thousands came to bathe in the sea, he readily imagined himself a kind of Moses: for he saw tens of thousands of Jews on the shore of a new Red Sea, which he was prepared to split, to bring them from bondage into freedom, into a land flowing with milk and honey, into the land of the church and the cross.

Ships arriving from Europe steamed close by Coney Island. Often they carried passengers spared from Hitler's murderous ghettos. (One may well recall Asch's "Jesus in the Ghetto," who "saved" the Jews.) So Asch hastened to Coney Island, to be first to greet the refugees from the ghettos, and to display to them *The Nazarene* and *The Apostle,* exclaiming: "These are thy gods, O Israel! These are the gods that brought you out of Hitler's Egypt and split the sea before you. To them must you now bow down; their laws shall ye observe."

And still another wall was so adorned in the City of New

264

York. All three appeared in 1943 and remained visible until about 1948.

O Sholem Asch! You erected a wall, and another and still another, but your house fell apart. And no matter how many walls you erect about you, you will forever remain without.

CHAPTER IX

With Back on Israel

Having estranged himself from Judaism and from the Jews, it
was perhaps logical for Sholem Asch to assume a negative attitude
towards the emergence of the state of Israel, which is the heart of
both the faith and the people.

That there is no compulsion for a Christian, because of his
Christianity, to be opposed to Israel, has been amply demonstrated
by experience. There have been many Christians who have nobly
assisted the Jewish state, both prior to and after its emergence,
despite a certain religious inhibition. Their broad humanity trans-
cended the narrow dogmatism which had doomed the Jew to
eternal statelessness and banishment from his sacred soil. But with
Christianized Jews it is a different matter; there is the long established adage that a meshumed is worse than a goy.

There is tragic irony in the fact that Sholem Asch, who for
many years stood close to Zionism, remained entirely on the side-
lines during that turbulent half decade beginning in 1945, which
marked the birth of Israel. In the heroic days of "Exodus 1947,"
when the Jewish remnants and refugees were storming the forbidden shores of the Jewish land; in the sublime days, when, at
the counsel tables of the United Nations, Jacob contended with
Esau for the holy land of Israel; in those days of wonders and
miracles, when Israel was won by the sword against the vast armies
of Ishmael; in all that period of unparalleled heroism and achievement which fired the imagination of all Jewish and even non-
Jewish writers, Sholem Asch remained aloof and apart. He was
not invited, and the spirit did not move him to come forward on
his own account. He knew he didn't belong.

In deference to old sentiment, or out of plain decency, Asch
should have clung to the position he had created for himself, that

266

of a stranger and an alien. Instead he elected the role of an opponent and open antagonist. He gave expression to his attitude in a letter to a friend, which the latter made public. It appeared in the "American Hebrew" of January 20, 1950, as part of an article by the British-Jewish writer, Joseph Leftwich.

Leftwich visited America late in 1949, and spoke with Asch, who voiced ideas and emotions which he later put in writing in a letter to Leftwich in England. From this letter came the quotation in the "American Hebrew" (surely not without the consent and authorization of its author).

Mr. Leftwich begins by saying: "Asch, who was at one time a lover of Eretz Israel has been drawn increasingly in recent years toward the European and American way of life." He tells of the Zionist Congress of 1929, when the Jewish Agency was created, and Sholem Asch was elected a member of it. Hailing from Poland, Asch was chosen to represent Polish Jewry—a choice which Shmaryahue Levin then called "symbolic." Asch himself addressed the historic gathering. It was a speech of acceptance. He spoke in the name of the Jews of Poland and said: "We are here, we Polish Jews are here, and Eretz Israel is the hope and joy that unites us."

But after the extermination of the Polish Jews, what then? Mr. Leftwich quotes: "My Jewish people, dear friend, has perished. Israel is not being built by my Jews, but by Orientals. To me it is becoming a land of Orientals. I am a European, and all that is near and dear and holy to the man of Europe is near and dear and holy to me."

Here we have a concise and clear expression of Sholem Asch's attitude toward the miracle called the State of Israel. He repudiates Israel and the people in it because they are mere "orientals." Not even oriental Jews, but just plain "orientals." He considers himself a member of the "higher race of Europeans."

The bitterness and resentment motivating Asch's attitude are concentrated in the single word, "orientals," which, to him, is synonymous with "Asiatics," which, in the old European tradition, is synonymous with "barbarians" or "savages."

Not so long ago, when Europe bestrode the world (including Asia and its peoples, which it oppressed and exploited and robbed) it sought to silence the voice of its own conscience by branding the Asiatics or orientals a kind of lower humanity, despite the fact that glorious civilizations existed in Asia long before Europe knew any.

267

Such is the contempt capsuled in the hated term, "orientals," employed by Asch against the Sephardic Jews—those of Arabia and Yemen, Irak and Morocco, and other Asiatic and African countries—who, with the founding of Israel, began to pour into the ancient homeland in the "ingatherings of the exiles" awaited by Israel for two thousand years! "These are not my Jews," sneers Sholem Asch, who will have no part of a land which they build. Ignoring his own pious strictures, vociferated in *The Nazarene*, against the sages who allegedly caused division in Jewry by separating Jews of old into "clean" and "unclean," he proffers instead a division into "Orientals" and "non-Orientals."

His own Jews have been exterminated, says Asch, mournfully and, alas, only too truly. But it was Europe that killed them all, and common sense dictates that he should have learned to hate Europe. But strangely enough, at this very time his love for that continent flowers forth in its fullest bloom.

Now let us look a little closer at the "orientals" Asch derides. Aren't we all orientals? Didn't Jewry originate in the East? All the anti-Semitic movements of glorious Europe were based on the assumption that Jews were orientals, with the mentality and character of barbarians; that therefore their place was not in Europe; and that therefore they must be massacred. But even Sholem Asch is an oriental, and so is his new god Jesus the Nazarene, and his prophet Saint Paul, and, of course, Mary.

This argument, however, never carried any weight with Christians and is obviously of no consequence to Sholem Asch either. This is perhaps the first time we have encountered such a violent segregation of Jew from Jew, by a Jew. Asch apparently would have preferred to discard the "oriental" Jews and leave them to their fate in the Arab wastelands. For Sholem Asch is far gone from us; the entire Jewish psychology has become something alien to him.

To us, all Jews are brothers; in a family sense as well as in a historical and theological sense they form one people throughout the world. And for the land of Israel, in the ingathering of the exiled, there is no selection of Jews. All Jews are equally precious.

Indeed, the "oriental" Jew is especially cherished in Israel. And the most oriental of all, the Yemenites, are distinguished for their wholehearted loyalty to their faith; for a loyalty which has never dimmed or diminished in all the years of their exile, which began even before the destruction of the first Temple. And who knows but that the Yemenite Jew is the one destined to foster a renascence of Israel, insomuch as he has never been gnawed by the vermin of European decadence.

The attainment of the "first million" was celebrated in Israel during Chanukah of 1950, and there was immediate reckoning and perturbation concerning the second million. Whence would the new immigration come? From the Arab lands, was the answer —from Yemen, Irak, and the others. How miraculous is the fact that the new return was to be from the very lands from which the first return to Zion took place after the Babylonian exile! In later centuries men will read of the present re-occupation with the same intoxication with which we today revel in the story of Ezra and Nehemiah. This whole era is filled with great mysticism! None may now fully comprehend the glory of the new race to evolve from the coming of so many classes of Jews from so many countries, climates, and cultures, in a new configuration.

After the cutting down of European Jewry, who dared belittle even the least among us? Every Jewish child, even from the most benighted and inaccessible region, became dearer to us than before. And now the possibilities inherent in the new life and form which Jewry is taking in the new land are so overpowering that one is filled with awe of the future.

The magnificence of the dawning epoch never touched Sholem Asch; it passed him by as he was wool-gathering in the church, rapt in the clouds of cloistered incense. And when he awoke, he remained silent, speechless, hushed, just as he did in the heroic days of the "Exodus 1947," and in the days of jubilation when the proclamation of the new State was heralded, and on the solemn day when Jewish blood was shed in conflict, and on the day when victory was hailed. But he finally spoke; and what he uttered was a curse. He offered no healing for the sorely wounded body of Israel—if anything, he deepened the wounds and widened the cut. But this need not surprise us if we gain an acquaintance with the background of his Christological fiction, and his Christian ideology as he himself expounds it. I have in mind a famous interview, one of a number on the subject, given by Asch to the noted American journalist, Frank S. Mead, and printed in the "Christian Herald," January, 1944.

Asch began by describing his adoration of the Christ-figure. "As you know," said he, "I grew up, you know, on the border of Poland and Russia, which isn't exactly the finest place in the world

269

for a Jew to sit down and write a life of Jesus Christ. Yet even through those years, the hope of doing just that fascinated me. I floundered a bit at first. I was seeking that something for which so many of us search—that surety, that faith, that spiritual content in my living, which would bring me peace and through which I might help bring some peace to others. I found it in the Nazarene.

"Jesus Christ," he said further in a passage already quoted, "to me, is the outstanding personality of all time and all history, both as son of God and son of Man. Everything he ever said or did has value for us today, and that is something you can say of no other man, alive or dead. . . . No other religious leader has ever become so personal a part of people as the Nazarene. When you understand Jesus, you understand that he came to save *you*, to come into *your* personality. It isn't just a case of a misty, uncertain relationship between a worshiper and an unseen God; that is abstract; Jesus is personal!"

Mr. Mead asked when Asch had begun writing *The Nazarene*.

"This was not a case of just writing," was the reply. "It was more of a question of getting the truth about Jesus, the Nazarene, straight and clear in my mind. There were years of hard thinking, of mental agony, before I picked up my pen. Frankly, while my writer's fingers itched to write this story, it never occurred to me to publish it. That would have been to attempt the impossible. My own people would have fought it, and Christians would have fought it. I could never have written *The Nazarene* and *The Apostle* had I not come to America.

"The final inspiration to write, the insistence that I write, came to me in Palestine. . . . ", he continued, revealing the true source of his perverted attitude toward the new land of Israel. "I saw," the account continues, "that I could never write about Jesus until I went to his homeland. So I went in 1907. There the story really came alive. The whole landscape of the Holy Land held his footprints; every bush and tree and stone was afire with Christ. I made more pilgrimages to Palestine, later, but if you want a date, it was in 1908 that the real writing began."

This is a portion of a long, very illuminating interview, the rest of which need not hold us here. All that was needed for our purpose is here laid out as on a platter: this is a true confession of Christian faith on the part of Sholem Asch.

From the words quoted it becomes clear that quite early

270

Asch was no longer in his heart a true member of the house of Israel, and that his interest in the land of Israel was not the interest and concern of a Jew. The land interested him only as the background for the Christian drama and it was chiefly for its setting that he repeatedly journeyed there, not for the building of a Jewish nation. As to the "Song of the Valley" it appears to have been just a by-product.

Asch seems to have had no moral qualm in telling his story with such illuminating frankness, entirely insensitive to the immeasurable depths of fraud, deceit and guile which for years he perpetrated upon a trusting people. He marched with the Zionists as a loyal member of the movement and from them he received honor and glory and treasure. But all along his heart was elsewhere—with the "son of God."

His duplicity soared to even greater heights when in 1929 he allowed himself to be elected to the Jewish Agency as a representative of Polish Jewry. He was then fully aware of the abyss lying between him and the people whom he now terms "my Jews." He knew, he admits, that it would have been impossible for him to write his book on Jesus while dwelling among the Polish Jews; that to be able to place his pen at the service of the Nazarene, he had to flee his country. He undertook, by his own admission, several trips to Palestine for no other purpose than to prostrate himself upon the grave of the Nazarene—to inhale the breath of the Jesus legend, as preparation for his Jesus opus. And then, after having harbored the secret of the Nazarene in his heart for nearly two decades, he permitted himself to stand up as a representative of the Polish Jews in the matter of Zionism and the Holy Land.

This will stand as the classic example of hypocrisy in the annals of Jewish literature.

One wonders what could have been the motive in back of such duplicity, by which Asch justified his two-faced behavior. Could it have been lust for notoriety, honor?

It was undoubtedly a great honor to be chosen a member of the Jewish Agency and above all to represent the great Polish Jewry. Yet all the while Asch harbored even loftier ambitions in his heart.

I am not aware whether any of this ever appeared in print, or reached the ear of a wide public in other ways; but in the inner circle about Asch, and especially in his immediate entour-

271

age, it was an open secret that the novelist flirted with the idea that one day, when the Zionist vision is realized and a Jewish state is arisen he would be chosen King. Fancy Sholem Asch sitting on the throne of Solomon and wielding the scepter of the royal house of Judah! He thought himself fully worthy of the honor, both because of his boundless vainglory as a writer and his imposing physical appearance—was he not, like Saul, "from his shoulders and upward. . . . higher than any of the people?"

And should the new state arise as a republic, he was prepared to be elected president. Something of that nature had taken place in Poland, before Asch's very eyes. The resurrected land of the Poles had given the high post of premier to its renowned wizard of the piano, Ignaz Paderewski. Indeed, Asch reasoned, since Poland had honored herself by offering this on to the great master of the keyboard, could the Jews do less for their greatest novelist?

Yet all the while deep in his heart he worshiped his newly discovered God and was ripening for his Christological endeavors: a king of Israel, nourishing in his soul a love for a strange God! But the years came and went, and there was no Jewish kingdom, and no Jewish crown for a King. Asch must have lost hope of ever mounting the throne of David. So, unable to become a king of the Jews, he became a slave of the gentiles. He turned away from Judaism. The Jews turned from him.

Then came the years of terror and of horror, of turmoil and chaos, and out of all the trials and suffering of the Nazi-holocaust emerged the long hoped for, the long dreamt of, State of Israel!

But Asch was now outside the fold.

The naive man had persuaded himself that the story of the man who declared himself a god constituted the greatest story ever told. No, the rise of the State of Israel, and the ingathering of Jews from all over the world, in short, the resurrection of a decapitated people, this is what constitutes the greatest miracle of the two thousand years of the Christian era!

But Asch could have no share in the miracle. For him, all ancient prophecies about Israel were fulfilled in the Nazarene. But we have seen the promises of the prophets fulfilled before our very eyes, in the true Servant of the Lord, in the people of Israel.

Let us turn to Isaiah: "But now thus saith the Lord that created thee, O Jacob, and He that formed thee, O Israel. . . . Fear not, for I am with thee; I will bring thy seed from the east, and

272

gather thee from the west; I will say to the north: 'Give up', and to the south: 'Keep not back.'" (xliii, 5, 6). Christological expositors maintain that this prophecy has been fulfilled with the return from the Babylonian exile. But when has this prophecy been fulfilled in such measure as in our day? When did the Jews come out of Yemen? At the return from the Babylonian exile, when Ezra sent emissaries to the Jews in Yemen, bidding them come, they refused, declaring that this was not yet the true redemption. Ezra rebuked them, and they rebuked him, and still they did not come. But today they have returned, "on the wings of eagles," as the prophecy foretold.

And not only from Yemen, but from Libya and Czechoslovakia, Ethiopia and India, Aden and Poland, Irak and Romania, from the sands of the Sahara and the pits of Iran, from Jabar and Lachlech, Jews, white, black, brown, and tan, came in answer to the ancient supplication: "Bring our scattered ones among the nations near unto Thee, and gather our dispersed from the ends of the earth."

Having blinded his eyes with false miracles, Asch was unable to recognize the true wonders when they came. Nevertheless he did apparently wish to take a proximate glance at the new phenomenon. In the fall of 1949 Sholem Asch journeyed abroad. His publicity agents announced his destination Israel. They gleefully rubbed their hands in happy anticipation of the magnificent reception he would surely receive there and of his ultimate triumph over his opponents.

He went to Paris, then to Rome, but a few hours from Tel Aviv by air, "on the wings of eagles." But he returned to America without completing his trip. Why? Is it possible that word came to him that he would not be crowned King of Israel after all? He made a second unsuccessful attempt and entered only at the third try, with mournful results (See Preface).

In turning his back on Israel Asch proved himself a reincarnation of Sanballat, the Horonite, of the time of the first return to Zion from the first exile, of whom Nehemia says:

"When Sanballat the Horonite, and Tobiah the servant, the Ammonite, and Geshem the Arabian, heard it, they laughed us to scorn, and despised us, and said: 'What is this thing that ye do?'" (Nehemia ii, 19).

Thus did Sholem Asch appear a Sanballat, who despised the people and laughed them to scorn—What is this thing that they

273

do? They are building up an "orientalism"—a frightening word, calculated to kill sympathy, to chill enthusiasm, to distort, to undermine, to destroy.

Asch thus aligned himself with the enemies. And what shall we say in reply? It is written in the same chapter:

"Then answered I them, and said unto them: 'The God of heaven, He will prosper us; therefore we His servants will arise and build; but ye have no portion, nor right, nor memorial, in Jerusalem.'"

The answer given to the ancient Sanballat applies equally to the Sanballat of the present day. For him there will be no memorial in Jerusalem. For he has torn himself away from all—from the faith of Israel, the people of Israel, and the land of Israel, the land which he aspired to rule. He could have been the anointed King of the realm of Jewish literature, had he remained a good and faithful servant to his people at the time of their greatest affliction. But Asch drifted away from his people and from the land of his fathers. He thrust his people away for a mess of pottage and a handful of glory.

There is a remarkable story concerning Nahmanides and a Jewish renegade. The renowned Rabbi of the Middle Ages, so the story goes, had a disciple who went over to Christianity. Once while promenading the sage encountered the convert, who was insolent enough to approach his former teacher and exclaim, "You may know, master, that it was because of you that I sought conversion!"

"Because of me!" returned the sage in amazement. "How do you mean?"

"I'll explain," said the other. "You have maintained that in the Pentateuchal portion 'Haazinu' are contained all things that exist in the world. Well, my name happens to be Abner, and it does not appear in that portion. So I began to doubt everything about my religion, and here I am."

"Why," replied the master, "you are mistaken. Your name is plainly writ there for all to see.

"Take the third letter of each word in the message 'Af'ehem ashbitah meenosh zichram'*—which means, 'I would make an end of them, I would make the remembrance of them cease from among men' (Deut. xxxii, 26). The four Hebrew letters thus gathered spell your name—Abner!"

* אפאיהם אשביתה מאנוש זכרם

274

When the convert heard this, he was seized by great fear and melancholy. He hied himself to the sea, seated himself in a small boat, pushed off, and drifted away; no one knows what became of him.

Astonishingly enough, Asch's name, too, is contained in that selfsame verse—the first letters of "ashbitah" would make the remembrance of them cease.

Such is the fate of our Jewish backsliders, deserters and detractors.

That it might be fulfilled which was spoken by the prophet, saying,

"Therefore as the tongue of the fire devoureth the stubble, and as the chaff is consumed in the flame, so their root shall be as rottenness, and their blossom shall go up as dust; *because they have rejected the Law of the Lord of hosts, and condemned the word of the Holy one of Israel.*" (Isa. v, 24)

Appendix
See page 24

For the benefit of those who have some understanding of Hebrew, I here give several examples of Asch's "expert" knowledge of Hebrew. (I quote from the second Yiddish edition of *The Nazarene*.)

He writes: "לא בחיל ולא בכח כי אם ברוח ה'" (p. 125) — misquoted. The correct quotation is: "לא בחיל ולא בכח כי אם ברוחי אמר ה' צבאות" (זכריה, ד,ז)

Proverbs 10, 27 reads: "שנות רשעים תקצרנה". Instead of "תקצרנה" Asch writes "תקצרנו" (p. 127). Bad elementary grammar.

He writes: "As the singer of Israel says: 'צדיק באמונתו יחיה' (p. 436)—incorrect: It is not the Singer of Israel—a designation for King David—who says this but the prophet Habakkuk (2, 4).

The scene is set in a synagogue on a Sabbath. Jesus is called up to the reading of the Law. And Asch writes:

"The reader called out the Rabbi's (Jesus') name with the addition of the title "רבּן": "מורנו רבן ר' ישוע בן ר' יוסף מבוקש לעולה לתורה" (p. 455): "לעולה" is an ear-grating error in grammar. The proper form is "לעלות". The three titles: "מורנו ר' רבּן" occurring together, are an incongruous combination never used and not heard anywhere.

He writes: "By this he means the Son of Man (בר-אנוש), the Ancient of Days (עתיק הימים), Him who dwells with God in Heaven from before as yet the world was created" (p. 458). This sentence is swarming with errors:
1) בר-אנוש: there is no such combination. He probably means: בר-אינשא or בּן-אנוש, or בר-נש. Perhaps בר-אדם. 2) עתיק הימים:—there is no such term. The proper form is: עתיק יומין or עתיק יומיא or עתיק יומין. 3) עתיק יומין is not an appellation of the Messiah, "who dwells with God in Heaven from before as yet the world was created" but is a name of God Himself. 4) That the Messiah existed prior to the creation of the

275

world is pure Christian theology. In Jewish tradition only the name of the Messiah was created prior to the creation of the world (P'sahim 54).

We read further in Asch: "They do the works of Zimra — "מעשי זמרה" — (p. 469) . Wrong. It should be: מעשה זמרי.

He writes: "It is stated in Scripture: 'כל הארץ מלאה כבודו' (The whole earth is full of His glory) " (p. 475) . Wrong. The verse is: מלא כל הארץ כבודו (Isaiah 6, 3).

When Asch, in the manner of the Nazarene, vituperates against the command of the Torah which prohibits bringing the hire of a harlot into the house of the Lord — a regular practice in temples of erotic cult among the pagans — he writes every time: "מתנת זונה" (p. 476) , where the Torah uses אתנז זונה.

At the trial of Jesus before the Sanhedrin, the advocate for Jesus, a member of the Sanhedrin, demands that the procedure follow the command of the Torah, that through no less than two witnesses shall a matter be juridically accredited, and he quotes aloud the command of the Torah, calling out: "על שני עדות יקום הדברו" (p. 618). Once thus, twice thus and thrice thus. But thrice is it in error. The text of the Torah reads: "על פי שני עדים או על פי שלשה עדים יקום דבר" (Deut. 19, 15) In the highest court of the land, a judge unable to quote the text of a basic law! And distorting its simple grammar at that! Only one who knows Hebrew can appreciate what a barbaric construction is this: "על שני עדות יקום הדבר".